WRITING FOR REAL

WRITING FOR REAL

A Handbook for Writers in Community Service

CAROLYN ROSS
Stanford University

ARDEL THOMAS
Stanford University

Longman

New York San Francisco Boston
London Toronto Sydney Tokyo Singapore Madrid
Mexico City Munich Paris Cape Town Hong Kong Montreal

Vice President/Editor-in-Chief: Joseph Terry
Acquisitions Editor: Erika Berg
Executive Marketing Manager: Ann Stypuloski
Production Manager: Eric Jorgensen
Project Coordination, Text Design, and Electronic Page Makeup:
    Electronic Publishing Services Inc., NYC
Cover Design Manager: John Callahan
Cover Designer: Maria Ilardi
Cover Photos: (top left) © 2002 Javier Pierini/Getty Images/PhotoDisc; (top middle)
    © 2002 Getty Images/Eyewire; (top right) © 2002 David Young Wolff/Getty Images/
    Stone; (bottom left) © 2002 Walter Hodges/Getty Images/Stone; (bottom middle) © 2002
    Andreas Pollock/Getty Images/Stone; (bottom right) © 2002 Javier Pierini/Getty Images/
    PhotoDisc
Manufacturing Buyer: Roy Pickering
Printer and Binder: Courier Corporation
Cover Printer: Coral Graphic Services, Inc.

Library of Congress Cataloging-in-Publication Data
Ross, Carolyn.
      Writing for real : a handbook for writers in community service / Carolyn Ross, Ardel
Thomas.-- 1st ed.
          p.   cm.
      Includes bibliographical references and index.
      ISBN 0-321-08911-1 (pbk.)
      1. English language--Rhetoric--Handbooks, manuals, etc. 2. Social service
literature--Authorship--Handbooks, manuals, etc. 3. Community and
college--Handbooks, manuals, etc. 4. Academic writing--Handbooks, manuals, etc. I.
Thomas, Ardel. II. Title.

PE1479.S62 R67 2003
808'.042--dc21   2002075429

Please visit our website at http://www.ablongman.com

ISBN 0-321-08911-1

2 3 4 5 6 7 8 9 10-CRS-05 04 03

To
my collaborators in life,
Caitlin, Ruffin, and Del
C.B.R.

To
Bari S Johnson
A.M.T.

Brief Contents

Detailed Contents

Preface

The service-learning classroom is an exciting, challenging, and sometimes confusing place, for instructors and students alike. As teachers committed to community-based teaching and learning, we know how much service-learning enriches students' practical and civic educations. We know how much students want to—and do—contribute tangibly to a better society when they practice what they learn, and learn what they practice, through classroom-based work in the community. Yet we have struggled, as many instructors have, to achieve a coherent community-based pedagogy, to manage the formidable logistics of the service-learning classroom, and to support our students in their unfamiliar roles as community-based learners and writers. *Writing for Real* arises from this commitment and through these struggles.

In *Writing for Real*, we have aimed to create a concise and practical handbook that will help students in any service-learning class, whatever its discipline, to conceptualize community-based writing assignments and to implement effective strategies in completing them. Virtually all students in service-learning courses across the curriculum write as part of their service-learning experience, whether it is about observations and ideas related to their community work or for the community agencies with which they work. Often, they are asked to do both. In *Writing for Real*, we address both kinds of writing—academic and practical—that students typically produce in service-learning classes. Beyond this, however, we integrate discussion of the two, since it is our belief that students' skills as academic writers enhance their skills as practical writers, and vice versa, just as what students learn about course content enhances their experience in the community, and vice versa. We focus on sharpening students' awareness of the audiences and purposes of academic and practical writing, and of the more specific writing forms and genres that exist within each of these two broad categories.

Writing for Real is certainly substantive enough to stand alone as a rhetoric, but we also hope that instructors will use it as a supplement to other texts and readings that are specific to the content of their courses. The variety that exists not only among disciplinary approaches and specific course content but also among instructors' individual approaches to teaching makes prescription of any single method of guiding student writers in service-learning courses as impossible as it would be ill-advised. Instead, the goal of *Writing for Real* is to provide a flexible, process-based, and resource-rich guide to writing in service-learning contexts. We hope that both experienced service-learning instructors and those for whom the implementation of a community-based pedagogy is a newer proposition will find what they and their students need in *Writing for Real*, in the balance it strikes between flexibility of approach and practical strategy.

APPROACHES TO WRITING IN SERVICE-LEARNING CONTEXTS

Several important premises account for the content and organization of *Writing for Real*.

- When students understand the fundamental educational and social principles behind service-learning, they better understand their roles in service-learning partnerships and are more fully invested in their work.

- The dual roles that students experience in service-learning as both learners and agents of change pose a productive conundrum, ultimately enhancing their authority in both roles.

- Collaboration—among students, agency mentors, community members, and instructors—is an inherent, complicated, and positive aspect of service-learning. Teaching and learning in service-learning are reciprocal.

- Important teaching and learning opportunities are lost when the problems and challenges of community-based learning are overlooked.

- Students' community-based experiences are enhanced through written reflection and classroom discussion.

- When students have a flexible understanding of audience and purpose, what they learn about research and writing in academic settings and research and writing in practical settings reinforces the quality of both.

- Service-learners are supported not only by instruction but also by example, through the experiences and familiar voices of other students and through the community-based writing that other students have produced.

Writing for Real is organized in three parts. Part I, Foundations (Chapters 1–3), provides context and a conceptual basis for students' work in service-learning classes. Chapter 1 provides a brief history of the service-learning movement in the United States, articulating its social and educational premises, and explains the importance of writing in service-learning classes across the disciplines. Chapter 2 establishes fundamental differences and similarities between the academic and practical writing that students in community-based classrooms do and introduces some of the specific types of writing that students are likely to encounter within each. Service-learning entails collaborations of many kinds and on many levels—between academic institutions and communities at large; among students, instructors, agency mentors, and other community members; among people of widely different backgrounds and experience. Chapter 3 helps students understand the importance of collaboration in the service-learning contact zone.

Part II, Groundwork (Chapters 4–8), helps students with some of the complex personal, social, and practical aspects of preparing to undertake a community-based writing project. In Chapter 4, we urge students to evaluate some of the problematic assumptions that are commonly attached to service, such as *noblesse oblige,* and to consider their own motivations for service. What roles will they take in the give-and-take of service-learning partnerships in communities beyond the classroom walls? With this foundation, we take students through the practical steps of establishing their community-based projects:

- Understanding community service within specific course contexts and requirements.
- Locating or selecting among service-learning placements.
- Working independently or in collaborative groups to set up initial meetings with agency mentors.
- Negotiating community-based assignments.
- Understanding academic and practical community-based writing assignments in terms of audience and rhetorical purpose.
- Considering time management in complicated community-based assignments and the differences in work styles that students might encounter in academic and community contexts.

The practical worksheets distributed throughout Part II will help students identify their interests, establish good matches with community organizations, and clearly define community-based projects.

Part III, Construction Zones (Chapters 9–14), serves as a practical guide for students as they fulfill their academic and practical community-based writing assignments. Discussion in Chapters 9, 10, 12, and 13 of researching, planning and drafting, documenting, and revising and editing integrates approaches to both academic and practical assignments in service-learning contexts, building one upon the other and moving from academic writing, which is generally more familiar to student writers, to practical writing, which is generally less so. Chapter 9 addresses in depth both primary and secondary research and includes strategies for interviewing, surveying, and evaluating print and online sources. Chapter 11, on formatting, provides special guidance and information about graphic design for students working on practical documents for their community agencies. Practical worksheets help students understand the audiences, purposes, and forms of practical documents, and provide guidelines for peer review of both academic and practical writing. In the final chapter of *Writing for Real* we pose the fundamental question, "How can you tell if a community-based writing project is successful?" When authority is shared among students, community mentors, and instructors, this question yields complex answers.

Although we include excerpts of student writing throughout *Writing for Real,* in the Appendix you will also find ten full-text examples of students' community-based writing in some of its most common forms. These examples include both academic and practical projects: a reflective journal, a reflective essay, a fact sheet, a brochure, a Web page, a report, a newsletter article, a grant letter, a brief documented essay, and a longer multiple-source research paper.

KEY FEATURES

- *Writing for Real* **is flexible.** This text is interdisciplinary and can be used in any service-learning course in which writing is required.
- *Writing for Real* **is practical.** This brief, accessible handbook is full of tips, strategies, and worksheets.
- *Writing for Real* **focuses on both academic and practical writing in service-learning contexts.** Discussions of academic and practical writing are integrated throughout.
- *Writing for Real* **is process-based.** It guides students step by step in understanding, preparing, and fulfilling community-based writing projects.
- *Writing for Real* **highlights student writing.** Examples of students' community-based writing, both academic and practical, are excerpted throughout the book; ten complete projects, in both academic and practical genres, are included in the Appendix.
- *Writing for Real* **features student voices.** Throughout the text, students speak of their experiences and express their thoughts as writers and service-learners.
- *Writing for Real* **is engaging.** Lively examples and compelling scenarios are a staple of the book; along with student writing and student voices, they bring community-based writing to life in the text.
- *Writing for Real* **encourages reflection.** Reflection brings students' work in the community back to the classroom. Reflective questions for journal-writing and class discussion end every chapter.
- *Writing for Real* **tackles the hard stuff.** The book is upbeat, but it also addresses head-on the challenges inherent in service-learning. A Troubleshooting section ends Chapters 4–14, providing constructive responses to real-world problems that students face when the community becomes the classroom, and the classroom becomes the community.

ACKNOWLEDGMENTS

Writing for Real has grown from a rich network of service-learning partnerships that we have developed over many years with academic colleagues, community agencies, community mentors and members, and students. So there are many people to thank.

Colleagues from around the country have provided us with invaluable help in shaping *Writing for Real* over the past two years. Thanks to our reviewers for their insights, perspectives, and cogent advice: Nora Bacon, University of Nebraska–Omaha; Susan Brown Carlton, Pacific Lutheran University; Sharon Hamilton, Indiana University–Purdue University Indianapolis; Peter Harris, Colby College; Glenn Hutchinson, University of North Carolina–Charlotte; Tobi Jacobi, Syracuse University; Michael Martin, San Francisco State University; Kathy Parrish, Southwestern University; Barbara Roswell, Goucher College; Maureen Rubin, California State University–Northridge; Kayann Short, University of Colorado; Frederic Stout, Stanford University; Amy Rupier Taggart, Texas Christian University; and Adrian Wurr, University of North Carolina–Greensboro. We owe special thanks to two of our reviewers: to Barbara Roswell for putting us in contact with some of her wonderful students, and to Frederic Stout for helping us extend our interdisciplinary network in the world of service-learning.

We would also like to thank Mindy Wright, of The Ohio State University, and her students for their enthusiasm and tolerance in piloting *Writing for Real* in unwieldy draft form in the Spring of 2002. We deeply appreciate their thoughtful assessments and constructive suggestions for final adjustments to the text.

We have been extremely fortunate to have benefited from a stimulating and ongoing discourse among our dedicated Stanford colleagues about the theory and practice of teaching writing and rhetoric. We extend our gratitude to Andrea Lunsford and Marvin Diogenes, Director and Associate Director of the Program in Writing and Rhetoric at Stanford, for their confidence in our work. Thanks to Corrine Arraez, Helen Blythe, Daniel Teodoro Contreras, Marjorie Ford, Wendy Goldberg, Michael Golston, Caroline Grant, Celia Marshik, Tim Maxwell, Teresa Pellinan-Chavez, Ron Rebholtz, Claude Reichard, John Tinker, Ann Watters, and Susan Wyle for so generously sharing with us their expertise, ideas, convictions, and wisdom about teaching writing in the academy and beyond.

However valuable the advice of fellow teachers has been, that of our student reviewers has been indispensable. Our thanks go to Stanford University students Nik Reed and Megan Vanneman, whose feedback kept us honest, and to Longman intern and Fordham University student Lauren Puccio, who gave our early manuscript the most thorough and perceptive review of them all and whose genuine commitment to the project inspired us all over again. Thanks, too, to Caitlin Bailey whose insights, from her dual perspective as Hampshire College student and summer intern at Children of Lesbians and Gays Everywhere (COLAGE), were extremely helpful.

Writing for Real, from inception to publication, has taken form as a consequence of the hard work of many people at Longman. We are grateful to all of them. We are blessed to have had Erika Berg as our editor. Her belief in *Writing for Real* has been unshakeable from the beginning, and we have relied on her experience, skill, intelligence, and common sense at every stage of the project. Our appreciation and admiration go as well to Eric Jorgensen, Production Manager for *Writing for Real,* and to Lake Lloyd, Project Editor, for their excellent work, not to mention their extraordinary patience. We'd like to extend a special thanks to editorial assistant Michele Cronin, without whose expert coordination of the details we would have been lost. (We came to depend on her smile—even though it was gathered only by phone and through email.)

We have, over the years, worked in partnership with so many wonderful community agencies and community mentors that it is impossible to enumerate them. The individual and cumulative impact of their dedication to social equity and to the communities that they serve has been an inspiration and a model to us and, more importantly, to our students. We would like to extend our deepest gratitude to Deborah Bartens of the Palo Alto Baylands Nature Interpretive Center and Junior Museum; Willard Davis of the Attitudinal Healing Network; Noreen Dowling of the Palo Alto Chapter of the American Red Cross; Dan Firth of the Palo Alto Fire Department, Environmental Division; Celia Harnett of Helping After Neonatal Death; Michelle Gassaway, Caryn Huberman, and Vince Yalon of the Stanford Blood Center; Kim Gelfend of Sustainable San Mateo County; Julie Maxim of the Mid-Peninsula YWCA Rape Crisis Center; Leslie Minot of the International Gay and Lesbian Human Rights Commission; and Geoffrey Skinner of The Trail Center. These people have not only generously guided our students and those of other instructors in their work and writing in the community, but they have also helped us substantively in developing this text.

We are extremely fortunate at Stanford to have had the Haas Center for Public Service as a resource for our work as service-learning instructors and researchers for the past twelve years. Without the ongoing support of Haas Center staff and programs, we would have developed neither the experience nor the insight that writing this book required. We would like to acknowledge the Haas Center staff's commitment to service-learning. In particular, we would like to thank Nadine Cruz, Kent Koth, Jon McConnell, Cari Pang, Jackie Schmidt-Posner, Timothy Stanton, and Nancy Vandenberg.

Most significantly, we are indebted to the students whose experiences and writing are featured in *Writing for Real*. These students are representative of many others to whom, although they are unnamed here, we also owe our thanks. We are continually impressed by the willingness of students to embrace the challenges that service-learning offers up and their hard work in doing so. We are most impressed by their optimism. *Writing for Real* is theirs.

Finally, we wish to thank our wonderful family, Caitlin and Ruffin, and our lovely friends for tolerating our individual and combined preoccupations these past two years. To each other we extend mutual gratitude, respect, love, and admiration.

CAROLYN ROSS
ARDEL THOMAS

PART I

Foundations: Conceptualizing Service-Learning

CHAPTER 1

Why Community-Based Writing?

Thought without practice is empty, practice without thought is blind.
—KWAME NKRUMAH, FORMER PRESIDENT OF GHANA

What is the relationship between education and society?

This morning, on your way to class, you head for the coffee shop on the corner. In the doorway of the building next door, a woman whose age you cannot guess asks, "Spare change?" She is worn and disheveled; behind her are a tarp, a blanket, and a garbage bag in which, you imagine, she carries all the rest of her possessions. You have barely enough money to buy yourself a cup of coffee, and you know that this will probably not be the last time you will be asked for money today. You can't help everybody, so you fix your gaze ahead and keep on walking. The topic of the lecture in your political theory class is democratic participation.

What is the tangible relationship between your education and the world you live in?

You and other students all over the country—all over the world—may wonder at times about the relevance of what you are learning in school. Sitting in a college lecture hall, you may feel a disconnection between the various aspects of your complex life—your academic life, your personal life, your work life, and your life as a member of your local community and of the larger society. Still, in an academic world of immediate concerns—of paper and problem-set deadlines, of tests to take and reading to do—this may not be a question in the forefront of your mind. Yet it is crucial.

What is the purpose of your education?

You have practical concerns. In a competitive society, you are probably hoping that your education, the skills you learn in school, will put you in a position to get a good job, one that will pay the bills and, at the same time, provide you with a sense of accomplishment and personal satisfaction.

*How will your education best prepare you for work in the world as well as life
in our society? On what basis will you measure success and personal satisfaction?*

Your involvement in a service-learning project is evidence that your university, your instructor, and key community members have recognized that both
you and society will benefit when your classroom learning is put to practice in
the world outside the university.

A BIT OF HISTORY: SERVICE-LEARNING
AND A DEMOCRATIC EDUCATION

Not long after the start of World War II, two great public intellectuals engaged in
a bitter war of words. The issue was the nature of a liberal education. One pro-
tagonist was Robert Maynard Hutchins, president of the University of Chicago, who
was on a crusade to transform the undergraduate curriculum around a canon of
"Great Books."... Hutchins claimed that the study of texts written by major West-
ern intellects would lead to a set of immutable first principles covering all aspects
of human life. On the other side, the renowned philosopher John Dewey argued
that this claim was dangerous nonsense—dangerous because the notion of fixed
truths requires a seal of authenticity from some human authority, which leads away
from democracy and towards fascism; and nonsense because purely intellectual
study should not be separated from practical study or from the great social problems confronting society. ...Study Aristotle, Plato, Aquinas, and the others, Dewey
urged, but recognize that contemporary learning from their writings requires the
application of their insights to contemporary issues....

At the time of the debate... leaders in higher education generally concurred
that Hutchins won the argument. The premise of service-learning ... is, however, that Dewey was right and Hutchins was wrong. Service-learning is the various
pedagogies that link community service and academic study so that each strength-
ens the other. ...Students learn best not by reading the Great Books in a closed
room but by opening the doors and windows of experience....

—*Thomas Ehrlich, "Foreword" to* Service-Learning in
Higher Education: Concepts and Practices. *Copyright © 1996 by Jossey-Bass Inc.,
Publishers. Reprinted by permission of John Wiley & Sons, Inc.*

Although John Dewey may have lost the crucial particulars of his argument in
1936 with Robert Maynard Hutchins, Dewey has contributed in a number of
extremely important ways to the evolution of educational practice in the United States.

Before the turn of the twentieth century, colleges in the United States saw
themselves as separate from the communities surrounding them and rejected
notions that they might have any role in contributing to the well-being of these
communities. Higher education was intended largely for the elite classes, and
students were seen as empty vessels to be filled with knowledge by those who
had been educated before them. The move toward liberal education began to challenge this isolation, although direct community involvement was slow to take hold.

Liberal education can be described as education that fosters the development of intellectual curiosity, critical intelligence, judgment, imagination, and sensitivity to the varieties of the human condition. It seeks to place students in the stream of history, to acquaint them with the methods of science, and to expose them to the power of the arts. At the same time it enhances in students an awareness of their own natures and motivations. In the United States its curriculum is often described as aimed at developing intellectual capacity through general knowledge, critical thinking, and problem solving. The way material is presented in liberal education programs is frequently cross-disciplinary, as one of its main concerns is to encourage students to make connections between branches of knowledge.

—Working definition for a conference on American-style liberal education in Budapest, 1996, from Nicholas H. Farnham, "Placing Liberal Education in the Service of Democracy."

Dewey was a firm believer in liberal education, but he had distinct and controversial views as to how a liberal education should be accomplished. For Dewey, there was much more than educational method at stake. He held that a liberal education was in fact crucial to the success of democracy because it encouraged both independent thought and social awareness. Furthermore, he argued, liberal education could best prepare citizens for life in a democracy if the educational process itself were democratic—that is, if students had an active role in shaping the content and direction of their own educations. Moreover, he was certain that students—indeed, all human beings—learn best by doing rather than by posing as the passive recipients of knowledge.

Clearly, Hutchins and many others disagreed. They had their own ideas about what a liberal education was, what its purpose and its best means of implementation might be, and their ideas largely held sway in twentieth-century education in the United States. Most of us have experienced the traditional paradigm of American education in which, contrary to Dewey's thoughts about a democratic education, the location of teaching and learning is fixed in the classroom; the object of teaching and learning is the textbook; and the authority in determining the content and direction of students' learning is placed exclusively in the hands of the teacher and the academic institution.

Education ... becomes an act of depositing, in which the students are the depositories and the teacher is the depositor. Instead of communicating, the teacher issues communiqués and makes deposits which the students patiently receive, memorize, and repeat. This is the "banking" concept of education, in which the scope of action allowed to the students extends only as far as receiving, filing, and storing the deposits.

—Paulo Freire, Pedagogy of the Oppressed

Most educators and social critics agree that with the great social movements and political upheavals of the 1960s, including the civil rights, women's, and antiwar movements, came fundamental challenges to mainstream thought about the nature, purpose, and direction of liberal education in the United States. There was a cry—especially from students themselves—for clearer political, social, and cultural relevance in American education.

Response to this demand for relevance has been awkward, sporadic, and slow to evolve, but changes in courses of study and educational methods are evident in American higher education today. The service-learning movement is one of these responses. John Dewey would no doubt have approved, since service-learning embraces many of his most fundamental educational philosophies.

The 1990 federal Commission on National and Community Service defines service-learning as an educational method

a. under which students learn and develop through active participation in carefully organized service experiences that meet actual community needs and that are coordinated in collaboration with the school and community;

b. that is integrated into the students' academic curriculum or provides structured time for the students to think, talk, or write about what the student did and saw during the actual service activity;

c. that provides students with opportunities to use newly acquired skills and knowledge in real-life situations in their own communities; and

d. that enhances what is taught in school by extending student learning beyond the classroom and into the community and helps to foster the development of a sense of caring for others.

—National and Community Service Trust Act of 1990

Although service-learning might seem like a new idea to you, in undertaking community work as part of your course work, you are enacting a long-standing educational philosophy. In service-learning, you will experience firsthand an approach to education in which the location of your learning will be the community as well as the classroom; in which you will learn by doing and reflecting upon your experience as well as by reading about the experiences and thoughts of intellectual authorities; and in which you will collaborate with diverse constituencies—staff and volunteers in nonprofit and public agencies, people whom these agencies serve, your instructor, and your peers—in a teaching and learning process.

SERVICE-LEARNING PARTNERSHIPS

The hyphen in service-learning is critical in that it symbolizes the symbiotic relationship between service and learning.

—Barbara Jacoby, "Service-Learning in Today's Higher Education" in Service-Learning in Higher Education: Concepts and Practices. *Copyright © 1996 by Jossey-Bass Inc., Publishers. Reprinted by permission of John Wiley & Sons, Inc.*

Who, exactly, benefits from service-learning partnerships?

You do.

Service-learning in a community setting will provide you with an opportunity to engage in real (as opposed to theoretical) problem solving, to apply in practical settings information and concepts that you have encountered in the classroom. You will not only learn how academic knowledge and skills apply in worlds outside the university, but you will also, in turn, learn how knowledge and skills at work in the community can enrich your academic study. You will probably find that your experiences in the community enliven your academic course work, lending it purpose and direction. Service-learning will offer you an important educational experience as well as an opportunity to contribute in concrete ways to a better society.

Nonprofit and public agencies do.

Students in service-learning placements generally work with community nonprofit organizations (which have been granted tax-exempt status and are funded primarily by donations and grants) or governmental agencies (which are funded by revenues from federal, state, or local taxes), not with for-profit businesses. In this respect, your service-learning placement may differ from other kinds of student internships with which you might be familiar. Internships promote students' learning in practical settings in many of the same ways that service-learning placements do, but since internships are often sponsored by businesses whose goal is to make a profit, they lack the community service aspect of the service-learning equation. Nonprofit organizations and governmental agencies are not concerned with profit-making; their goal is to serve the public interest and promote the welfare of communities in the most effective way possible. Through the service that you provide to a nonprofit or governmental agency in your service-learning placement, you will be one of many people, including paid staff and community volunteers, helping to promote that agency's work in the community. In a service-learning context you are not, strictly speaking, a volunteer; rather, in helping your agency to accomplish its work, you are exchanging your services for a learning opportunity and a chance to be of use.

The people whom nonprofit and public agencies serve do.

Although the agency with which you work in a service-learning partnership will benefit from your participation, ultimately, of course, the more important beneficiaries are the people whom your agency serves. Whatever kind of nonprofit or public agency you work with, and whatever kind of work you do with your agency, the objective is to better the lives of people in the community who rely on your agency's programs and services. Just as certainly as these people will benefit from the service that you provide, you will benefit from the opportunity to provide this service.

COMMUNITY AND COMMUNICATION:
LINKING SERVICE-LEARNING AND WRITING

Service-learning projects take many different forms and, depending on the course that sponsors them, can serve many—and often multiple—educational and practical purposes. In hands-on work in a sociology class, for instance, you might take on a service-learning project with a social service agency targeting at-risk youth, the elderly, the homeless, or immigrant populations. As a member of a biology class, you might work on a creek restoration project with a local environmental organization. In a business course, you and your classmates might help as advisors in a neighborhood program encouraging start-up businesses in impoverished areas. You and other students in nursing or in medicine might undertake projects at an AIDS clinic. In a computer science class, you might work in an after-school program that gives economically disadvantaged children access to computers and teaches them how to use them. The possibilities of partnership and collaboration are abundant and exciting.

Growing numbers of students are also enrolled in college writing courses with service-learning components. In these classes, students learn through both practical and academic community-based writing projects. Whether your assignment is to write a practical document for a local nonprofit agency or an essay related to your service-learning experience for class—or both—the primary course objective is that you learn something specific and worthwhile about writing.

Actually, whatever the specific course objective or academic discipline might be, in virtually any class with a service-learning component, writing is likely to be an important means by which you will document, reflect upon, analyze, extend, and share your thoughts and experiences.

KINDS OF WRITING IN SERVICE-LEARNING

The two most fundamental kinds of writing that you are likely to encounter as part of your service-learning experience are (1) practical writing for nonprofit or public agencies and the communities that they serve, and (2) academic writing about service-learning experiences or topics related to them for an academic audience. Because academic writing projects that are closely tied to students' community work tend to be so directly relevant to community issues and the work of community agencies, very often service-learning students share academic projects with readers in the community, even though their primary readers are their instructors.

Practical Writing

In a practical project, you will research and write a document that the agency you are working with will use to further its work in the community. The community agency, rather than your instructor, will probably assign the project to you, or work closely with you to develop it, since what you write will accord to agency needs. Although your community writing project will fulfill a need for the agency that you work with, it will also fulfill a writing requirement for your class.

In order to accomplish their work, public agencies and community nonprofits need researchers and writers to complete various writing tasks for educational, political, public relations, or fundraising purposes. These documents take numerous forms—for example, brochures, fact sheets, newsletter articles, press releases, reports, policy statements, proposals, fundraising appeals, and various kinds of writing for organizations' Web sites—and they target a wide variety of readers.

In practical writing, rhetorical purpose is directly related to practical purpose. For example, the primary rhetorical purpose of a practical document in a community setting might be to inform readers of agency programs, or to explain political candidates' positions on issues relevant to agency work, or to persuade readers to donate money to the agency or its causes. These rhetorical purposes—to inform, to explain, and to persuade—might be familiar to you, since the most essential purposes of academic writing, including reports, analyses, and arguments, are the same.

However, the audiences for public documents as compared to academic essays are quite different; just as the purposes of public documents are more varied and particular, so are their audiences. The readers of a fact sheet that you write could be elementary school children, and the purpose could be to instruct them about fire safety in the home. An article that you write might target adult readers of an environmental newsletter, and your purpose might be to explain the complex nuances of pending environmental legislation. Or a flyer that you write might address teen mothers, and its purpose might be to inform them about a series of parenting workshops and persuade them to sign up. You can see how your approach in writing each of these documents would differ vastly, depending on the specific audience and purpose of each.

The kinds of practical projects that you could undertake in service-learning vary not only according to audience and purpose, but also according to practical genre. *Genre* refers to a particular sort, kind, or category of writing. In the pragmatic types of writing that writers encounter in workplace or community settings, genre has to do with rhetorical purpose; it also relates to the form the document takes and the means by which it reaches its reader. For example, a reader might encounter what you write in the form of a brochure or flyer, or as an article printed in a newsletter or newspaper or posted on a Web site, or as a typed report for in-house use. The forms and formats in which readers encounter writing can be understood as *practical genres.* Therefore, as a community-based writer, you will conceive, research, organize, write, and format your practical project in careful consideration not only of audience and purpose, but also of the form and circumstances in which the reader will encounter your writing.

One source of students' great excitement, satisfaction, and apprehension is that in practical projects their writing will be distributed to a much broader readership than college writers are generally accustomed to, and it will have a real impact in the community. The writing that you produce for your organization, if it is good enough according to the agency's standards, may appear in print or be used in important in-house documents or programs. Clearly, much more than your grade on the project or in the course is at stake. Your community agency and your readers will be relying on your authority, your credibility, and the clarity and effectiveness of your writing to communicate something of real consequence to your readers. Your work will contribute in important ways to the goals of the agency you are working with and hence to the well-being of the community.

Academic Writing

A crucial part of the educational value of your service-learning experience will involve the ways in which you digest what you learn in the community and integrate it with what you learn in class. Although no doubt some of your reflection and analysis will occur in class discussions and informal conversations with other students, your agency mentor, and your instructor, much of it is likely to be articulated in writing.

Some of the writing that you do about your work in the community will probably be informal. For instance, your instructor may ask you to keep field notes, a log, or a journal in which to record what you experience, observe, or think during your community service or your reflections after the fact. Some instructors will want to read these informal writings while others will not. These types of assignments, although they may have no other audience than yourself, play an important role in your learning. When you record your observations and experiences, you will probably remember them more completely. Furthermore, since writing is a form of focused and articulate thinking, when you reflect upon the meaning of your experiences and attempt to explain your thoughts, even if just to yourself in informal writing, you will begin to make connections between experience and thought that you might not have made in less focused or more random thinking. Another important consideration is that often your informal writing will serve as the basis—the raw material—for later, more formal, academic writing.

The formal assignments that you encounter in a service-learning context may include various kinds of academic writing. For example, you may be asked to write an experiential or reflective essay in which you describe your experiences in the community and ponder their consequences. In expository writing, you may be asked to explain events, issues, policies, or procedures that you encounter in your community work and relate them to ideas and concepts that you learn in the classroom or through outside reading. You could be asked to articulate a written argument about issues and policies related to your agency's work or the community it serves. If you are asked to write a documented research paper on a topic related to your service-learning experience, you might integrate any or all of these forms of writing into your paper.

Since their topics will relate directly to your work in the community, these kinds of academic writing assignments might prove to be more interesting and compelling than many, more traditional academic assignments you have received. In fact, you may find that the direct relevance of community-based academic writing breathes new life into your engagement in academic discourse in general.

Both practical and academic writing assignments arising from service-learning work will ask you to engage tangible rather than abstract issues in the community at large, infusing your writing with purpose. This is *writing for real*.

REFLECTIVE QUESTIONS
FOR JOURNAL-WRITING AND CLASS DISCUSSION

1. Go back and look at the debate between Robert Maynard Hutchins and John Dewey as well as the quote from Paulo Friere. In light of their views, what edu-

cational philosophies seem to have been most widely enacted in your own educational experience?

2. Some students are required to take service-learning courses, others are placed at random in classes with service-learning components, and many elect to take service-learning courses. What compelled you to enroll in your current service-learning class? How might various motives for students' participation in service-learning affect their experience?

3. Most of us have had experience, in some form or another, as writers of practical documents. You may have written a memo in a work context, or you may have created a flyer to advertise a car for sale, or perhaps you have designed and written a personal Web page. Choose an example of a practical document that you have written. To what extent and in what ways did your understanding of your audience and purpose inform your approach in styling this document? Do you think your document was successful? How do you know? If you were to work on this document again, what adjustments might you make? Why would you make these changes?

4. In service-learning, much more is at stake than students' grades. Community agencies rely on students to contribute to the work they do in real and substantial ways, which may include hands-on work in the agency or in the community, or researching and writing practical documents for agency use. Do you feel confident in taking on these kinds of tasks and responsibilities? If you have concerns or apprehensions, what are they? What would help resolve them?

5. What do you think the most important consequence of your service-learning work will be?

CHAPTER 2

Writing in College
and Writing in the Community

In academic writing, the audience reads your paper because they have to or are deeply interested in the topic. This is not necessarily the case with community writing where your aim may be to attract the person's attention or persuade someone once you do have the precious few minutes of his or her attention.

—ANH BUI, FOURTH-YEAR STUDENT

This morning, you have an appointment with your writing instructor to discuss the polished draft of your research paper, which you have been working on for a full month. It feels like forever that you have been researching, planning, and drafting. This is your third draft! The paper has come a long way from the first draft where you were just beginning to work out your ideas on paper. A part of you wishes that you had chosen an easier topic—one that was more straightforward, less complicated; it would be nice to feel that you had found *the* correct answer in your paper. But if it had been an easy topic, the whole research and writing process might not have interested you as much as it has, and the essay certainly wouldn't have been worth three drafts. You know that you're close to finishing. In this draft you think that you have finally succeeded in communicating your ideas on your complex subject. You hope that the information and ideas you have drawn from your outside sources in research haven't overwhelmed your own ideas. You hope that your instructor accepts your argument as valid and interesting. You hope that the way you have expressed yourself will be not only clear, but also memorable.

Later today, you have an appointment with your agency mentor at the Disability Rights Center to discuss the two fact sheets that you have been working on for the agency. For one of them, you researched city laws concerning wheelchair accessibility in government buildings; this fact sheet targets people working in government offices so they can recommend renovations that will make their offices accessible to everyone, in compliance with the law. For the other fact sheet, you researched and wrote about minimum wage and workers' rights. This second fact sheet will be given to people who are mentally or psychologically challenged and are seeking employment. Although there has been little room for your personal voice in conveying information in these fact sheets, you had to be both careful and creative about the way that you presented the information, balancing concise content with appealing layout and graphics in order to capture and sustain your reader's interest and, above all, making sure that the information is accurate. After sending drafts via email to your agency mentor and revising according to her comments, you are excited to bring the finished products to her this afternoon. You hope that each of these fact sheets achieves its distinct purpose with each set of readers. You hope that you will make a difference in people's lives.

WHAT IS ACADEMIC WRITING?

Throughout your career as a student, regardless of your major, you produce written documents on a regular basis. In fact, during your time in college, writing for school may be the only kind of writing that you do in any ongoing way, with the exceptions of the private journal you may keep or the personal email correspondence you carry on. You may be doggedly familiar with the various kinds of writing that you work with at school. But you probably haven't thought of them, together, as a genre.

You may recall your high school or college teachers' use of the term "genre" to help categorize the work of important authors in fiction, drama, and poetry. So it is likely that you think of genre in connection with the literature that you have read in your English classes. The novels of Charles Dickens and Toni Morrison fall within the genre of fiction; William Shakespeare and Tennessee Williams's plays exist within the genre of drama; and writers from Walt Whitman to Adrienne Rich have worked in the genre of poetry.

Although when most people think of literary genres, they tend to think of fiction, drama, or poetry, the most widely encompassing literary genre is actually nonfiction prose. Included in this category are essays and book-length works that are *true to fact*. These works may be autobiographical or biographical—about or related to the author's own life and experiences or someone else's. They may be instructional, as in the textbooks you read for class. They may report, as news articles do. They may analyze and persuade, offering clear interpretations and arguments. Or they may employ a combination of these approaches.

More writers work in the genre of nonfiction prose than in any other genre, and the subgenres of nonfiction prose are so various and pervasive that they are often considered to be genres themselves. Journalism, for example, is generally considered to be a genre within the even larger genre of nonfiction prose, and what characterizes it as a genre has a lot to do with the purposes it serves and the forms it takes. Academic writing may be considered a genre as well, with many distinctive subgenres, and its functions and formats are determined by the academic context in which it exists.

When you write a lab report for a science class or a research paper for a humanities class, you probably don't think, "I have just worked within the genre of academic writing." But that *is* nonetheless what you have done. Students are not only readers of genres; they are also genre-based writers. As an academic writer, you are a writer of nonfiction prose, and you specialize in academic writing.

Academic writing comes with numerous variations and overlaps, but it definitely has a specialized purpose and tends to have certain characteristics of organization, tone, and style that we recognize as inherent. Andrea Lunsford and Robert Connors offer five characteristics of academic writing:

- *standard academic English*, characterized by the conventional use of grammar, spelling, punctuation, and mechanics;

- *reader-friendly organization*, which introduces and links ideas clearly so that readers can easily follow the text—or hypertext;

- *a clearly stated claim supported by various kinds of information*, including examples, statistics, personal experiences, anecdotes, and authority;

- *conventional academic formats*, among them lab reports, literature reviews, and research essays;

- *a conventional and easy-to-read font size and typeface.*
  —*The New St. Martin's Handbook*

Although these general characteristics apply to most academic writing, we could probably all think of notable exceptions, specific pieces of writing that we have encountered in an academic context that don't conform to all of these conventions, or that conform only to a degree. For example, one essay by Gloria Anzaldúa, "How to Tame a Wild Tongue," has been widely anthologized in college textbooks. Anzaldúa employs many of the conventions of academic writing that Lunsford and Connors cite, but certainly not all of them.

> "We're going to have to control your tongue," the dentist says, pulling out all the metal from my mouth. Silver bits plop and tinkle into the basin. My mouth is a motherlode.
>
> The dentist is cleaning out my roots. I get a whiff of the stench when I gasp. "I can't cap that tooth yet, you're still draining," he says.
>
> "We're going to have to do something about your tongue," I hear the anger rising in his voice. My tongue keeps pushing out the wads of cotton, pushing back the drills, the long thin needles. "I've never seen anything as strong or as stubborn," he says. And I think, how do you tame a wild tongue, train it to be quiet, how do you bridle and saddle it? How do you make it lie down?
>
> Who is to say that robbing a people of
> its language is less violent than war?
>
> —Ray Gwyn Smith, *Moorland Is Cold Country*, unpublished book.
>
> I remember being caught speaking Spanish at recess—that was good for three licks on the knuckles with a sharp ruler. I remember being sent to the corner of the classroom for "talking back" to the Anglo teacher when all I was trying to do was to tell her how to pronounce my name. "If you want to be American, speak 'American.' If you don't like it, go back to Mexico where you belong."

"I want you to speak English. *Pa' hallar buen trabajo tienes que saber hablar el inglés bien. Qué vale toda tu educación si todavía hablas inglés con un 'accent,'*" my mother would say, mortified that I spoke English like a Mexican. At Pan American University, I and all Chicano students were required to take two speech classes. Their purpose: to get rid of our accents.

Attacks on one's form of expression with the intent to censor are a violation of the First Amendment. *El Anglo con cara de inocente nost arrancó la lengua.* Wild tongues can't be tamed, they can only be cut out.

— Gloria Anzaldúa, "How to Tame a Wild Tongue"

This is how Anzaldúa begins her essay. Throughout the essay, as she does here, she embeds words, phrases, and sentences in Chicano Spanish within her English text—definitely not a hallmark of "standard academic English." The reason that she does this is perhaps apparent in the content of her opening: this is an essay that is itself about "standard English" and the extent to which Chicano people have been marginalized through their use of language. How could Anzaldúa have written this essay in any other way? In "How to Tame a Wild Tongue," Anzaldúa also draws on many of the other standard conventions of academic writing, including, for example, footnotes that document the outside sources she uses. The point is that in academic writing, writers often defy conventions when doing so serves their specific rhetorical purposes.

Established academic writers—for example, professional academics—probably feel freer to take these kinds of rhetorical risks in their writing than most student writers do. However, the freedom to defy convention is crucial in most academic writing *because* its overriding purpose is educational.

Purposes in Academic Writing

What purposes do a lab report and a humanities research paper serve? Practically speaking, of course, each fulfills a requirement in a particular class. Writing assignments make up a significant portion of your academic work, and completing them satisfactorily is essential to earning your academic degree. Presumably, though, there is more to your college education than simply meeting the requirements for graduation. For all its considerable variety, which depends upon the discipline of study and the specific class that inspires it, the writing that you do in your college courses serves a unique primary purpose: it furthers your education.

In some of your classes, you may have to memorize facts and figures that you repeat on an exam, and this is one way of learning about a particular topic. However, each time you are asked to study a topic in depth and articulate the results in writing, as in a science lab report or a humanities research essay, you are learning through a process of discovery, synthesis, and analysis. Chances are that because you wrote the lab report, you will remember the process and outcome of your biology experiment better than you will the specifics of a memorized biological process like the Krebs Cycle given to you on an exam. While you may remember specific dates in history for your mid-term, you are much more likely to remember the causes and effects of a significant historical event if you have researched and written about it at length. In these ways, academic writing offers you a way to be actively involved with your own learning process that passively memorizing material does not. Furthermore, it provides you with opportunities to develop your writing skills and to interact with the discourse surrounding your topic and the discipline in which you are working.

Although both a lab report and a research essay are examples of academic writing, they have distinctive forms and styles dependent upon disciplinary and rhetorical purpose. The logic of a lab report's organization and style allows other researchers to distinguish clearly between the *facts* of the experiment and the *interpretation* of the experiment's results. Therefore, the format of a lab report clearly distinguishes between the factual "Materials and Methods" and "Results" sections and the interpretive "Discussion" section. A research essay in the humanities, on the other hand, often grants the writer much more leeway for originality in both organization and style. Although your humanities research paper should conform to a reasonable degree to fundamental academic writing standards, your instructor will also appreciate originality in your thinking and your style of writing. A research paper in history would lose much of its impact and the argument would not be as compelling if it were put into the objective style of a lab report. We would get all of the facts about the topic, but the rhetorical purpose would be diminished. On the other hand, if a biology lab report were articulated in the style of a research paper in the humanities, the topic might be interesting, but the emphasis would likely be less on a set of intriguing *facts* than on an intriguing *idea*.

In academic writing, learning is key. As an academic writer, however, exactly what you learn, how you communicate what you learn, and to what end will vary—from discipline to discipline, class to class, and project to project.

Audiences in Academic Writing

Audiences for writing are defined by purposes of writing. Since the overriding purpose of academic writing is educational, academic audiences—especially for student writers—are generally severely limited. Usually, as an academic writer you are writing for an audience of one: your instructor, whose job it is to evaluate your progress and to help you improve your ability to express yourself clearly and effectively in the academic discipline in which you are working. In an academic setting, you know the measure of your success through your primary reader's reaction. In other words, your instructor will assign a grade or in some other way evaluate your work. In this way, academic writing tends to be impelled by academic authority (that is, your instructor's), and your success is measured to some extent subjectively, by the response of one reader, however well qualified that reader might be.

Many students find that they have a fairly uninspired and relatively stagnant relationship with their academic writing. Grades are certainly an incentive to perform well. So is your sincere wish to challenge and improve yourself as a writer. But these incentives may not always provide you with the concrete sense of purpose that you need to stretch and grow significantly in your development as a writer.

Many instructors are aware that this limited writer/audience dynamic often impedes students' progress as writers, and they take important steps to broaden students' audiences in order to motivate and legitimize their writing. You may have been in classes in which peer review or writing workshops open your audience to include other students as well as your instructor. Peer review and writing workshops are both wonderful ways to help you feel less isolated and more real in your writing process. They provide you with important opportunities to hear from more than one reader—and from more than one kind of reader—how your writing affects them; furthermore, you can improve your own writing skills significantly by observing the strengths and weaknesses of others' writing, especially your peers'. Still, because academic peer review and workshops take place in an academic setting, the fundamental frame of reference for your audience, although it may be an expanded audience, stays pretty much the same: your lab report and your research essay will generally be read and scrutinized only by members of the academic community.

WHAT IS COMMUNITY-BASED WRITING?

> No writer can participate in a discourse community without adopting the genres of that community.
>
> —*Anne Beaufort*, Writing the Organization's Way: The Life of Writers in the Workplace

Most community-based writing can be described as being primarily practical in nature or primarily academic in nature. This is not to say that academic writing serves no practical purpose—of course it does. It helps you to develop practical knowledge and skills. Nor are we saying that practical writing serves no academic purpose; clearly in a service-learning context it does. A practical writing project that you take on in the community is part of your course work and helps form your academic learning experience.

In referring to community-based writing that is "practical," we mean documents that serve a practical purpose for the people who need them (for example, staff at community agencies) and the people who read them (members of the communities that these agencies serve). In referring to community-based writing that is "academic," we mean student writing that arises from classroom assignments rather than from explicit agency or community needs, but in which students integrate what they learn in the community with what they learn in the classroom.

Community-based writing—whether it is practical or academic—is *writing for real*. It engages tangible issues, uniting thought and action, and it calls for new approaches to writing.

Practical Writing in a Service-Learning Context

If your service-learning placement calls upon you to write for a community agency, the practical writing genres that you encounter will probably be much less familiar to you, at least as a writer, than academic writing genres are. However, these practical genres are no doubt very familiar to you as a reader. Did you read a newspaper this week? How many fliers have you scanned lately on bulletin boards or in the mail? Did you read any advertisements today, on the side of a bus or in a magazine? News articles, fliers, and advertising copy adhere to different formats, but they are all practical writing genres.

Remember that *practical genre* refers to both the purpose of the writing and the form it takes. In practical writing, genre is directly determined by a writing's pragmatic purpose, and the success of writing in the community, whatever its format, depends positively on the writer's clear and unambiguous understanding both of the document's goals and of the identity, assumptions, and needs of its reader. Practical writing, as compared to academic writing, comes with an entirely different set of audience expectations, purposes, forms, and conventions. Unlike academic writing, when a practical document targeting a community-based audience fails, it tends to do so flatly and categorically because it *just doesn't work*; it is not credible, clear, or appealing to its reader. From a reader's point of view, you know why: you toss aside practical documents all the time when they seem irrelevant or are unappealing to you.

Even though any practical writing that you do for a nonprofit agency will eventually wind up in the academic classroom, your primary audience will not be academic readers; rather your readers will be people in the community, and writing for this audience will present you with new challenges. For example, you might work with an environmental group that needs you to construct a casually informative self-guided nature walk aimed at a general teenage to adult population.

STATION TEN: The abundance of pickleweed you may notice before you indicates that you are back in the high tide zone. This zone is the favorite habitat of the **Salt Marsh Harvest Mouse,** who, as you may remember, loves to feed on pickleweed. Listed as an endangered species, this mouse is found nowhere else in the world but in these saltwater marshes. Unfortunately, you probably will not see this mouse since not only are they rare, but they are also nocturnal animals. Weighing only as much as three copper pennies, the mouse has a relatively large appetite, feeding on plants and seeds. It is one of the few animals in the world that can drink the salty, brackish bay water. During high tides, the mouse moves out of the pickleweed zone and into the higher grasslands where it can hide in safety. However, as these grasslands have gradually been destroyed, the salt marsh harvest mouse has been left exposed to predators during high tides; thus, the mouse population has been decreasing rapidly.

—*Sharon Chen, first-year student writing for Baylands Nature Interpretive Center*

Or you could be asked to write a brochure for a rape crisis center that targets friends and family who want to help support a survivor of sexual assault.

**DO YOU KNOW SOMEONE
WHO IS A SURVIVOR
OF SEXUAL ASSAULT?**

Would you like to help,
but don't know how?

Let them know:

They WILL live.

TELL THEM:

They are not alone.
It was not their fault.
You believe them.
You support them.
They are strong.

BUT PLEASE:

Don't accuse them.
Don't disbelieve them.
Don't trivialize their pain.
Don't back away—survivors need you.
Don't tell them not to talk about it.
Don't tell them to forget about it.
Don't assume you know what is best for them.
Don't be afraid.

Survivors need time to heal.
Be there for them during that time.

*—Brochure by Terri Iwata and Nicole Louie,
first-year students writing for the mid-Peninsula YWCA Rape Crisis Center*

Or you could be asked to write to a corporate or public funder to request grant money for the agency with which you are working.

Dear Grants Management Board,

I am writing on behalf of the organization HAND (Helping After Neonatal Death) of the Peninsula. HAND's mission is to provide support for families in the North County, Mid County, South County, and Coastside

(continued)

(continued)

regions of the San Francisco Peninsula who have suffered the death of a child before, during, or after birth. These deaths result from miscarriages, genetic terminations of much-wanted babies, stillbirths, "preemies" too little to survive, neonatal deaths due to congenital abnormalities, or sudden infant death. The loss of the child is often very unexpected, and the parents who had anticipated such joy are suddenly faced with extreme grief, complicated by feelings of guilt, confusion, and isolation.

At the time when parents are most in need of support, they often do not find it. The bereaved couple no longer attends prenatal or parenting classes and is unable to find solace among other expectant couples and new parents. In our mobile society, many couples are far away from their relatives and have no extended family to offer them support. Additionally, for young couples, the loss of a baby may be their first exposure to a death in the family. They find themselves in a bewildering situation that they could never have foreseen—they are forced to choose a casket at a time when they expected to be choosing a crib.

HAND of the Peninsula is a community based nonprofit 501(c)3 organization. We have been offering support to bereaved parents since 1981, and we have established a very successful long-term record and an excellent reputation within the community. We are the only organization in the Peninsula offering these services....

A donation from the Foundation of $3500 to obtain this vital technology (or a donation of the technology itself if that is preferable) would greatly benefit the organization. With the help of the Foundation, HAND may more effectively maintain records, financial and otherwise, in order to continue providing education, aid and emotional support to the unfortunate families who have suffered the death of an infant.

—Adryon Burton, first-year student writing a grant letter
on behalf of Helping After Neonatal Death

Although all of these pieces of writing come under the heading of "practical genres," their content, tones, styles, conventions, and forms vary markedly, according to their audiences and purposes.

The self-guided nature walk does not need to come to the reader with an "emergency" sign on it. Presumably, the reader who takes this walk will want to learn more about local flora and fauna. She or he might be on a school field trip or sharing this special place with visiting family or friends. Whether the reader is an ardent nature lover or not, the tone of the self-guided tour is inviting; it has the feel of a casual Sunday afternoon. "Station Ten" provides the kind of information walkers can expect at each station along the way—in this case, about the Salt Marsh Harvest Mouse, its habitat and diet. There is a mini-argument about the Salt Marsh Harvest Mouse's classification as an endangered species; other stations provide other arguments about the importance of preservation of various plants and other animals found in the marshlands. This student consulted numerous biology and environmental texts in her research, but her tone here comes across as relaxed. This material about the Salt Marsh Harvest Mouse could have read like a lab report, but if it did, it would risk alienating the general public for whom it was written.

The brochure needs to offer supportive advice to people who are in a very delicate situation. In the excerpt from the brochure you will notice a lot of short commands—the do's and don'ts. But the tone remains hopeful, even upbeat, which helps encourage those in a position to support victims of sexual assault and rape. The "brochure style" grabs your attention as a reader with bolded fonts and font variations strategically placed. The information in the text is presented and articulated in a way that is easy to take in at a glance. Clearly, had the authors of this brochure taken an academic approach to styling this document, their readers would not have gotten the crucial information and encouragement they needed, appropriate to the circumstances of their reading.

As do the brochure and the self-guided walk, the grant letter exemplifies a "practical genre." (Please see the Appendix for the full text of the letter.) In the other two examples, the audience is composed of the public that the agency serves; readers could be many kinds of people. The audience for the grant letter, however, is quite different, and quite specific: the "Grants Management Board" of a foundation that awards nonprofit agencies grant money annually, to whom the agency is appealing for financial support. While appealing to the sentiments of individual board members, all professional people in a position of authority, the author must make the case that the agency's mission and the work it does in the community are in line with the views and goals of the foundation. In the excerpt above, and certainly in the full text of this grant letter that is included in the Appendix, you might begin to appreciate the very specific formula that grant-writing generally follows. Just as a science lab report is organized, articulated, and formatted in a particular way that accommodates the needs of its specialized audience and purpose, so is the grant proposal.

In spite of crucial differences, especially related to audience and purpose, between practical and academic discourse, the fundamental information resources and rhetorical devices that you use to discover, develop, and articulate information and ideas in each are perhaps surprisingly similar. Clear and effective writing shares many of the same characteristics in both discourse communities. What you learn about research, organization, analysis, and articulation in a community writing context can inform your approaches to these tasks in an academic context, and vice versa.

Academic Writing in a Service-Learning Context

One of the great advantages of academic writing in a service-learning context is that, since community-based academic writing topics are anchored in the real life and issues of the community, the writing is infused with a clearer relevance than most academic writing is. As a service-learner, when you connect your own observations and direct experience in the community with the broader, more theoretical perspectives often provided in academic courses, regardless of their discipline or specific subject, the results are often a poignant learning experience.

In her service-learning placement, Katie Cameron worked with the Arbor Free Clinic. When she was asked by her instructor to research and write an academic essay in which she took a stand on an issue directly related to her agency's work, Katie chose to write about the consequences of inadequate health insurance coverage that she witnessed firsthand through her work with the clinic.

The Arbor Free Clinic: Filling the Gaps between Medicaid

and Private Health Insurance

During the last decade, the rising cost of health insurance in the United States has forced many Americans to go without medical care. Those who cannot afford private health coverage can sometimes qualify for Medicaid, a government-provided health insurance. This program, however, limits the patient's choices of health care providers and also does not necessarily pay for all medical care. Between 1996 and 1998 an additional 2.6 million Americans became uninsured, increasing the total national number to 44.3 million ("Go Directly to Work" 9). Because of the insufficiencies in managed health care, the uninsured must rely on free health care providers such as the Arbor Free Clinic. Arbor volunteer Jeannie Chang voiced a common concern among ... local health nonprofit organizations, whether the work done is "creating or serving a need" (interview). The Arbor Free Clinic provides crucial primary health care services to the under-served communities in this county.

In the county, eighty-two percent of those without medical insurance are from working families; over half of those families are headed by one or more full-time, full-year employees (Brown 3). Federal medical insurance provides services for people whose incomes fall below the poverty line. However, nearly ninety percent of the uninsured working families in the county do not qualify for this government aid, as their incomes place them above the poverty line (Brown 4); they are uninsured because they either cannot afford health insurance or are not provided it from their employers. These people need subsidies to be able to afford private health insurance. It is in this "gap" between the federal poverty line and the ability to afford private health insurance that the majority of patients at the Arbor Free Clinic fall....

* * *

Though organizations like the Arbor Free Clinic serve the need for health care for many, institutional changes need to be made. The situation in our county is representative of the current state of health insurance provision across the state and the nation. In recent political elections a common issue was the expansion of government-provided health insurance to cover more Americans. Through legislation and new programs this goal can be achieved. The undeniable need for affordable health care must be met.

—Katie Cameron, first-year student

In these two opening paragraphs and the closing paragraph of her essay, it is evident that Katie is both knowledgeable and passionate about her academic topic. Katie's knowledge, as you can surmise, comes not only from secondary but also from primary sources; she has read a great deal about her topic, but she has also spoken to a volunteer at the clinic in order to learn more, firsthand, about her subject. Her passion comes from the fact that she worked at the Arbor Free Clinic as part of a service-learning experience in one of her classes. The people whom the clinic serves are not just statistical entities for her; she came to know them, and their problems, personally in her work at the clinic. This student's passion motivated her learning; therefore, both knowledge and passion motivate her writing. You will probably notice the same combination of authority and authenticy in Rebecca Freeland's community-based academic argument, "Grass or Astroturf: Environmental Groups and Corporate Sponsorship" (see the Appendix), a research essay that came from her work with Bay Area Action, a nonprofit environmental group.

Jessica Gray's research paper, "Landmines: Distant Killers," is another, more complex example of community-based academic writing. Jessica wrote this paper in connection with her service-learning work with a local chapter of the American Red Cross. As part of an earlier assignment for her class, she researched and wrote a brochure for the Red Cross on "Landmine Awareness" (included with her research paper in the Appendix). Jessica's agency was thrilled to have the brochure that Jessica produced, and it was quickly published and distributed. Her interest in the landmine topic compelled her further research and writing, and the result was "Landmines: Distant Killers," the research paper she wrote for class.

When Jessica finished her paper, she was as anxious to get a copy of it to her mentor at the Red Cross as she was to get a copy of it to her instructor, even though strictly speaking it was an academic rather than a practical community project.

The American Red Cross is now using her research paper as a resource from which it plans to generate further educational materials.

REFLECTIVE QUESTIONS
FOR JOURNAL-WRITING AND CLASS DISCUSSION

1. Estimate how many academic writing projects you undertake in one quarter or semester. Which type of academic writing are you most comfortable with? Why?

2. Have you written an essay for a class that you think might also make a good newspaper article or opinion-editorial piece? What qualities or characteristics of the essay make it workable in both contexts?

3. What kinds of practical writing possibilities excite you most? Why? For example, if you are excited about the prospect of working on Web writing, is it because you are comfortable with computers and technology, or is it because you are uncomfortable and want to get over your apprehensions and learn?

4. What do you think are the similarities and differences between academic and practical writing genres? For example, in what ways are academic arguments similar to and different from grant proposals?

CHAPTER 3

Collaborations

Just how deeply entrenched in our culture is the assumption that authorship is an individual enterprise? The absence of discussion of collaborative writing in our freshman composition texts and the well-established image of the writer as an isolated, often alienated, hero provide just two examples of this phenomenon.
—ANDREA LUNSFORD AND LISA EDE, *SINGULAR TEXTS/PLURAL AUTHORS*

How often have you felt alone as you worked on an essay for class, staring at the page or screen, wracking your brain over how to finish—or start? Surely we have all experienced the feeling of being the isolated writer, even when we are surrounded by other writers in a crowded library or computer lab. But perhaps there have also been times when you have experienced a feeling of community during your writing process, brainstorming with a friend, a classmate, a tutor, or a teacher about your writing ideas, troubleshooting problems together.

Thinking and writing collaboratively can enhance and extend everyone's learning experience significantly. Collaborations often result in more complex and dynamic finished products than isolated efforts can produce. But in calling writers out of isolation and into active engagement within a community of writers, collaborations also require a more complex and dynamic writing process.

COLLABORATIONS IN THE ACADEMIC COMMUNITY

In the academic community, the sciences have traditionally enjoyed a collaborative component to learning and work in the field. In science labs, students often conduct experiments together and frequently collaborate on writing up findings. However, in most writing-intensive courses, especially in the humanities, active encouragement of group work and collaboration on writing assignments has tended to be a relatively recent development.

If you have participated in peer review—in which students exchange their work and provide feedback on each other's writing—you have already experienced one of the forms of collaboration most widely practiced in academic communities. Peer review partnerships provide an opportunity for students to learn from each other, especially in reviewing drafts prior to revision. You benefit when you engage with and respond to the best advice of another writer, and you benefit when you apply to your own revision process the lessons you have learned as a peer editor. Many writers have experienced being too close to their writing to revise effectively; in fact, it is often easier for writers to recognize problems, and to propose solutions to them, in someone else's writing than in their own. After having given and received a peer review, you will probably return to your writing not only with new ideas about revision strategies and some sound editorial advice, but also with a new understanding of how your writing reads to others.

The advice of your peer reviewers will be helpful to you, just as your advice to them will aid them in their revisions. In peer review, you will see that your classmates experience the same sorts of writing challenges that you do. Since you are all involved in the same writing process and are sharing this experience with one another, you will feel less isolated and more a vital member of a community of writers. These sorts of collaborations help to build community within your academic setting.

In some courses, you may be asked to collaborate on writing projects with other students not just in revision, but from the beginning of the writing process. These full-fledged writing collaborations often pose a whole new set of problems and possibilities, especially in course contexts in which students must work hard to decide on their fundamental approach to the writing task.

In collaborating to write a lab report, you will find that you and your peers have a well-defined organizational structure to follow. You may pool your notes and observations, then sit down with the others in your group and piece together what you have learned, articulating your findings in a traditional lab report format. Since a scientific lab report follows a relatively straightforward format, many important writer's questions are already answered. In most other kinds of academic writing—in essays with extended or subtle arguments, for example—you are working without the aid of a standard writing formula or format. You and your fellow collaborators must answer several questions together in order for the piece to read smoothly and coherently:

- What tone do we strike?
- How do we introduce our topic?
- Where do we put the thesis?
- How do we organize our argument?
- How do we move toward a conclusion?

These are difficult enough questions for a solitary writer to resolve; in a collaborative project, writers must agree on a common approach to writing.

Students working in collaboration are able to take on more complicated and often more worthwhile writing projects than they would on their own, and ideally the collaborative process will escalate inquiry, learning, and acquisition of skills as students energize and inspire one another. In a collaborative project, you are not alone, even if you are individually responsible for parts of the whole writing task.

One of the purposes of a collaborative project in an academic context is to help you learn to work within a community of writers. A collaborative project moves all of you toward working out an egalitarian relationship. This is, of course, where collaborative projects are also challenging, because each person must do his or her part if the collaboration is to be a success. In collaboration, you have to work well with your peers if everyone is to have a good experience and if your project is to receive a positive evaluation.

Collaborative projects in the academic community help to prepare you for the world of work, where much is accomplished through collaborative effort. If a student collaboration fails in an academic setting, the consequences are a feeling of failure within your group and a poor grade. When collaborations fail in the workplace—or in a community setting—consequences can be much more serious. The stakes are much higher than a grade.

COLLABORATIONS IN A SERVICE-LEARNING CONTEXT

As difficult and demanding as it is, collaboration is a necessary part of service-learning, laying the groundwork for trust and community building that is inclusive and reciprocal.

—*Barbara Jacoby, "Service-Learning in Today's Higher Education" from* Service-Learning in Higher Education: Concepts and Practices. *Copyright © 1996 by Jossey-Bass Inc., Publishers. Reprinted by permission of John Wiley & Sons, Inc.*

In collaborations with instructors and peers in an academic setting, you participate in a process of community building, but only within that setting. Relationships between collaborators are limited by the collaborators' roles and relative authority. Although academic collaboration gives you and other students a real opportunity to extend and to share authority, you are still the student, and your instructor retains the traditional position as the final authority on your academic projects. Here is a graphic depiction of a traditional academic teaching and learning model, illustrating the generally inflexible and limiting relationship between the student writer and the teacher:

AN ACADEMIC WRITING MODEL

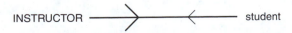

INSTRUCTOR ⟶ ⟵ student

Service-learning, on the other hand, opens up new teaching and learning possibilities, including new relationships between writers and readers, by adding community members to the equation and adjusting the relative authority of *all* members of the service-learning partnership—students, teachers, and community members alike. Your role as the student in a community-based writing scenario enhances your authority, just as it redefines your instructor's role, asking her or him to share authority with you and with your mentors in the community. In service-learning, you will take the community-building skills that you have learned in academic collaborations with instructors and peers "to the streets." The minute that you walk into the nonprofit agency that you will be working with, you begin to build a bridge between the academic community and the community at large.

A COMMUNITY-BASED WRITING MODEL

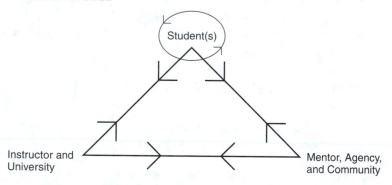

Community-based writing in the context of an academic class involves a three-way partnership among students, agency mentors, and instructors. In community-based writing, you will encounter unfamiliar roles and kinds of collaborations in working with your peers, your instructors, and your agency mentors.

Collaborations among Peers

The project was a collaboration between myself and my partner, Suzy. We divided the task so that we each covered half of the pertinent issues. For example, she researched the park's significance to visitors other than San Franciscans, and I focused on the significance that the AIDS Memorial Grove occupies within the immediate community. The collaborative part of the paper was difficult in that it required extra organization and we had to weave our parts together to make a unified whole. In the end, though, the partnership was quite fun.

—*Nik Reed, third-year student*

Community-based writing requires cooperation and collaborations of many kinds and on many levels. Before you even contact the nonprofit organization that you will be working with, the process of collaboration begins in the classroom among you and your peers.

If you have already experienced collaborating with peers in this or other classes, or if you have collaborated on a project with someone at work, you may come to community-based writing with an idea about how positive, challenging, and at times frustrating collaborations can be. If community-based writing offers you your first experience with collaboration, then you are in for a rich learning experience—just be prepared to communicate and to listen well.

> Having a partner gave me faith in the effectiveness of collaboration. Until this project, I had shied away from working in groups, afraid that I would end up doing all of the group's work myself. However, Mark and I were able to work as a team. With two people to brainstorm, writing was much more efficient. I gained confidence in my writing abilities; Mark and I motivated each other to work hard and to write well. Often, one of us was able to correctly phrase an idea that the other was thinking but could not clearly convey.
>
> —Katie Braden, first-year student

Perhaps it is obvious, but collaborative writing entails more than the production of a written document. If you work with one or more of your peers on a community-based writing project, you will find yourself collaborating in negotiating placements, logistics, and assignments, as well as in researching, planning, writing, revising, and editing these projects. In collaborating on a community-based writing project, the group should start out with an agreement that all work will be divided equally.

You will have to consider logistical questions together and early in the collaborative process:

- Who will make the initial contact with the agency mentor?
- How will you coordinate your school and work schedules so that you can attend at least the first meeting with the agency mentor as a group?
- How will you handle transportation to and from the agency?

You will want to make sure that you come up with a fair distribution of the logistical work involved in your service-learning project, and take care not to make assumptions about one member of your group being more or less responsible than any other.

In some practical writing scenarios, students will be offered various projects within the same agency. In this case, you will need to work as a group to figure out who will work on which project. Two of you might work together on a medi-um-sized project while the other three people in your group take on a different, larger project. Or each student might work on a smaller individual project.

If your service-learning placement involves a collaborative practical writing project, your peer collaboration will have just begun. Before you start research-ing, planning, and writing your project, you will need to make sure that every-one in the group understands the project in the same way. You will want to discuss the project in detail together:

- What type of document has the agency asked you to produce?
- What sections or parts will the document include?
- What format will the document take?

If your group agrees early on in its initial conception of the project, your collab-orative efforts will be better unified and much more efficient.

In most community-based writing projects, research in advance of writing will be essential. There are many ways in which a group can divide research equitably among its members. For example, one person might research background, while another could research one aspect of the specific topic, and another person could research another aspect. If your group's research entails interviews, these interviews might be divided equally among group members. It will be crucial, of course, that the group come together to share and to analyze what everyone has learned through his or her research.

In a collaborative writing project, whether the assignment is to produce a prac-tical document or an academic essay, you will probably not write together sentence by sentence, especially if there are more than two writers involved. This does not mean, however, that one person in the collaboration should carry more weight than another when it comes to writing; group members may contribute differently, but they should contribute equally to the writing.

As with research, there are many ways to plan and organize an effective writ-ing collaboration. If your group decides to divide the writing into sections, each group member may draft one section. When your group comes together to fuse these sections into a unified piece of writing, you may focus on collaboratively writing introductions, transitions, and conclusions. You will also want to focus on editing the whole so that voice, tone, and writing style are consistent. You will work together on formatting the document so that it suits its audience and purpose.

Or your group may decide to take a different approach to the collaborative writing process, one based on group members' relative strengths and weaknesses as organizers and writers, building on each other's strengths. For example, the per-son in your group who seems to have the best organizational skills might draft an outline of the project, after input from the entire group, and the person who is most confident in writing a draft might take the first stab at drafting the whole. After gathering input from all group members on the draft, a third group mem-ber, who may have strong editing skills, might undertake the first revision, to be reviewed, again, by the entire group. Whatever strategy you and your group members choose, bear in mind that while it is fine to capitalize on the individual strengths of each group member, no one member should contribute more or less than any other.

In addition to organizational and writing skills, members of your group may have other skills that could enhance your collaboration. For example, one person may have an eye for graphic design but no significant experience with computer graphics, while another has extensive experience with computer software but no particular talent for design. Put these qualities together, and you may have a winning combination when it comes to project presentation—and a terrific learning experience. Consider how contributions like these might feature in the overall collaboration.

Of course, peer review in a community writing context is yet another form of collaboration. Whatever the specific arrangement, remember that students who have placements in the same agency make wonderful peer reviewers. Even if you are not all working together on the same specific project, you know the context of each other's projects well. For that matter, students in your class whose service-learning placements are with other agencies can also serve as excellent peer reviewers; while they understand the course context, the fact that they are not specifically familiar with your placement and project may be an excellent test of your clarity.

Collaborations between Students and Agency Mentors

> It was good to collaborate because Mark [the agency mentor] gave me guidance when I needed it. Still, my actual writing happened independently, and I appreciated the freedom.
>
> —Anamaria Nino-Murcia, second-year student

Regardless of the distance—whether across the street or across town—between your college campus and the community in which you find your service-learning placement, it is in your power to help construct a bridge between the academic community and the community at large. Agency mentors look to you and other service-learning students as people with academic writing skills, knowledge, and resources that will benefit their agencies and their communities. Likewise, you will no doubt look to your mentor as an experienced person with practical, community-based skills, knowledge, and resources from which you can benefit.

A student who works with other students on a writing project for an agency may find herself participating in a collaborative group that includes students, the agency mentor, and perhaps other agency staff or volunteers. Many students enjoy the dynamic energy of these large working groups, although they can also feel unwieldy at times. In other situations, a student may be the only person in his or her class to work with a particular agency, or may be the only student at work on a particular project at an agency where other students may also be working. Even if your project does not call upon you to collaborate with your peers in research and writing, there will be lots of collaboration with your agency mentor and perhaps with other people at your agency. Many students like these one-on-one relationships with community agencies or with mentors. Jessica Gray's brochure, "Landmine Awareness" (see the Appendix), was created through her one-on-one collaboration with her agency mentor. Jessica did not work with a peer from her class, but she was certainly not alone in her writing process.

> The contributions of the students are very important to us at the Chapter. They are able to extend our efforts and I do believe that their exposure to the organization is valuable to them as well. I and WE appreciate the collaboration.
> —Noreen Dowling, agency mentor, Palo Alto Chapter of the American Red Cross

In your relationship with your agency and your agency mentor, you will have perspectives of both an "outsider" and an "insider," which will limit as well as enhance your participation. Some students work with agencies and in communities with which they are already familiar, and this helps them to feel like insiders. Most students, however, work with agencies and in communities with which they are not familiar, sometimes specifically to broaden their own horizons. Furthermore, although students' associations with their agencies may be intensive, they are usually temporary. These facts contribute to many students' feelings of being outsiders.

Generally speaking, the more closely you work with your agency, the more you will feel that you belong with the agency, contributing as an important member of that community. Depending on the agency and the work that it does, you might have to go through at least one training session or staff meeting before you participate in hands-on work or in a practical writing project. These kinds of activities will deepen your understanding of the agency, and they will help you feel more like an agency insider. Your work with your agency may also require an understanding of important community issues, and in order to develop this understanding, you may be asked to attend certain community events, such as town meetings. Your participation in community affairs not only constitutes important research—research that you will apply to your work in the community and your work in the classroom—but it also inspires feelings of community membership.

If you are writing about the community or your agency's work there, these town meetings would be critical to your understanding not only of community issues, but also of how community members feel about these issues. Without this understanding, you would be unable to articulate the agency's goals or to describe the kinds and levels of community participation, both of which are likely to be crucial considerations in a community-based academic writing assignment.

No one likes feeling like an outsider, and there is no reason, ultimately, that you shouldn't feel like an insider in your work with your agency and in the community. But remember, too, that having an outside perspective is not necessarily a bad thing. The fact that you might not be a permanent fixture at your agency or a permanent resident of the community may provide you with a fresh perspective that many agency mentors value highly. Students in service-learning placements often contribute terrific ideas in collaborating with agency mentors in hands-on or practical writing projects, ideas that might never have occurred to people who work more closely or consistently with the agency because they are too close to the problem.

Your outside perspective will also serve you well in your community-based academic writing, where it is quite often your job to analyze situations with some degree of detachment. As someone who has access to both inside and outside perspectives as a service-learner, you can enjoy the best of both worlds.

Collaborations among Students, Instructors, and Agency Mentors

In service-learning, you are both learner and teacher. You and your peers bring what you learn in the community back to the classroom, and your instructors' specific involvement with community agencies takes place primarily through your projects. Your instructor looks to you to bring into the classroom not only the experience of service-learning, but also the perspective of community-based writing.

Just as your role and authority as a student shifts in a service-learning scenario, the role and relative authority of your instructor will shift as well, in some interesting and sometimes unsettling ways, especially in service-learning situations that involve writing. For instance, in fulfilling a practical writing need in the community, you will have to accept the agency mentor rather than your instructor as the primary authority; your instructor's role shifts to that of facilitator or editor. Your mentor knows what sort of written document the agency needs. Brochures, for example, are a practical genre that looks nothing like most college writing. Your instructor can give you advice or help you edit as you compose and revise your brochure, but beyond that, as with many other practical writing projects, your instructor will need to get feedback from your agency mentor in order to know on what basis to evaluate your project.

In a community-based academic writing project, you will find that the primary authority will be your instructor. However, depending on the nature of this project, your agency mentor could also have an important role in terms of authority. For instance, if your community-based academic essay describes the agency and its mission, you will rely heavily on your agency mentor's input, particularly as a source of credible information. On the other hand, if your academic assignment focuses primarily on relating your experiences in working with a nonprofit agency to ideas encountered in course readings, class discussions, and academic research, your instructor will likely have primary authority.

Some instructors have relatively little ongoing contact with the agency mentors with whom their students work, preferring that the students serve as the link between the classroom and the community; others enjoy an active exchange of questions, comments, and points of view with agency mentors. Whatever your instructor's and your mentor's relationship may be, and whether you are writing for or writing about a community or a community agency, you and your work become the conduit through which the connections between the academic community and the community at large combine and flow.

COLLABORATIONS IN THE "CONTACT ZONE"

> I use this term ["contact zone"] to refer to social spaces where cultures meet, clash, and grapple with each other, often in contexts of highly asymmetrical relations of power, such as colonialism, slavery, or their aftermaths as they are lived out in many parts of the world today. Eventually I will use this term to reconsider the models of community that many of us rely on in teaching and theorizing and that are under challenge today.
>
> —Mary Louise Pratt, "Arts of the Contact Zone"

The term "contact zone" as it applies to both historical and contemporary encounters between cultures gives us an important framework in which to understand service-learning. In her essay "Arts of the Contact Zone," Mary Louise Pratt describes a letter, written in 1613 by an indigenous Andean of Inca descent, Felipe Guaman Poma de Ayala, to King Philip III of Spain. The letter, titled *The First New Chronicle and Good Government,* is twelve hundred pages long and is written in two languages, Spanish and Quechua, Guaman Poma's native tongue. In this remarkable letter, Guaman Poma attempted to communicate to King Philip an understanding of Inca and pre-Inca history and a vision, in Pratt's words, of "a Christian world with Andean rather than European peoples at the center of it." He further argues, Pratt tells us, that "the Spanish conquest ... should have been a peaceful encounter of equals with the potential for benefiting both, but for the mindless greed of the Spanish." The manuscript was discovered in the Danish Royal Archive in 1908, prior to which Quechua was not thought to have been a written language. In spite of Guaman Poma's impressive efforts, King Philip never received the letter. In fact, the letter was, from a European perspective, unreadable.

The fact that Guaman Poma's letter, which Pratt describes as being "truly a product of the contact zone," was considered incomprehensible is not just a matter of language; it goes deeper than that. Throughout history, colonial conquests have resulted in the domination of indigenous worldviews. With Europeans' "discovery" of the Americas and Africa, the religious beliefs, cultural practices, and social structures of innumerable native peoples were subsumed by the dominant culture's assumption of the veracity of its own beliefs and the innate superiority of its own customs and practices, including language. Guaman Poma's letter to King Philip was incomprehensible because it articulated a marginalized worldview.

Of course, most of us would maintain that considerable progress in cross-cultural understanding has been made since the *conquistadores'* conquests of Peru and Mexico or Columbus's "discovery" of "America." Today, the United States—and indeed much of the rest of the world—is increasingly multicultural, and in a multicultural society, contact zones abound, as Pratt defines them: "social spaces where cultures meet, clash, and grapple with each other." We enter contact zones in classrooms and workplaces; in restaurants and movie theatres; as we walk down the street, read the newspaper, and vote. Although there are far, far too many exceptions, there has been a general increase in multicultural awareness, a more prevalent attitude of mutual tolerance and respect for the differences that exist among us, and a mounting interest in learning from one another. We have also begun to understand "culture" in broader terms than in the past. Culture, to a large extent, is community, and the communities with which we each identify overlap and vary widely: they may be based on nationality, regional or ethnic identity, occupation, gender, religion, political affiliation, economic standing, or educational level, among many other possible factors. In service-learning, you will travel between and within various communities, moving in and out of various contact zones.

It is important to remember the crucial qualifier in Pratt's definition: contact zones are "social spaces where cultures meet, clash, and grapple with each other, *often in contexts of highly asymmetrical relations of power.*" Even where attitudes of mutual tolerance and good intentions prevail, contact zones still tend to exist within contexts of dominant and marginalized cultures. We can see evidence of this imbalance of power in various ways. For example, since most nonprofit organizations exist in order to fill a perceived void in information or services or in opposition to mainstream policies or practices, the nonprofit agency with which you work in your service-learning placement, as well as the constituency it serves, is likely to be marginalized in some respect. The organization's engagement with the dominant culture creates a powerful and dynamic contact zone, one in which change is possible.

These "highly asymmetrical relations of power" may also take more subtle or intimate forms that might be difficult for some students to recognize or accept. Dominant culture denotes privilege, and privilege can take many forms. In our society, privilege may be economic; it may have to do with race, ethnicity, gender, sexual preference, or disability. Education itself is a powerful form of privilege since it provides access to information and knowledge that are sanctioned by mainstream culture.

[An] important goal of service learning [is] the role that students can play as change agents…. For students to see themselves as agents of social change, often it is necessary to have contact with diverse individuals and groups whose struggles might in some way connect to the lives of the students.

—Robert A. Rhoads, *"Critical Multiculturalism and Service Learning"*

If through your service-learning placement you work in a community that is unfamiliar to you, you may at first feel that the agency mentor or the people aided by the organization are "other," entirely different from yourself. Even if you undertake work in a community that feels like home to you, you may feel some degree of separateness; if nothing else, your role as a student in higher education may to some extent set you apart. Over the course of your experience, however—as you and the people you encounter in the service-learning contact zone come to know each other through collaboration—you will begin to establish important connections, recognizing commonalities and learning through differences.

To offer a tangible example, let's say that you and two of your classmates have chosen to work with a soup kitchen near your college campus. The agency mentor with whom you are working has asked that the three of you create an issue of the agency's bimonthly newsletter. This will be a collaborative project with your student partners and your agency mentor. As a group, you decide that each student will write one article explaining a specific aspect of the agency's work. Your article will describe how and why people come to the agency for help as well as how and why other people volunteer their time there. You decide to help serve the evening meal so that you can interview both clients and volunteers.

Imagine your surprise when you hand two slices of bread to the woman who had asked you for spare change early that morning. She is one of the people you interview and will write about. In talking with her, you find that, although her immediate situation is quite different from yours, the two of you have quite a lot in common. She was born and raised in a town very near where you grew up. Like you, she has family who still live in the area—in her case, two grown children and several grandchildren. When the retail store she had worked in for nearly twenty years went out of business, she lost her job, then her apartment. She thought that she could live out of her car until she got another job, but without a home and a permanent address, a new job proved impossible to find. When the city impounded her car, she found herself on the streets. You realize the unthinkable: you too live paycheck to paycheck; it is not inconceivable that a similar sequence of events could happen to you.

After you talk together for a while, this homeless woman no longer seems so different from you. She has taught you that homelessness has a face and a personal story. You have taught her that there are people outside her immediate community who care to listen.

On a later visit to the soup kitchen, you will give your agency mentor the finished newsletter that your group has produced. Your mentor will distribute copies of the newsletter to community members, political leaders, potential funders, other agencies, and staff and clients at the soup kitchen, including the woman you interviewed. Your instructor will also ask that your group distribute the newsletter to the members of your class. Through these various contact zones, you will have brought the academic classroom to the community. At the same time, you will have brought the realities of the soup kitchen into your classroom, and hence, to the academy as a whole.

The ideal of the service-learning contact zone is that it be "a peaceful encounter of equals with the potential for benefiting both." Service-learning is, certainly, a tangible means by which the academic community attempts to address issues of social and cultural inequity. But it is also an acceptance of the proposition that all actors in service-learning partnerships have something to teach and something to learn, that knowledge, whatever its source, is valuable. Service-learning is all about collaboration, about engaging the potential for mutual learning and positive change that is inherent in any contact zone.

REFLECTIVE QUESTIONS
FOR JOURNAL-WRITING AND CLASS DISCUSSION

1. Have your experiences with collaboration in the past—in school, at work, or in the community—been positive or negative?

2. In what situations would you rather work alone on a piece of writing, and in what situations would you rather collaborate?

3. Look at the Academic Writing Model and the Community-Based Writing Model presented in this chapter. Describe the kind of relationship you think you would have with your instructor in each. Assuming that you have had more experience with the Academic Writing Model, what are some of your hopes and fears about the changes in this relationship depicted in the Community-Based Writing Model?

4. What do you expect of your relationship with your agency mentor?

5. What are some of the power dynamics related to authority that you see at work in the academic community? Compare these to some of the power dynamics you see at work in the community at large.

PART II

Ground Work: Understanding Your Service-Learning Project

CHAPTER 4

Understanding Service

We are all individuals, we are all members of communities. Once, these concepts were commonly presented as an either-or proposition. An earlier politics, born of the conditions of modernism, demanded an allegiance to one or the other poles of identity and commitment. But as strict modernist conceptions of social life have given way to more fluid post-modernist ways of understanding the world and our place in it, individuality and communality have become intertwined and interdependent. Our individual autonomy, we now understand, is enhanced and supported by the power of community membership. And the authenticity of our communities is measured by the health and independence of the individual lives they support.
—FREDERIC STOUT, THE PROGRAM ON URBAN STUDIES, STANFORD UNIVERSITY

Whether in a collective response to a national tragedy or through an individual calling, more and more of us find ways to incorporate community service into our lives. In the academic arena, student interest and enrollment in courses and programs that offer service-learning components are on the rise, and this enthusiasm about community service in education is encouraging. However generous and apparently straightforward the impulse to serve might be, though, *service* can actually be a rather complicated proposition.

Students will need to examine their preconceptions about the very nature of service before embarking on a service-learning project. Misguided assumptions can bias research and limit opportunities for learning. Likewise, your preconceptions about service, and even about what constitutes a community, will directly impact your relationships with the people you work with in the community. Beginning to understand assumptions that may underlie your idea of service and allowing any new understanding to affect the way in which you approach it can, in fact, be a large part of what you learn.

Before you begin your service-learning project, consider these fundamental questions:

- What does "community" mean to you?
- What comes to mind when you hear the term "service"?
- What do you understand *community service* to be?
- How do you envision your role in a service-learning scenario?

You might want to respond to these questions in informal writing, even if a service-learning log or journal is not required in your class. Your community-based learning experience will probably be a new one for you, and having a place to record your observations and ideas, a place to reflect honestly on your service-learning work, can help you keep track of and process this experience. Discuss your responses with other students in your class. You will probably find that people's definitions of service and community and their motivations to serve are varied and quite personal, although you will no doubt discover commonalities too.

THE POWER EQUATION IN "SERVICE"

To me, community service is an issue of servanthood. Being a servant is the only way for me to really make any important differences in the lives of people.
—A first-year student

The desire to serve is admirable. Consider, though, what motivates this desire. One of the assumptions that some students in service-learning make is that servers function only as active providers and those served function only as passive recipients. Furthermore, as service-learning scholar Lori Varlotta points out, the assumption is often that this "power relationship between server and servee is linear, monolithic, and static." It is not. Perhaps part of the misconception arises with the term "service." The fact that you can provide a service means that you do have something—perhaps something unique—that an individual or a group needs. Great! There is nothing wrong with this. However, you will limit your opportunities if you do not realize that you, too, will gain in tangible ways from community service.

If you ask dedicated volunteers or professionals in the nonprofit sector what motivates them to serve, you will no doubt get a range of specific answers, but people devoted to service will generally tell you that they get as much as they give in serving people in their communities. In service in general, and in service-learning in particular, the teaching/learning relationship should be reciprocal. You will give something to others, and they will give something to you, contributing to your concrete knowledge and experience, to your learning process, and to your development as a human being. Difficulties arise when you go into service thinking that you are merely giving and those you are serving are merely taking. This attitude assumes that the one serving holds all of the power while the one served has none.

> Community service is volunteering to help people who have some community bond with me. I would not call building houses in Costa Rica community service even though it is a good deed for a community; it is not done to a group that shares more than the most basic bond to me. But helping people who live nearby, who share the same land, laws, government, and weather moves me to have a concern for their well-being; that is community service. In a sense, it is helping myself by improving the general situation around me, which affects me in so many visible and not visible ways.
>
> *–A first-year student*

This student defines community service as volunteering to help people in his local community, rather than communities removed from him. In and of itself, there is certainly nothing wrong with wanting to serve your home community; the wish to do so makes perfect sense. However, if we understand community service only in terms of a narrow definition of community, excluding anyone who falls outside of that particular realm, we find ourselves sliding down a slippery slope.

In the latter part of the twentieth century, many activists have urged people to "Think globally; act locally." Through slogans like this, we have become more and more aware that our everyday activities *do* affect others around the world. For instance, we know that there is a direct link between fast-food hamburger consumption in the United States and the depletion of the Amazon rain forest. We do live in the "global community," but unfortunately the student quoted above envisions a distant community not only as one that is geographically removed from his but also as one whose members do not share his values.

When considered on an even more local level, does this imply that people who live on the other side of town or who may differ from us racially, ethnically, socioeconomically, spiritually, or culturally are not part of our community and, therefore, not deserving of our service? To define community so narrowly severely curtails both community service and learning opportunities. The student quoted above does not see community service as a way of learning about people who are different from him, nor does he seem to appreciate that this new knowledge might help him understand himself better. Instead, it appears that his sense of community service is tied up with his own desire to be comfortable in his individual world. This is a limited and self-serving motivation for community service.

> Community service is volunteer work done for a deserving group of people. Though these people live in close proximity to you, you would most likely not get to know them if it weren't for your affiliation with the service organization.
>
> *—A first-year student*

One of the more problematic aspects of community service has to do with one's power to decide who is "deserving" of service, and on what basis they are deserving. The idea that some people deserve your help while others do not demonstrates very directly the way that power can come into play in community-service situations. What does this student mean by "deserving"? Why does she make an assumption that there is an authority (possibly herself) who determines criteria for who is and who is not deserving of help? The idea that the server will always remain in the position to give and that the servee will never move beyond the role of the one who needs to take sets up a perpetual power imbalance in the relationship between the student in community service and the agency and the people it serves. Even though the people "live in close proximity" to her, the student acknowledges that she would not get to know them if they were not affiliated with the service agency. Precisely *because* the people working at the agency and the people the agency helps fall into her equation of those who are "deserving," she distances herself from an entire group of people in her home community.

Here are two basic considerations to help you think about, work through, and get beyond this power dynamic:

Begin by writing down your assumptions. Acknowledging and understanding your preconceived notions about service, as the students cited above did, are the first steps in rethinking and changing them. Even if you are going to be working in your "home" community, you may still have some ideas that need to be examined before you actually engage in your community work.

Remember that your community service work is service-learning. Because the work that you will be doing is part of a class (part of a learning process), you need to remember that your time in the community working with the nonprofit agency should, as Lori Varlotta reminds us, "accentuate reciprocity—a 'doing with' instead of a 'doing for'—that depends on constant and meaningful exchange between those serving and those being served." You learn from your agency mentor as well as the people in the community who utilize the agency's services. At the same time, they also learn from you.

Community service means reaching out to other people and acknowledging that your position in the world is not the only one. You can make a positive difference in the lives of others if you put in a little effort.

—Emily Dawson, first-year student

Emily makes a critical point: her position in the world is not the only one. Whether you will work in a community with which you are familiar or unfamiliar, keep in mind that communities comprise individuals who, in one way or another, have a position in the world that is dissimilar to yours—intrinsically no better or worse, just different.

Some differences may seem more obvious than others, which is why you will want to look in depth beyond your assumptions. Imagine that you are an African American man in your senior year at an Ivy League university. For your final project in a business class, you choose to work with a nonprofit organization that teaches business skills to recent Eastern European immigrants. The most obvious differences between you and the people you are serving involve race, ethnicity, nationality, culture, and educational privilege or status. Your position in coming from a prestigious American university is clearly different from the position of the people coming to the agency to learn business skills. In understanding the students in the agency's program, you will have to be careful not to make blanket assumptions. Although they have their enrollment in the agency's business workshop in common, these individuals come from a variety of backgrounds and positions in the countries they left. Some may have no business experience—in fact, this is your assumption. However, some may have owned successful businesses in their home countries and are anxious to learn ways of conducting business in the United States, in which case they will have more hands-on business experience than you do. It is important to acknowledge and respect these individual differences, both between you and the people you work with in the community, and among the individuals you work with there.

Each person involved in a community service-learning project meets in the contact zone that we described in Chapter 3. Within this space you, the agency mentor, and the people in the larger community whom the agency serves each become the "server" and the "servee" at different times during the relationship. If you are working for a pre-college outreach program for teenagers in low-income communities, you might learn about the very real ways that socioeconomic privilege and disadvantage work in the United States. You will probably learn more firsthand from your teachers in this situation—the agency mentor and the agency's clients—than you would listening to a lecture in your Economics 101 class. In this way, you learn from your community agency and the people it serves. If part of your work at the agency is to create an agency Web site that will feature information and news articles, during this process you might teach various people at the agency how to create a Web site. Here, you become the teacher.

Regardless of the length of your time with the agency—whether you work there for only a quarter or a semester, for the entire academic year, or perhaps even longer—you will most likely find that the give and take fluctuates. Whatever you thought your role was going to be when you embarked on this adventure, it will invariably involve more roles than one, and these roles will vary.

NOBLESSE OBLIGE

> You perform community service because you feel fortunate and able to help out someone else.
>
> *—A first-year student*
>
> Recognizing and overcoming *noblesse oblige*—the obligation assumed by those in "privileged" positions to behave nobly toward those judged less fortunate—should be an ongoing concern for teachers and administrators of service-learning programs.
>
> *—B. Cole Bennett, "The Best of Intentions: Service-Learning and* Noblesse Oblige *at a Christian College"*

Assuming that you had a choice in the matter (and not all students do), part of the reason that you have taken a class with a service-learning component is presumably because you want to help make the world a better place. You see yourself as someone with the power to make change—and you are! However, it is important to consider why and how you will go about doing this.

Some students feel that they are going into the community, undertaking their work with a community agency, to "save the day." This attitude may come from feeling empowered by a fortunate situation, which is the case with the student quoted above. Because she feels fortunate, she wants to help those who are "less fortunate." She sees herself as the server and the people with whom the agency works as the servees; in her mind, she becomes the benevolent giver to people who are in a position only to take. An imbalanced power dynamic is at work.

One of the more problematic implications of *noblesse oblige* is the idea that some people are inherently privileged, while others are inherently underprivileged. There are several versions of *noblesse oblige,* and they have to do with what might constitute "advantage" or "privilege": socioeconomic status, level of education, race and ethnicity, and physical ability, to name only a few.

Educator Ellen Cushman has noted that some students in service-learning situations see people whom the nonprofit agency assists as "passive victims who have created their own fates." An attitude of *noblesse oblige* often employs a patronizing "blame the victim" mentality. For instance, imagine a student interested in pursuing a medical career who chooses to work with an organization that helps physically challenged people live independently. When the student interviews one of the clients—a quadriplegic survivor of a diving accident—he cannot help but think about how the woman sitting across from him in the wheelchair should have known better than to dive into a murky lake. In another situation, an Anglo student from an upper-middle-class suburban neighborhood chooses to work in an inner-city after-school program that serves predominantly African American and Latino/Latina middle school students who live in a city housing project. Here, the student recognizes only differences: she is older; the students are from different ethnic backgrounds; they are living in low-income city housing. She views the kids' parents as people who lack the motivation to pull themselves up by the bootstraps and work themselves out of poverty. She assumes that there is some magic pathway out of the cycle of poverty and that these families have failed because they have not found the correct route. The assumptions of *noblesse oblige* combined with often deeply buried attitudes of blaming the victim serve to distance service-learners from the people whom they are trying to help.

Even if you are working in your home community, there are still numerous ways in which you may find yourself distanced from the agency and the people who go there for help if you adopt an attitude of *noblesse oblige.* For example, imagine yourself returning to your old inner-city neighborhood to work with a late-night basketball league. In your time away from your old home, one of the many changes you embraced was becoming an Evangelical Christian. You may see yourself in a position to give love and support unconditionally both through your religious beliefs and your connections to your home community. But if part of your personal mission is to impose your religious beliefs on the children with whom you are working, despite your best intentions and regardless of the fact that you are working in your home community, you will have distanced yourself from them by setting up a power imbalance: you see yourself as someone who knows what is best for them.

When you distance yourself from the community-service agency and from the people in the community, you miss out on a vital part of your education in the service-learning scenario. You are not the only person in the situation who has the power to give. Whether you are creating a written document for your agency or participating in a hands-on project, you are gaining knowledge about the agency, the community, and issues that impact us all. Your interactions with people whom you see as different from you are opportunities for all concerned to learn about different lives, differing points of view, and the ways in which we each contribute to the complex culture.

One of the first steps away from *noblesse oblige* is to become aware of it. Self-reflective journal writing will help you think about the assumptions that you may have about your role in community service. Your journal becomes a safe place to explore your thoughts without having to worry about being criticized for your ideas and opinions or how you express them. Think about the different people that you have met or will meet, and consider these questions when you sit down to write in your journal:

- In what ways might you consciously or unconsciously distance yourself from the agency mentor and the clients?
- What will you learn from them?
- What will they learn from you?

Service-learning is learning for all who are part of the process. The more that all parties involved remember that they are each teachers and students, the richer the service-learning scenario will be.

OUTSIDER OR INSIDER?

> As a freshman coming from the Midwest to California, I thought that working in a community-service group would give me a good idea of what sort of social issues exist in this area and how they differ from the Chicagoland area.
>
> —Cindy Yuchin Lin, third-year student
>
> Since I am from the area, I was able to continue an already established relationship with Breast Cancer Action while attending college. I had volunteered with BCA once a week for five hours during the previous summer, so I had a good connection with their resources and staff members.
>
> —Megan Vanneman, second-year student

The ways that you identify yourself as an "outsider," "insider," or some combination of both will play a major part in helping you formulate and understand your role in the community in general as well as in the community agency in particular. You might initially see yourself as an outsider in the community in which you are working. On the other hand, you could work within your home community or one that feels like home because you strongly identify with the people there; this makes you feel like an insider.

Imagine that you are a young woman from Singapore who has arrived in the United States just a week prior to the beginning of school at the large midwestern state university that you have chosen to attend. Not only are you challenged in negotiating all of the various aspects of social culture shock (meeting your roommate from Chicago who has pink hair and listens to punk rock, for example, and adjusting to the idea of eating "chicken fried steak") but of academic culture shock as well (finding your way around a huge campus and attempting to understand all of the course requirements and syllabi in English, which is not your first language). Imagine, then, that a requirement for your writing class is to travel off-campus to work with a nonprofit agency in the community to produce a monthly newsletter. You would probably feel like the epitome of an outsider.

Now imagine that you are a young man attending a small college in your hometown on the East Coast. For your service-learning project, you have chosen to work with an organization that focuses on supporting children with leukemia. You are familiar with the organization because you volunteered there during high school. In fact, you are intimately familiar with the disease because your younger brother has leukemia, which is a large part of your reason for choosing this organization. Your home community, your academic community, and your agency community all feel like home to you, and you feel like an insider.

Even outsider/insider scenarios that appear extreme may not be. If you are like most people and have some degree of choice in the matter, you will probably work with a particular agency because you have an affinity for the type of work that it does or the type of community that it serves. For example, the young woman from Singapore may decide to work with an agency that provides support to Asian immigrant communities. The affinity that she feels for the agency's work and the people whom the agency serves will help her feel more like an insider, even early on. This feeling of connection will deepen as she becomes more specifically involved in her agency's work and with the community. On the other hand, if you work with an agency or a community that you know or that feels quite familiar to you, you may discover as your work there develops that you are more of an outsider than you thought you would be. Perhaps the young man with a service-learning project at a known agency in his home community will find, once he is more deeply involved in agency politics, that his ideas about how to best serve people with leukemia differ radically from those of the executive director. It's important not to make too many assumptions about outsider or insider status.

Assumptions that some insiders make based on their own experience can be particularly misleading, especially if they act without examining these assumptions. Imagine that you are a Chicana in your second year at a large university in the city where you grew up in the desert Southwest. For the service-learning component of your education class, you choose to work with children at the bilingual elementary school where you went as a child. Through culture and education, you have a lot in common with these children, and you identify closely with them: it has only been ten years since you lived in this neighborhood and were a student at this school, and you are bilingual in Spanish and English, as your young students are aspiring to become. The most obvious difference between you and your students is that you are older and successfully pursuing a college degree. You are well aware that this fact, along with the background you and your students share, is likely to ensure that you will be a role model for them. Here, in spite of the obvious age and achievement differences, similarities seem to dominate.

However, even in this home community scenario, there are important differences to consider. In the decade since you lived in this neighborhood and were a student at this school, the demographics have changed. No longer are 80% of the student body in this school Chicano/Chicana, like you, with the remaining 20% almost entirely Caucasian. Now the student body is much more diverse: roughly 40% are Chicano/Chicana, 20% are Latino/Latina from Central or South America, 20% are East Asian, 10% are African American, and 10% are Caucasian. In terms of specific ethnicity, you were in the majority population when you went to school here, and now other Chicano/Chicana students are in the minority population. You will have to work harder than you thought, and avoid assumptions based on your own experience, in helping the students become bilingual in Spanish and English.

To some degree, each of you will embody the position of outsider *and* insider in a community-service context. The mere fact that you are in a college may set you apart from many community agencies and many of the communities that they serve, because higher education is still seen as a privilege in this country. Even if your school is located in the middle of a city or town, the campus is often a community apart from the greater community. This sense of separation can cause problems in a community service-learning scenario. It is important to keep in mind these often fluctuating and problematic ideas of outsider and insider when you are thinking about your role in the community-service context.

GIVING BACK

> Community service is a way that one (myself) can give back to a world that has privileged him so much.
>
> *—Kent Anderson, first-year student*

The desire to give back is one of the major reasons that people decide to participate in community service. We all have very personal definitions of what giving back means. Above, Kent talks about giving back not to a specific community but rather to a more generalized, perhaps global, community. For many of you, however, the notion of giving back will be related to a very specific home community, or variations of what you have come to understand as your home community.

> I vividly remember my first day working with the Upward Bound program, when I introduced myself to the parents of the Upward Bound students. As I spoke about myself and my background, I saw the hope in their eyes as they thought of their children's possibilities. They saw a young Latino man who came from a background similar to that of their children and who had "made it," to a certain degree. They looked at the Upward Bound staff as if we held the key to their children's success; it was an overwhelming feeling to know that people entrusted you with their children's futures and believed that you could help them be successful both in school and in life.
>
> *—Steven Lopez, fourth-year student, "Building Bridges"*

In the example above, Steven and the Upward Bound students are not technically from the same community. However, because he is Latino and from a socioeconomic background similar to theirs, the parents of the teenagers embrace him. He symbolizes the possibility of their own children's success. For him, there is a need to give back to a community that stood behind him, and although it is not his home community in a geographic sense, he adopts them.

Although giving back may seem completely positive, it issues its own kinds of challenges. Whether he likes it or not, Steven has been handed a powerful position because, somehow, he must have "The Key." What kind of pressure must he feel with this responsibility? Will it be hard for him to draw boundaries when he has given all that he feels he can give? Does he have expectations of the parents and students that they may not be able to meet? Does he push the students hard enough? Does he push them too hard? All of these questions reflect issues of power in the service-learning contact zone—even in the act of giving back to one's home community.

Giving back involves both give and take. In supporting the work of agencies in communities familiar and unfamiliar, service-learners *give* their time, energy, skills, and talents to those in need of them. They answer hotlines; they construct wheelchair-accessible trails; they teach adults to read; they develop new agency programs. In practical research and writing projects, they produce agency brochures, newsletter articles, grant proposals, Web sites, and educational displays.

In working through the challenges that service invariably poses, service-learners also *take* in the powerful lessons—intellectual, practical, and personal—that community-based learning provides. Experience brings academic concepts to life in ways that even the most engaging textbook could not. Practical experience reveals new ways of knowing and new approaches to writing. Your work as a service-learner will help you develop a deeper understanding of yourself and the ways in which you can contribute actively—to your community and to your education. In this way, give and take will come full circle.

REFLECTIVE QUESTIONS
FOR JOURNAL-WRITING AND CLASS DISCUSSION

1. Do you think that acting locally helps the global community? If so, how and why? If not, why?

2. Do you think that truly selfless motives for service exist? Think of examples that support your answer.

3. We mentioned socioeconomics, race, ethnicity, education, and physical ability as areas in which people might be viewed as either "privileged" or "disadvantaged." Can you think of others? How might assumptions of *noblesse oblige* be expressed in community-service scenarios involving any of these bases of so-called privilege and disadvantage? Try role-playing some of these scenarios in class.

4. Describe a situation in which you felt like an insider. Among many possibilities, this could be a situation you have encountered as a member of a sports team, sorority or fraternity, church, or school group, or in a particular location in your neighborhood. In attitudes and behavior, how did you and other insiders in this situation relate to outsiders? You might want to role-play some of these situations in class. What do you think accounts for insider attitudes and behaviors?

5. Describe a situation in which you felt like an outsider. This could mean that you were the only person present of a particular ethnicity, religious affiliation, socioeconomic position, level of physical ability, gender, age, or sexual orientation, or who spoke a particular language. How did it feel to be on the outside? Did your feelings persist, or were they addressed? Consider role-playing some of these scenarios in class.

6. Many people, especially people who identify with these groups, hold a very strong preference for the following terms in reference to race, ethnicity, sexual orientation, or physical and mental ability:

   - Asian (or specific nationality such as Chinese, Japanese, Korean, Vietnamese, Filipino)
   - African American
   - Latino or Latina; Chicano or Chicana (for people of Mexican descent)
   - Native American
   - Gay; lesbian; bisexual; transgendered person
   - Physically challenged
   - Mentally challenged

   Do you use these terms? Do you think that there are acceptable alternatives to them? What does your use of these terms, and your feelings about using them, have to do with your position as an insider or an outsider in any of these groups?

TROUBLESHOOTING

WHAT IF...

you did not have much choice in signing up for a class that required community service and you feel like a "forced volunteer"?

TRY TO...

take a different class if you are dead set against performing community service as part of your course work and if service-learning is elective, not required, at your school. A student's resentments about community service in education can be a recipe for disaster for everyone involved in a service-learning partnership. Agency mentors can feel it when a student comes in with a bad attitude, and this can make completion of a successful project nearly impossible.

keep an open mind, especially if service-learning or community service is required at your school. If you have concerns about "forced volunteerism," discuss these feelings with other students and your instructor openly in class.

focus on the positive. If, in spite of concerns, you are inclined to give service-learning a try, remember that this experience is part of your overall college education. Although you may not be particularly interested in working with a nonprofit agency, try to see this experience as a unique educational opportunity. You will no doubt learn something worthwhile—and quite possibly something completely unexpected. Remember, too, that your service-learning work will be a valuable addition to your résumé; because it demonstrates that you have put your knowledge and skills to work in the "real" world, service-learning experience will very likely impress potential employers.

WHAT IF...

working in the service-learning contact zone raises all sorts of uncomfortable and sometimes seemingly ridiculous issues about political correctness?

TRY TO...

develop a sensitivity to what underlies issues of "political correctness," but try not to let the pressure to be politically correct overwhelm you with either self-consciousness or cynicism. We understand political correctness to be a set of responses assumed to be liberal, automatic, and unexamined, to politically, culturally, or socially charged situations. The rhetoric attached to political correctness is often interpreted as self-conscious, awkward, and even silly. There is a lot of cynical talk about people (especially in academic communities) being too "P.C.," but political correctness does have a purpose, for example, when it comes to the ways in which groups and individuals wish to be identified. Identifying people according to their wishes is a sign of respect.

WHAT IF...

you hear people in a certain group refer to themselves in ways that you consider completely inappropriate?

TRY TO...

distinguish between insider and outsider identifications. It might feel a bit confusing if, for example, you work with injured veterans and you hear them refer to each other as "gimps." Coming from someone who is not physically challenged, the term would be incredibly insensitive. On the other hand, the term "physically challenged" might feel awkward and overly formal to you. If one of the veterans with whom you work laughs and asks you to just go ahead and say "handicapped," use the term if you are comfortable with it. The important thing to do is to listen: *how do people within a certain group of which you are not a member refer to themselves when speaking to you?*

CHAPTER 5

Making Connections

A minority of students really make the effort to get involved off-campus.
It is very easy to get wrapped up in academic/social life and forget about the rest
of the world that (truly) isn't that far away at all.
—ANAMARIA NINO-MURCIA, SECOND-YEAR STUDENT

Students' relationships with and attitudes about the communities in which their schools are located range widely. If you go to college in your hometown or your own neighborhood, you will feel differently about that community than would a classmate whose home community is far away. If you live on campus, "downtown" might feel like another world, whereas if you commute to school, it is your campus that may feel distant. Schools' institutional relationships with surrounding communities also vary. The degree to which a school is involved or uninvolved in community affairs will depend on what kind of school it is, what its relationship with the community has historically been, and to what extent it sees its place in the community as a matter of mere location or its role as participatory in community affairs.

A smaller city college is apt to draw many of its students from the very community that serves as its home; therefore, both the students and the school are likely to recognize their roles as invested and active community members. On the other hand, a private liberal arts college will probably draw most of its students from areas farther away; therefore, both students and the institution might find it harder to identify with the home community. This poses a challenge to attain and maintain active community involvement. Many large universities that attract students from both far and near are so big that they function like small, self-contained cities. Even students from the immediate area may feel somewhat isolated from the home community when they enter the university setting.

Your own college may have a relatively engaged relationship with its home community, or it may not. You yourself may very closely identify with the community in which you attend school, or you may not. However, whether or not it is deserved, universities have a fairly widespread reputation as being "Ivory Towers," detached from community life and the real issues and problems that exist "out there." Even though a college education is widely valued, people involved in higher education are often stereotyped as being out of touch with life's realities, and you often hear allusions to an uncomfortable division between "town" and "gown."

These assumptions and stereotypes are understandable if you consider the history of education in the United States (see Chapter 1). In the past, people viewed a college education as an elite aspiration, a luxury. These days, however, people see a college education more as a practical necessity. Even though we have not yet succeeded in sending everyone to college who wants to go, regardless of ability to pay, we no longer assume that college attendance equates to privileged socioeconomic status. What students learn in college today tends to relate more clearly and closely to real-life issues and the acquisition of practical skills. Nevertheless, long-standing divisions between the university and the community often persist in the attitudes of all concerned, and changing them can be difficult.

The fact that your school offers the service-learning course in which you are now enrolled signals that your institution and your instructor believe in taking an active role in community affairs and that connecting the classroom and the community will enrich your education, the school, and the community. Your participation in a community-based class indicates your desire to put to practice what you learn in school, and to reap the educational and personal benefits of doing so. It also demonstrates your willingness to help build the bridge between your school and the community. This bridge will allow ideas, experience, knowledge, and skills to move freely back and forth in a mutually enlightening and beneficial arrangement.

UNDERSTANDING THE COURSE CONTEXT

> Academic writing is seen in the context of the education the school offers; so even though in a community-based writing project one might be writing a newsletter article about child abuse, it has some sort of link to the class one is taking, and hence to one's education.
>
> —*Terence Chia, second-year student*

Before you become involved in your community-based project—before you meet your agency mentor, before you even decide what community agency you will be working with—it is important that you understand your service-learning experience clearly within its course context. Remember that in this particular community work, the enhancement of your education is the primary objective. Here are a few points worth reflecting on and perhaps discussing with your instructor and your classmates before your project gets underway:

Service-learning is not volunteer work. Although through your service-learning project you will perform a service for the community, your academic course work provides the occasion for this service. You will find that service-learning differs from volunteer work in several specific ways:

- Strictly speaking, you are *not* volunteering, since your services are required as part of your course work, as other fieldwork, writing, or reading might be.

- You undertake a community-service project in order to learn something specifically related to the course content; in the process, you enter into a give-and-take relationship with your agency and the community it serves.

- Even though your instructor may seek input from your agency mentor about your performance in a service-learning project, ultimately, your community-based work will be evaluated by your instructor, along with your other work for the course, according to criteria and standards of performance that he or she will determine.

Community-based learning has different educational purposes in different course contexts. In order to understand the educational relevance of your service-learning experience, make sure that you understand both the course content and your instructor's specific expectations and goals.

- Primary learning objectives will vary according to the academic discipline or the department offering the course. For instance, a community-based learning component of a biology course will clearly emphasize learning something about biology, while a service-learning component in a composition class will focus on learning about writing.

- Some courses will have multiple objectives. For example, an upper division biology course with an emphasis on writing in that major will stress learning about both biology and writing in that discipline. A composition course with a specific theme—for example, civil liberties—may, through community-based writing assignments, present students with opportunities to learn about writing as well as civil liberties.

Depending on course contexts and instructors' goals, students may be engaged in fundamentally different kinds of service. The community service that you provide in your community-based project may involve hands-on work or fieldwork with the agency, writing practical documents for the agency, or a combination of both. Make sure that you understand early on what kinds of service will be expected in your service-learning class.

- *Hands-on work* might entail your serving meals at a homeless shelter, taking part in a low-income housing project workday, helping with patient intake at a neighborhood free clinic, or participating in the organization of a community farmers' market. Hands-on work with a community agency may have you working directly with the people aided by the agency, collaborating with other community members on local community improvement projects, or helping the agency with organizational and administrative tasks.

- Many service-learning projects involve *writing practical documents* for the agency. Much of the work that nonprofit and governmental agencies do demands writing in one form or another. Agencies often need help in creating informational and public relations documents such as brochures, flyers, press releases, Web-site content, and newsletters, or analytic and persuasive documents such as position statements, letters to the editor, and grant proposals. Very often agencies identify generation of these materials as the tasks with which they need the most outside help. In taking on these kinds of research and writing projects for an agency, you perform an important service.

- Many community-based projects that arise from academic classes will involve *a combination of hands-on work and writing* for the agency. In fact, in order to understand enough about the agency's work to write for the agency, students often *must* be involved in a hands-on capacity.

Community-based writing may involve fundamentally different kinds of writing. The kinds of writing that you undertake in community-based projects writing can vary fundamentally in terms of learning objectives, audiences, and specific purposes. The most basic variation is between practical and academic writing projects. Many instructors who teach community-based classes require both academic and practical writing projects. Make sure that you understand early on what kinds of writing will be expected in your class.

- In *practical writing projects*, you write documents explicitly for your agency's use in accomplishing its mission and work in the community. Of course, you will find tremendous variation among practical writing genres. For example, a newsletter article is a very different practical genre from a brochure or a grant proposal. Collaborative work—including research and writing—with your agency mentor, other agency staff, or members of the community is inherent in many practical writing projects. For example, your agency mentor might ask for your help in writing a grant proposal. You might be in an excellent position to contribute sections that explain the agency's mission, describe the community it serves, and argue the importance of the project for which the agency is seeking funding. Agency staff might be in a better position to contribute other sections, including those that relate to agency staffing and budget. In another example, you might collaborate with middle school students to write and produce a play.

- In *academic writing projects*, you will not produce documents for explicit use by your agency; rather, you will write about subjects related to both your service-learning experience and the academic course content, for your-self and for your class. Academic writing enterprises vary widely, from field notes and reflective journals to experiential, argumentative, or research essays. You may find that your academic writing also involves working directly with agency staff or community members. For example, if your instructor assigns a research paper that focuses on an issue related to your community work, you may well want to interview people in your agency or in the community it serves.

ASSESSING YOUR INTERESTS, VALUES, AND LIMITATIONS

As you begin the process of locating a nonprofit agency with which you would like to work, first consider your interests, values, and limitations. If your interests lie in the sciences, you might rather work with a blood bank than an after-school reading program at the local library. If you are opposed to abortion, you would prob-ably be uncomfortable working with a women's health clinic that performs the procedure; instead, you might prefer working at an after-school reading program. It is also important to be aware of and honest about your limitations. For instance, if you do not have a car and a good public transit system does not exist in your area, you might want to choose an agency within biking or walking distance from your home or campus.

Exploring your own background and taking into account the practical con-siderations of your life will help you to discover what criteria are most impor-tant to you as you contemplate your placement options. As an exercise in self-clarification, try responding to the questions posed in the "Self-Assessment Worksheet" provided on the following page.

LOCATING POTENTIAL PLACEMENTS AND PROJECTS

You can find service-learning placements in several ways, depending on the extent to which institutional support for service-learning exists, or does not exist, on your campus.

Prepared Placements

If a volunteer clearinghouse, a service-learning center, or a community-service writ-ing program exists on your campus, you will have concrete resources and help avail-able to you as you research potential placements, establish contact with community agencies, and begin your service-learning project.

- *Volunteer centers or clearinghouses* on many college campuses provide stu-dents with listings of nonprofit agencies seeking volunteer help. Although not specifically geared toward service-learning or community-based writing, volunteer clearinghouses may be able to suggest placements that would nonetheless relate well to your course context.

SELF-ASSESSMENT WORKSHEET

Background

Think about the ways in which you identify yourself. For each of the following categories that seems relevant to you, write a couple of sentences to describe yourself.

Race/ethnicity	Language
Class	Family Background
Gender	Military Service
Physical Challenges	Education
Geography (For example, urban, suburban, rural? Regional?)	Age
	Work
Nationality	Community Service
Sexual Orientation	Other?

Values

How would you briefly describe your values in the following areas?

Religious or spiritual	Economic
Political	Community Service
Cultural	Other?
Educational	

Interests and Goals

Briefly describe your specific interests in the following areas. What are your goals related to these interests?

Personal	Professional
Cultural	Volunteer Work
Political	Other?
Academic/Educational	

Practical Issues

Consider any limitations that you might have in any of these areas of your life.

- Does physical ability limit you in any way?
- What is your work schedule? How flexible or inflexible is it?
- What is your academic schedule? How flexible or inflexible is it?
- If you are involved in a sport, what is your athletic schedule? How flexible or inflexible is it?
- What are your commitments to family? How flexible or inflexible are they?
- To what extent do other commitments (for example, to volunteer work or political work, participation in school or extracurricular activities) take up your time? How flexible or inflexible are these?
- What kind of transportation access do you have? Do you have a car? How readily available is public transportation to your home and school?
- Other?

- Some colleges sponsor on-campus *service-learning programs or centers* that exist specifically to help faculty and students in various disciplines develop service-learning placements with local nonprofit agencies.
- Increasingly, college composition departments include *community-service writing programs*. If community writing has been formalized at your college, the people who coordinate the program will help you locate nonprofit agencies that specifically need help with writing tasks.

If your college does not have a formal volunteer or service-learning infrastructure, your instructor may have developed placements for you and your peers. Independently, she or he may have established relationships with community agencies and mentors and discussed with them what needs they have for student assistance. In this case, you might be asked to select among them or to work with the entire class in one agency. Even if your instructor has not made direct contact with community agencies, she or he may have put together a list of nonprofit or governmental agencies in your area from which you can identify and pursue potential placements on your own.

Self-Developed Placements

The fact that your college may not have a volunteer clearinghouse, a service-learning center, or a community-service writing program, or that your instructor may not have developed placements for your class, does not mean that service-learning placements are impossible to make. In fact, as part of the course requirement, some instructors choose to leave the research and the development of service-learning placements up to you, the student. This can be an important part of your learning experience. In the process of developing your own placement, you will learn a lot about your community, its problems and issues, how they are being addressed, and by whom.

If part of your service-learning experience involves locating and developing your own placement with a community agency, you may be wondering how and where to begin. Remember that you are not looking for a job; rather, you are seeking a service-learning placement, with the emphasis on service *and* learning. This means that you will search for a placement with a community nonprofit or governmental organization—that is, an agency, whether independent or government-sponsored, whose purpose is to provide a public service, not to make a profit. Your instructor will provide specific guidance, but here are some ideas that might help you begin the process of locating a potential placement:

Consider how your personal interests might intersect with nonprofit work in the community. Before you begin to look for specific agencies, you can narrow your search by pinpointing what kind of community work you would like to do. Look back at the "Self-Assessment Worksheet" (page 59). What social or political issues do you feel passionately about? Homelessness? Environmental justice? Legal aid? Healthcare? Education? Disability rights? What do you love? Children? Sports? Art? Which nonprofit agencies in the community provide services that relate well to your interests?

Ask around. Ask friends, family, other students in your class, and your instructor what nonprofit or governmental agencies they know of in your area and what kinds of work these agencies do. Write down their suggestions. Consider them in light of your interests.

Notice what's going on in your neighborhood. In addition to asking around, look around. Notice what agencies exist in your area. Which agencies respond in times of need? Who helps out when natural disasters such as floods or tornadoes hit? Who works to feed the hungry and house the homeless? Who administers social programs or community health services? Many nonprofit agencies that fulfill these roles in the community will have local offices, and many of the governmental agencies concerned with public welfare, education, and safety will be housed in government buildings, at city hall or in county administration buildings.

Contact local civic groups, schools, and churches. Local civic groups (e.g., the Kiwanis Club or the League of Women Voters), schools, churches, synagogues, temples, or mosques can be excellent starting points as you begin researching social service organizations in your area. Many of these groups sponsor such programs themselves or will be able to refer you to other community agencies with which they have established relationships.

Check out the telephone book. The phone book can be a valuable information resource and might provide you with important information about nonprofit and governmental agencies near you. Take a look at the local area pages where you may find listings under headings such as "Community Programs" or "Community Services." These could provide you with names, addresses, and phone numbers of community nonprofits and governmental agencies involved in public service. Among these, you might find an agency that interests you and with which you could develop a service-learning placement.

Search the Internet. With one of the widely available search engines such as Yahoo! (http://www.yahoo.com) or Google (http://www.google.com), you can search the Internet for community agencies and volunteer opportunities in your area. Try searching for your location—e.g., your county or city—then search using the key words "volunteer," "social service," or "community service."

We can offer one very productive Internet search for volunteer opportunities. Go to the Yahoo! home page (http://www.yahoo.com) and select the

"Society and Culture" category. There, you will find a number of more specific categories, including "Issues and Causes." If you select "Issues and Causes," you will have further specific choices, including "Philanthropy." Finally, under "Philanthropy," you will find "Community Service and Volunteerism."

Clicking on "Community Service and Volunteerism" will provide a wealth of information in the form of links to Web sites that match individuals and community agencies according to geographic location and mutual interests. One such site is VolunteerMatch (http://www.VolunteerMatch.org). From the Volunteer-Match home page, you can search for volunteer opportunities and information about the community agencies that provide them. You can search by specific location: once you select a region within the United States, you will be asked to enter the number of miles—anywhere between 1 and 100—you are willing to travel to the agency. You can search by areas of interest, including "Environment," "Health," and "Race/Ethnicity" to name a few, as well as within categories of "ongoing" and "one-time" service. Other Web sites with similar features include PlanetVolunteer (http://www.PlanetVolunteer.org), VolunteerWeb (http://www.VolunteerWeb.org), and Action Without Borders (http://www.idealist.org).

As you browse these directories, keep in mind that most of the opportunities posted are for "volunteers," and, as we have pointed out, a volunteer is not exactly what you are as a service-learner. Furthermore, although some of the postings may mention writing opportunities, most will not. Neither fact means, however, that the agencies listed would not welcome either service-learning students or student writers who want to help them accomplish their work. The best way to use these listings is to consider their potential in yielding contacts for service-learning placements.

Within these directories, you will find links to organizations' Web sites where you can research their work in depth. Here's a tip: Web sites for private nonprofit organizations will end in ".org" and those for public nonprofit, or governmental, agencies will end in ".gov." You will also find essential contact information, including agencies' addresses and phone numbers, as well as names and email addresses of people to contact at the organizations so that you can make further inquiries about potential service-learning placements.

Organizing Your Information

Whether you are choosing from among prepared placements or self-developed placements, as you begin to identify which possibilities seem most promising for you, you might want to keep track of what you find out about each agency and potential projects as you go. Try filling out a "Placement and Project Assessment Worksheet" for each potential placement. (See the following page.)

Contacting the Agency Directly
If You Need More Information

If you are choosing among prepared placements, you can assume that whoever has prepared the placements for your class has already been in touch with the agen-

PLACEMENT AND PROJECT ASSESSMENT WORKSHEET

What do you know about the agency and about possible projects with the agency?

Agency

Name of Agency:

Agency Address:

Agency Email Address:

Agency Phone Number:

Agency Web Site URL:

(Note whether this agency is private non-profit, with a Web site ending in ".org" or governmental, with a Web site ending in ".gov.")

Contact Person or Agency Mentor

Name of Contact/Mentor:

Phone:

Email:

Agency's Work in the Community

- What is the agency's mission? (Look up the agency's mission statement on its Web site or in pamphlets, brochures, newsletters or other printed materials.)
- Where is the agency located? How far from your home or school?
- Would you have access to public transportation available to and from the agency?
- What do you know about the community in which the agency is located?
- Whom does the agency serve? Is the agency's clientele related to its location? If so, how?

Possible Projects

- What is the nature of the hands-on work you might do with this agency?
- What writing projects are available for the agency's use, if any and if known?
- Who will the audiences be for practical documents that you write? In what forms would they reach their audiences?
- What academic writing projects for your class might arise from your placement with this agency?

cies. He or she has collected necessary contact information (including addresses, phone numbers, and email addresses) and has probably identified mentors at the agencies with whom students will be working directly. You can also assume that these agency mentors will understand something about the academic context of your service-learning placement.

However, if you are developing your own placement, you will have to do this initial work. If the work of a specific agency interests you, get in touch with that agency to find out more.

If you have only a general phone number or email address, call or email the agency and ask to be connected with the Volunteer Coordinator or, if there is no such position, the Executive Director of the agency. If in your research you discovered a contact person at the agency, get in touch with him or her by phone or email. These contacts at the agency should be able to answer your questions.

Explain what you want. You will want to let the contact person at the agency know that you are looking for a service-learning placement. Make sure that the agency contact knows that you are exploring potential placements. Be prepared to explain how service-learning works at your school and in your specific course as well as what kinds of service are expected of students in the class. If you are looking for hands-on work with the agency, let the contact person know what you are most interested in doing. If you are looking for a placement that involves writing for the agency instead of or in addition to hands-on work, specify what you mean by writing projects; mention brochures, newsletters, grant proposals, flyers, and fact sheets as some of the possibilities. Most importantly, you want to find out (1) if the agency is interested in working with you in a service-learning context, and (2) what work or projects might be available.

Find out more about the agency and its work. This initial contact provides an opportunity for you to ask questions about the agency, its mission, how it operates, the people it serves, and its projects in the community. Before you call or email, compose a list of questions to refer to.

Identify potential projects. Although the agency contact may not yet have a clear or specific idea about how she or he might make the best use of your services, take this opportunity to brainstorm potential projects, whether these involve hands-on work, writing, or both. If you are seeking a practical writing project, ask what kinds of writing the organization might need and which among them are most pressing. For instance, an agency might like to have a new brochure, but a grant proposal deadline is six weeks away.

Identify a potential mentor at the agency. Perhaps the mentor you would work with at the agency is the person with whom you have established this initial contact. However, depending on the kind of service-learning project you are interested in, the size of the agency, and who would be in the best position to work with students, your mentor might be someone else. Ask your contact person whom you would likely be working with in a service-learning placement. Write down that person's name, phone number, and email address so that you can communicate directly with him or her.

Offer to provide further information. Your agency contact might appreciate more information, either general information about service-learning at your school or specific information about your course. Offer to mail, fax, email, or drop off a copy of your course syllabus or other relevant information to the agency contact.

If you feel ready to commit to working with this agency, set up a time and place (preferably at the agency) for an in-person meeting in which you can discuss in more detail the project that you will undertake. (See Chapter 6, Negotiating Community-Based Assignments.) If you are exploring several potential placements, or if you need more time to think, tell the person at the agency that you will get back in touch within a specific time period to let him or her know your plans—and stick to that promise.

FINDING A GOOD MATCH

I have a personal connection with the organization I worked with. I have lost both my uncles and a best friend to AIDS. The AIDS Memorial Grove has been part of my life for many years. I had been visiting the Grove as a community member and in fact had organized and led a high school group that participated in the monthly workdays.

—Nik Reed, third-year student

I chose to work with my agency precisely because I had never worked with or been involved with Native American issues before. As an international student in the USA, I felt it would be very instructive and educational to work with an agency that helped Native Americans and to see how this particular ethnic group was adapting to the changes imposed by urbanization and "Americanization."

—Terence Chia, second-year student

I was interested in community service; I was interested in the sciences. I was glad to be able to meld the two with my work for the nature interpretive center. I learned skills that I know I will apply in the future.

—Anh Bui, fourth-year student

To the extent that you will have a choice in your service-learning placement, it is important that you achieve the best match possible between you and the nonprofit agency that you work with. As you can gather from the comments above, students identify a good match according to many different criteria.

Whether you are selecting your service-learning placement from possibilities provided to you through on-campus services or by your instructor, or from a list of agencies that you yourself have researched and compiled, chances are that you have found quite a few agencies that look interesting. Now it's time to narrow your search. Two good ways to accomplish this are by analyzing agency mission statements and by gathering information from outside sources.

Analyzing Mission Statements

Since an agency's mission statement provides to the public the clearest articulation of its identity and goals, it will probably be published in the agency's brochures and newsletters and on its Web site. As you will see in the following examples, a mission statement—though often only one sentence long—reveals a great deal about an organization.

> The mission of the Beaver Lake Nature Center is to foster local and global stewardship of nature through diverse recreational and educational opportunities that enhance visitors' awareness, appreciation and understanding of the natural world.
>
> —*Mission statement of the Beaver Lake Nature Center,*
> *Baldwinsville, New York*

> Rainforest Action Network (RAN) works to protect the Earth's rainforests and support the rights of their inhabitants through education, grassroots organizing, and non-violent direct action.
>
> —*Mission statement of Rainforest Action Network,*
> *San Francisco, California*

If the focus of your service-learning course were on environmental issues, your instructor or community service coordinator might select organizations very much like these two. In conducting your own search for a service-learning placement, you might also come across organizations similar to these. From these brief statements, you can gather not only important information about the agencies' goals and programs, but you might also begin to form an impression of their respective characters and values. Take a close look at the key words of each of these statements, and compare them.

Beaver Lake Nature Center	**Rainforest Action Network**
Nouns	*Nouns*
stewardship	rainforests
nature	rights
opportunities	inhabitants
awareness	education
appreciation	organizing
understanding	action
world	
Adjectives	*Adjectives*
local	Earth's
global	grassroots
diverse	non-violent
recreational	direct
educational	
visitors'	
natural	

Verbs	*Verbs*
foster	works
enhance	protect
	support

Now read the two mission statements again, and ask yourself these questions:

- To what extent is the mission of each organization educational?
- To what extent is it recreational?
- To what extent is the work of each organization political?
- In what ways does each value "environment" and "nature"?
- What role does each organization take within the larger community?

Both mission statements mention bringing about environmental awareness through education. Environmental education is a goal that they share, but beyond that, the missions of these two agencies and the tones of their statements differ in significant ways.

The Beaver Lake Nature Center functions as a visitors' center. If you are familiar with the area, you will know that Baldwinsville is a rural community not far from Syracuse. At Beaver Lake, visitors find "recreational and educational opportunities": people come to the lake for recreation, to relax and enjoy the day in a natural setting; they come to the Nature Center to learn more about nature and the environment. If you took on a community-service project with this organization, you might work as a docent leading groups—from senior citizens to elementary school children—on tours of the center and in the surrounding park. You might find yourself taking part in a weekend volunteer workday of clean-up, trail building, or tree planting, or you might participate in a springtime seminar on native wildflowers. The Beaver Lake Nature Center is both fun and constructive. The community that the center serves is not just the one in the closest town, but neighboring communities both large and small. People from all walks of life come to Beaver Lake, and in this way the center serves to bring diverse people from various communities together into one larger community of people who want to enjoy and to learn more about nature.

Rainforest Action Network's mission, on the other hand, is much more political. RAN enacts its mission not only though education but through "grassroots organizing, and non-violent direct action." This agency is composed of committed environmental activists. In one sense, the community that RAN serves exists far away from its organizational home; it is unlikely that, as a service-learning student, you would come into direct contact with RAN's primary constituency, which are the Earth's rainforests and the indigenous people who live there. In another sense, of course, the community that RAN serves is global, since in working to preserve rainforest ecosystems worldwide, the organization serves our collective environmental and cultural interests. If you were to work for this agency—perhaps in researching and writing about corporate destruction of rain-forests and indigenous cultures—staff and volunteers would expect an activist spirit from you, in support of the agency's mission.

Working with the Beaver Lake Nature Center, you would be involved in a relatively quiet, intimate form of environmental work; working with RAN, you would be involved in more politically charged, global environmental action. Which organization would be the better match for you?

Gathering Information from Other Sources

In addition to reading mission statements closely in order to learn about agencies and their communities, you might see if information about them exists elsewhere. You can learn a lot about an agency if it has been written about in national, local, or campus newspapers or magazines, or if its activities have been featured in television or radio news reports. These types of sources—ones not produced directly by the agency—can help you come to a fuller understanding of how the agency's work, as well as the issues the agency deals with, are seen within a larger community.

In conducting a search for records of an agency's activities, try targeting a specific periodical or newscast. For example, especially if the agency you're interested in is entirely local, conduct a key word search of the name of the agency in back issues of your campus or city newspaper, if these exist online. If they don't, call the papers and find out how you can search past issues for reports on or related to the agency's activities. If the agency you are interested in is a national or international organization (you may be considering working in a local chapter), it is likely to have been mentioned in the national press. In this case, try key word searches of *Time, Newsweek,* the *New York Times,* the *Washington Post,* or other news publications online. Similarly, transcripts of National Public Radio and Television reports are accessible online; try key word searches there as well. Call local television and radio stations for advice on locating transcripts.

You can take the same approach in conducting key word or subject searches on the issues and the communities with which the agency works, although results of these kinds of searches are likely to be much more general. Always remember, too, that reference librarians at your school or public library can advise you on how best to go about these kinds of searches.

When you are well informed about the agencies that you have identified as potential placements and their work in the community, and you understand well how this work relates to your interests and circumstances, you will probably feel ready to commit to working with a particular community agency. If you are still undecided, responding to the "Connections Worksheet" provided on the following page might help you reach a final decision.

We have just one last word of advice. In making your choice, consider not only the advantages of working within your comfort zone, but also what you might gain by stretching it a bit. In other words, consider not only obvious compatibilities, but also the ways in which undertaking work with a less familiar agency might enlarge your service-learning experience.

CONNECTIONS WORKSHEET

For each category below, write a paragraph in which you articulate how your identity, interests, and practical limitations intersect with the agency's work and expectations.

Background

How do your background and your identity intersect with the agency's work and the community it serves? Are you interested in pursuing work with this agency because of similarities between the agency's work and your background? Because of differences between them? Because of a combination of similarities and differences? What are they?

Values

How do your values resonate with the agency's values, as reflected in its mission statement? Are your values substantially similar to or different from the agency's values as you understand them? If so, how? To what extent, and in what ways, do you think any differences in values could be a problem or an asset in your work with the agency?

Interests and Goals

Specifically, how could your work with the agency further your interests and goals?

Practical Issues

In what ways would your working with this agency be a natural or a challenging match, given your practical limitations? How far are you able or willing to stretch in order to accommodate such factors as the agency's location (distance and transportation), its hours of operation, your mentor's schedule?

THERE WILL BE SURPRISES

Understanding a community cannot be attained through secondary sources. One must know its past, interact with its people, experience life in the community, and see what the future possibly holds for that community. Understanding is a complex knowledge of the community from every aspect; disregarding any feature is disregarding the community as a whole.

—*Greg Camarillo, first-year student*

Even if you have completed the three worksheets in this chapter and have planned for your service-learning experience as carefully as possible, your interactions with the people that you will encounter and your responses to the situations in which you will find yourself are likely to produce some surprises. As Greg observes, you cannot fully understand a community through research; you have to experience it directly. Despite all of your preparations, *expect the unexpected.*

When you go into the community, remember to keep an open mind. Try to put yourself in the shoes of your agency mentor, the other people who work there, and the people whom the agency serves. If you will be working in your home community, this probably will be relatively easy to do. If you will be venturing into a new community, remember your reasons for picking this particular agency. Try to see and feel from the community's perspective; establish empathy. This will be especially important in the more challenging scenarios that some of you could encounter. One key to empathy is to remember the cultural context, which includes the sense of history that Greg talks about above. Some of you may already have a grasp of the community's history, but many of you will have to consider broader cultural and historical factors that you might not have thought about at all.

For example, imagine that you are a young woman from Nigeria who, in a health and public policy course at a Catholic college in southern Louisiana, decides to work with an AIDS organization. You have focused on AIDS because the disease has decimated the town in which you grew up; you have lost loved ones to the pandemic. The organization that you have chosen helps people with AIDS make various legal decisions and arrangements. Now you find yourself in the part of New Orleans' French Quarter known to be the heart of the gay community. Hesitatingly, you walk into the AIDS organization's office and are greeted by the person who will be your mentor, an African American man sporting a colorful rainbow tee shirt that reads, "Gay and Proud."

Looking around the office at all the rainbow flags and gay pride posters, you wonder what all of this has to do with AIDS as you know it, a disease decimating many African countries' populations—men, women, and children equally. In Nigeria, AIDS is a heterosexual disease. Furthermore, in your home culture, there is a deafening silence surrounding homosexuality; notions of gay and lesbian culture and pride do not exist.

In this situation, some research on AIDS in the United States might help you form an historical understanding of how AIDS has been perceived in American culture. We now know that anyone can contract AIDS. However, it is important to understand that homophobia in both mainstream society and the American medical community caused people with AIDS to be shunned, especially early on in the epidemic, on the moral and religious grounds that AIDS was a "gay disease." Consequently, many of the first groups to respond to the crisis were gay men's health networks. Currently, many AIDS organizations are still predominantly run by people in the gay, lesbian, bisexual, and transgender communities.

If you are the young woman from Nigeria, what do you do in this situation?

- *Remember the importance of communication.* The man who greets you at the AIDS organization may be just as shocked about you as you are about him. Be open with him about your experience with the AIDS pandemic. Furthermore, don't be afraid to ask questions.
- *Remember why you chose this particular organization.* AIDS devastates people—all people. You can look into the eyes of the man at the front desk and recognize an ally in the same struggle.

- *Look for the common ground.* You were not entirely prepared for this situation; he may not have been either. He will be mentoring someone who may not initially understand how particular social and political issues in the gay community affect his agency's work. Maybe you lost your boyfriend to AIDS. Maybe he lost his. Once you locate common ground, it will be easier and feel safer to explore the areas where you differ—in culture, sexual orientation, gender, and many other ways that are not so visible.

This is the contact zone that you both need to enter, and in the end, you will both come away with new ideas about two cultures that, on the surface, may seem to have little in common.

Now let's take a different example in which an agency mentor's cultural bias or ignorance might slap you in the face. For your semester-long project in your education class, you and your classmate decide to work with an adult night-school program that teaches English as a second language. Students in the class are predominantly Vietnamese and Korean, with a few students from Mexico, Nicaragua, and Guatemala. You are bilingual in Spanish and English and you are Chicano, although many people mistake you for Anglo. Your classmate is bilingual in Vietnamese and English, and he is the son of Vietnamese refugees. Part of the reason you decided to work together with this program is that you are both interested in bilingual education and in the ways that immigrant communities are often stigmatized and marginalized.

After you have met with the coordinator of the program, you go together to meet the woman who will be your direct mentor—the instructor of the class. An hour before class, you find yourself chatting with her in her office. She begins to talk to you about the students and what you might expect from them. She looks directly at you and says, "Well, you know, no matter what I do, the Mexicans seem to have a hard time staying motivated and staying awake in class. Now these Asian students," she says and glances over at your classmate, "are always on time and they are always eager to learn."

There are so many different levels of racism operating in this incident that it is probably difficult for you to figure out where to begin. Obviously she assumes that you are, like her, Anglo, so she has indulged in the conspiratorial "we're all white here" attitude. She has also lumped all of the students from Mexico, Nicaragua, and Guatemala together under one umbrella and stereotyped them as "lazy Mexicans." She has then looked at your classmate and trotted out another racist stereotype—the one about Asians as a model minority.

What do you do? Few would blame either of you for standing up and walking out. Again, in a sticky situation like this one, it is crucial for you to remember why you chose this particular community-service organization: you wanted to use your bilingual skills to help teach people English. This could be a terrific opportunity to help educate not only the students in the class, but also the instructor. If you feel comfortable with it, you might want to explain to her that you are Chicano and that you do not appreciate her stereotypes. You and your classmate can both engage with her in the contact zone. Although it may be more difficult in this situation than in the previous one, do attempt to look beyond her objectionable attitudes; as difficult as it might be, try to sympathize with her as another human being. Can she be teaching this class if she truly does not care about the students? Is she just having a bad day? Does she feel defeated by this particular educational situation? She truly may be having problems keeping the students engaged; some of them may be falling asleep in class because they have come from a full day of work. Think of the ways in which this may be a learning opportunity for all of you. Most importantly, remember all of those adult students waiting to meet you and learn from you (and teach you in turn).

Let's take a look at one last scenario. Say you are an Anglo woman in your first year at a prestigious university. You grew up in a poor neighborhood in a city on the opposite coast from this university, and you have earned a full scholarship. You and your best friend, an African American woman who grew up near the university in a wealthy neighborhood, are taking a core requirement course on society and politics with a service-learning component. You have chosen a placement together in a small grassroots nonprofit that works with environmental and social justice issues. For your initial meeting with the agency, the two of you take the bus across town. As you watch out the window, you see large, expensive homes with perfectly manicured lawns give way to increasingly small, rundown dwellings. Some of the houses, you note, have bars protecting doors and windows. As you pass by, you catch the shouts and laughter of children as they run from one balding yard to another, playing kickball.

You notice that this neighborhood looks a lot like yours back home. Your friend, who had been very animated in pointing out the homes of her high school friends in the earlier part of the ride, has now become quiet. You get off the bus at the stop your mentor mentioned in her directions. Half-way down the block, you locate your agency; it occupies a small storefront tucked between a discount liquor store and a barber shop. When you open the door and walk in, you are greeted by the four people who work for the organization. They are all African American. You look over at your friend, and suddenly you feel very white.

What do you do in this situation? Again, remember empathy. Also remember your own point of reference. You chose this agency because it works with environmental and social justice issues that impact this community. Part of what compelled you was that residents of your neighborhood suffer a disproportionately high rate of cancer, and this alarming fact has been related to a toxic waste site near your home. You want to examine some of the tangible ways that class oppression harms people in this country. On one level, you might feel very much like an insider in this situation since you come from a socioeconomic background similar to that of the community that this organization serves. On the other hand, you may feel like a complete outsider because everyone in this community setting is African American.

What is your friend thinking about at this time? Perhaps she feels included because of her ethnicity. At the same time, she may feel excluded because of her socioeconomic position. Her impulse may be to reach out to you as a friend; it may be to distance herself from you. No matter what happens in this situation, it is a prime opportunity for everyone involved to try to understand and learn about each other. You will need to understand how both race and class operate in this community context.

When you walk out of your classroom, into your agency, and begin to establish relationships in the community, you will encounter new ways of learning that will change your life. How will what you learn there inform what you learn in school from that moment on? How will this alter your sense of belonging in the academic community and beyond?

REFLECTIVE QUESTIONS
FOR JOURNAL-WRITING AND CLASS DISCUSSION

1. Have you done community volunteer work before? If so, what have these experiences been? In what ways do you anticipate that community work in a service-learning context will differ from volunteer work?

2. This one is for your journal. In considering how your background, values, and limitations might influence your choice of a service-learning placement, think what kinds of personal information you might want to share with others in the service-learning partnership (your instructor, classmates, and agency mentor) and what you might want to keep private. You might be comfortable sharing certain information about yourself with some people, and not with others. For example, a student who is working with an agency that provides counseling services to bereaved families and whose own mother has recently died might not feel like talking about his personal loss with his instructor or classmates, but he might feel quite comfortable talking about it with his agency mentor.

3. Analyze the following mission statements. Read closely! In what ways are these agencies and their missions similar? How are they different?

    The mission of the Southeast Asian Center (SEAC) is to empower the Southeast Asian—Vietnamese, Hmong, Laotian, and Cambodian—communities of Syracuse, which total 3000 individuals and are growing steadily. SEAC works to overcome isolation of individuals and families through various supportive community building activities and programs, and to increase independence to overcome the overwhelmingly disempowering refugee experience.

    —*Mission statement of the Southeast Asian Center, Syracuse, New York*

    The Spanish Action League was established to provide comprehensive services to the Latino community and to address the unique needs arising from language and cultural barriers. The SAL has opportunities for service in our Youth Center, help in writing grants, organizing educational seminars or classes, fundraising, special events and various other tasks.

    —*Mission statement of the Spanish Action League in Syracuse, New York*

4. In the "There Will Be Surprises" section of this chapter, we mentioned a few awkward service-learning, contact-zone scenarios. Brainstorm other challenging situations that you and your classmates could encounter. Try role-playing the parts in these scenarios.

TROUBLESHOOTING

WHAT IF…

you decide to call an agency because your analysis of its mission statement doesn't give you a clear sense of the work that it does and you can't locate any reference to the organization in any outside sources? What questions do you ask?

TRY TO…

develop a clear sense of the kind of organization you would like to work with before you call. If, for example, you want to work with an organization dedicated to improving health care access, would you be more comfortable with a group that works within the system or with one that challenges the system? Either preference is fine, but you should be clear with yourself about what your preference is before talking to someone at the agency.

be direct when you ask someone at the agency not only about the agency's mission, but also about its methods and specific values. People working at nonprofits are used to these kinds of questions. If this agency is not a good match for you, the person you speak with might be able to recommend one that suits you better.

WHAT IF…

you are unsure about who your agency mentor will be, especially if you are developing your own placement?

TRY TO…

speak with the agency's volunteer coordinator. Most agencies have one. This person will know whom you should contact in the agency about a specific project. If there is not a volunteer coordinator, ask to speak with the agency's executive director. Don't let the title frighten you. Addressing questions such as yours will be part of this person's job.

WHAT IF…

you feel shy about making a cold call to an agency, or about talking on the phone to strangers?

TRY TO…

look at your call from the agency's point of view. Your call is nothing but good news to the person you will be speaking with. After all, you are calling to explore the possibility that you will offer your services to the agency. Really, what have you got to worry about? Besides, if you come out of this with improved confidence and phone skills, that's just another benefit of service-learning!

WHAT IF…

you initially tell one agency that you will work there, but then something better comes along?

TRY TO…

follow through: stick to your original commitment. It's only right. On the other hand, be careful not to commit yourself to working with a particular agency if you aren't really ready, or if you have doubts. If you are still exploring your options, be clear and honest about that with the person you speak with at the agency. Once you are committed to an agency, you could very well come across another agency that you think would be cool to work with. Keep in mind that you might be able to work for this second organization later, in another service-learning class or as a volunteer.

CHAPTER 6

Negotiating Community-Based Assignments

A good initial meeting is a way to set yourself up for a good working relationship.
—SHANNAH METZ, FIRST-YEAR STUDENT

When you meet with your agency mentor to receive and discuss the details of your assignment, you may feel excited, nervous, or both. This meeting will likely be your first face-to-face contact. Although you have come to know something of the agency in the process of your advance work, you probably have a lot of questions going through your mind, questions that will only be answered through experience. *What kind of person will your mentor be? What will she or he think of you? What will the office be like? Who will be working there? What will they be working on?*

If your participation with your agency will involve hands-on work, you may have an idea of what kind of work you will be doing, or you may not. If you will be taking on a practical writing task for your agency, you may have some sense of what your assignment will be, or you may have no idea. If there will be academic writing assignments related to your community and agency work, you may know what these assignments are in advance, or you may not. You do know, however, that whether you will be working with your agency in a hands-on capacity or as a writer, your agency will be counting on you to deliver.

WHY MEETING AT YOUR AGENCY IS SO IMPORTANT

A large part of our first meeting was getting an introduction to the agency, looking at the exhibits, taking a tour, and learning about the programs it offers to the community.

—Anh Bui, fourth-year student

An in-person meeting at your agency's office is really the best circumstance in which to clarify your assignment. Although it would be possible for your agency mentor to dictate your assignment over the phone or by email, you would be missing an important part of the service-learning experience with this detached means of delivery. It is as important for you to meet your mentor as it is for your mentor to meet you. Your relationship should not be merely practical; it should have a personal dimension.

A meeting at the agency will allow you and your mentor to get to know one another, to talk in both structured and unstructured ways about the work the agency does and about your assignment. In visiting your agency, you have an opportunity to acquaint yourself with other people in the office and to understand the work culture there. You will be able to observe, ask questions, and get answers on the spot. Discovering your agency on its home turf will also serve as an important introduction to the community, since, in most cases, the community in which the agency is located is also the community it serves. If you want to get everything you can out of your service-learning experience, *be there*, and be prepared to return on a regular basis.

In service-learning projects, it is essential that you do more than simply receive and complete an assignment. You must understand the context in which you are working in order to do a good job, as well as to gain everything you can from the experience. Community-based projects require background understanding, of both your agency and the community.

Imagine trying to write a grant proposal for your agency without understanding your agency's unique contribution to the community. Without a specific understanding of your agency's work and the particular needs of the community, how would you be able to argue effectively for agency funding? Could you write an essay about your agency and its community without having visited either of them? Whether you undertake a practical or an academic writing project, whether the agency is located in your home community or far away, and whether the people of the community are geographically, socioeconomically, ethnically, or culturally similar to you or dissimilar, you need to discover the agency, its work, and the community firsthand. The best place to do this is at your agency's office, and the best time to begin is during your initial meeting with your mentor.

ARRANGING THE INITIAL MEETING

Arranging an initial meeting with your agency mentor in order to define your assignment may seem like an easy enough task, but the logistics can be complicated. Here are some tips that might help making contact and arranging an initial meeting with your agency mentor easier:

- *Before you contact your mentor to arrange a meeting, review your schedule and identify several possible meeting days and times.*

- *If you are working with a group of students in a placement with one agency and one mentor, choose one student to serve as the contact person.* Each student calling and making separate arrangements would be more complicated and time-consuming for your mentor. Review your schedules together and come up with several possible meeting days and times when all members of the group could attend. Remember that the student who agrees to serve as the contact person in this particular instance has no more or less ongoing responsibility in the project than any other student in the group: this is a collaboration.

- *First, try contacting your mentor by phone.* If you succeed in speaking with him or her personally on the first try, great! If you need to leave a message, try to leave one on your mentor's voice mail instead of with someone else in the office, since details can get lost. Be aware, though, that not all agencies have voicemail.

- *In your messages, be specific.* Leave your name, your telephone number, and the best times to reach you, along with your email address. Remind your mentor that you are a service-learning student from "X" class at "X" University. Be clear and specific about the reason you are calling: you would like to speak with your mentor about arranging a day and time to meet in order to discuss your assignment for the agency. Mention the specific days and times that would work for you and that you look forward to hearing back from, and meeting with, your mentor soon.

- *If your mentor does not return your call right away, don't take it personally. Your mentor is a busy person.* Be politely persistent. If you do not hear back the same day, call again the next day. If you have to leave another message, leave the same details again.

- *If you do not hear back from your mentor within a day, try sending an email with the same content as your phone message.* (But be aware that although most agencies and mentors do use email, some don't.) Some people check their email more frequently than they check their phone messages. Your phone message might have gotten mixed up with other general office voice mail, and your mentor may not have heard it.

- *If you do not hear back from your mentor within a few days, try talking to someone else in the agency office.* Is your mentor out of town? Is there a better phone number to try?

- *If talking to someone else in the office does not produce results, ask your instructor for help or advice.*

- *When you speak to your mentor in person, remind him or her of who you are and why you are calling:* to arrange a meeting, preferably at the agency office, to discuss the details of your project. Let your mentor know what days and times would work for you or your group, and ask what would work for him or her. Especially if a group of students is involved, it can be a challenge to find a day and time that works for everyone. But be persistent, and be as flexible as you can possibly be. You will find a time to meet.

- *Be sure to get specific directions to your agency.* If you will be using public transportation, get your mentor's advice on which subway, train, or bus route to take.

WRITING A LETTER OF INTRODUCTION

Once you have committed to work with a particular agency, your mentor should have the opportunity to learn more about you. A letter of introduction is a good way to provide this information. Writing this letter is more than an exercise; your letter is a practical document. Its purpose is to help you initiate a positive working relationship with your mentor.

Composing this letter will require you to consider nuances of audience and purpose. Your agency mentor is the person at the agency with whom, and for whom, you will be working over the course of your project and to whom you will look for direction and guidance. This person has knowledge, experience, expertise, and authority related to your project that you do not have and clearly is deserving of your respect. Of course, you are deserving of your mentor's respect as well, since you are undertaking important work that supports the agency's mission.

What are your specific purposes, then, in introducing yourself to your agency mentor? What might your mentor need or want to know about you in order for you to work together to develop the most worthwhile project—for you and for the agency? The specific content of the letter is a matter for your own judgment. So is its style. But there are some things that your agency mentor might be particularly interested in knowing about you. To help you plan your letter, consider the questions posed on the following page.

Although there is no correct or incorrect form, length, or style for your letter of introduction, there are certainly more or less appropriate and inappropriate ways to present yourself. The style of your letter will not only say something implicit about who you are as an individual, but it will also suggest the kind of relationship you want or expect with your mentor. Your letter of introduction is an opportunity to set the tone of that relationship. How formal or informal do you want it to be? You probably don't want your letter to be overly formal. You would probably prefer a friendly and open relationship with your mentor, so the style of your letter should convey this hope. But—and this is important—you don't want your letter to sound overly familiar; after all, you probably have not met your mentor yet and you want to convey your respect.

Try to strike a comfortable balance between formality and informality, between deference and friendliness in the tone and style of your letter of introduction. Be sure that you check your letter very carefully for grammatical, spelling, and

---

**QUESTIONS TO CONSIDER IN WRITING
YOUR LETTER OF INTRODUCTION**

- Who are you? Where are you from? What are your academic and potential professional interests?
- What does "community" mean to you? What are your feelings about your home community (that is, where you are from) and about your new community, if you are attending college away from home?
- Why do you want to "serve"? Why are you participating in a service-learning class? Have you done other service work in the past? Is any of your past work related specifically to the agency's mission?
- What is your understanding about the work that your agency does in the community? What is your understanding of the nature of that community or the clientele that your agency serves? How does your agency's work intersect with your background, experience, and interests?
- Do you have any questions about your agency's work or the community or clientele it serves that you look forward to asking when you meet with your mentor?
- What are you looking forward to in your community-based writing in comparison to other writing (academic, practical, or personal) that you've done?
- Do you have any special skills or interests that you hope to bring to your work with the agency? For example, are you bilingual? Do you have Web authoring skills?

---

typing errors before you send or deliver it! You certainly don't want to give the impression that you are careless in your work. If you are thoughtful, straightforward, and careful, what you say about yourself and how you say it will set the stage for an honest and mutually respectful relationship with your mentor.

Letters of introduction are as various as the students who write them. Still, you might appreciate reading examples of letters in which other students in community-based writing classes have introduced themselves to their mentors.

Dear Ms. Ronda Rutledge,

I wanted to thank you for giving me the opportunity to work at the American Indian Child Resource Center. I am truly excited to be working with AICRC because nonprofit work is precisely what I want to do with my life.

On campus, I am part of the activist community. I am a member of the Labor Action Coalition, which is a coalition between students, faculty, and university workers that works to combat labor injustice both on and off campus. Activism is difficult and often unrecognized work but it is also incredibly satisfying because you are devoting so much of your time and energy to fighting histories of inequity and discrimination.

Along with my enthusiasm for activism, I am intensely interested in studying race relations and urban development and this is another reason I was drawn to AICRC. At one point in my high school career, I wanted to be a shrewd businesswoman but then I attended a class on Race and Ethnicity and my ambitions were completely turned around. This class helped me to make the realization that the reason people end up where they are is dependent more on circumstance than on actual ability. Also, I began to understand how racism and socioeconomics are closely intertwined. Working with AICRC seemed like a great opportunity to study firsthand how past and current systematic racism in America influences minority communities, especially the development of minority children.

Along with my interest in race studies, I really enjoy writing. While I usually write editorials and performance pieces, working for AICRC will allow me to learn writing skills that are essential for my future occupation as a nonprofit worker. I recognize that learning how to write a convincing grant is just as difficult as writing an essay for English class—they are both skills that must be developed. I am eager to begin learning these specific writing skills at AICRC.

Thank you once again for the chance to work with you at AICRC. I know that this will be an amazing experience and I look forward to writing for you.

Sincerely,
Meghana Reddy

Meghana has done an excellent job in her letter of explaining how important work in the nonprofit sector is to her, since it is work that she is interested in pursuing after she graduates from college. She also has a very clear idea of how the work the agency does in the community relates to the areas of academic study and political work she is involved in. Because she does a good job of articulating the connections between her personal, political, and academic life with the mission of the organization she will be working for, she has introduced herself to her mentor as someone who will be highly motivated and highly compatible with the agency's work.

However, you and many other students undertaking service-learning and community-based writing placements may not have the explicit connections with your agency that Meghana has with hers. Rebecca Freeland writes an effective letter of introduction in which she emphasizes other motives for her work with her agency.

Dear Mr. Drekmeyer,

I'm really looking forward to working with Bay Area Action and the Peninsula Conservation Center Foundation.

I'm from Oakland, so I'm pretty familiar with the area in general, but I haven't spent much time off campus since I moved to the Peninsula. My primary academic interests are history and English, and I'm especially interested in writing. Hopefully, whatever I end up doing—possibly teaching or some form of journalism—will give me the opportunity to pursue that interest.

I signed up for the Community Service Writing program because it seemed like a good way to make my writing actually <u>do</u> something. One of my most rewarding experiences during high school was volunteering as a teaching assistant at a summer school for junior high kids. Teaching writing skills was one way to put my academic interests to good use; CSW seems like another chance to do the same thing.

I'll admit that I've never really done environmental service work before, and I don't know a whole lot about environmental issues. But I think that may make this project all the more interesting for me: I'll be trying out a new writing style (different from the style of, say, an English essay) and learning about unfamiliar, but definitely important, subjects. I'm particularly interested in the concept of sustainable communities. I still don't quite understand what the term means (!), but I like the idea of figuring out ways to integrate environmental awareness into daily life. And it sounds like BAA/PCCF really promotes that idea in a variety of ways. In addition, as an area resident, I feel that I have a personal interest in maintaining natural spaces all around the bay, especially in my new home on the Peninsula.

I should probably add that I have basically no experience in webpage design or anything like it. I understand that the project will primarily consist of research and writing, but that it will ultimately be posted on the Web. I thought I should warn you.

I'm really excited about getting involved in local activism and maybe doing something to help promote it. I look forward to working with BAA/PCCF and its members. Thank you.

Sincerely,
Rebecca Freeland

Rebecca's past experience, current interests, and future aspirations do not have a strong connection with her agency's work. However, in her letter of introduction to her mentor, she is still able to articulate the ways in which she does relate to the agency's work and why she is interested: she is from the area, and therefore has a personal stake in its environmental health, and she is interested in environmental issues, even though she doesn't know much about them. It is clear that she welcomes her placement with a local environmental organization as an opportunity to learn more and to do something to promote environmental values in her enlarged neighborhood. Rebecca conveys, both through content and style, that she is honest, motivated, and looking forward to an interesting, active learning experience.

Remember as you compose your letter of introduction it is important for you to make a real connection with your community mentor and the agency as your project begins.

PREPARING FOR YOUR MEETING

> Prepare lots of questions. Start thinking about how you would want to shape the project individually so that you can discuss your ideas with them then.
>
> —*Meena Ramachandran, first-year student*

Before you keep your first appointment with your agency mentor, make sure that you are prepared in practical terms:

- *If you haven't done so already, send your letter of introduction to your agency mentor, or plan to bring it with you to your initial meeting.* If you have a résumé, attach that to your letter.

- *Write up questions for your mentor in advance.* You might have questions beyond those answered by your preliminary research on your agency and the community that it serves. You might also have questions about work in the nonprofit sector. Of course, you will have questions about your project. What is its subject? Who are its readers? What is its purpose? What kind of document will it be—a brochure, a fact sheet, a flyer, an article? When is the deadline? How will it be published or distributed? What format will it have? Your meeting will provide a good opportunity for you to ask your mentor for examples of the kind of writing you will be doing.

- *Brainstorm a list of your specific interests and skills; they might be relevant to work with your agency.* How might your academic interests (for example, in biology, economics, education, journalism, law, or health) relate to a project with your agency? How about your personal interests (the fact that you love children or sports, for example)? Has any of your past work, including volunteer work, stemmed from or provided you with special interests or skills (for example, as a reading tutor or hospital volunteer)? Do you have any technical or artistic skills that might be applied to your work with the agency (for example, in Web authoring or graphic design)? Are you bilingual (many agencies really appreciate bilingual skills)? There are many ways in which these kinds of skills could be valuable assets in specific practical writing projects. Your mentor will appreciate knowing what your particular interests and skills are because most mentors want to establish the best match possible between a particular student and a particular project.

- *Make sure that you know not only how you will get to your agency meeting, but also how long it will take you to get there.* It's definitely not a good idea to be late. Make sure to allow enough time, especially if your meeting happens to be scheduled around rush hour. (We know of several occasions when students were stuck in unanticipated traffic and missed the agency mentor entirely.) Remember that many public forms of transportation (especially buses) require exact change in coins.

- *It may be time to do your laundry!* There's no need to dress up, but you definitely want to make a good impression, so plan to dress nicely.

AGREEING ON A PROJECT

> Think about what you expect of the project, what responsibilities you expect your mentor to have, and what responsibilities you expect to have yourself.
>
> —*Katie Cameron, first-year student*

Not only is the first meeting with your agency mentor important so that you can meet one another face to face, but it is also crucial because this is probably the time and place in which you will agree on and commit to a specific project. In hands-on work, which may be directly related to an academic writing assignment in your service-learning class, this could mean that you agree to spend a certain amount of time at the agency each week distributing information to people who stop by. Or you might agree to read to a group of blind children on a particular afternoon each week. In order to fulfill most academic community-based assignments, you will probably spend a fair amount of time, and on a regular basis, at the agency; therefore, you will probably see your agency mentor more frequently than you will if you are given a practical writing assignment.

If yours is a practical writing assignment, your initial meeting may very well be one of the few opportunities that you have to meet with your mentor face to face. Many students send drafts of projects and receive feedback via email rather than through meetings. Since direct contact might not be regular, it is crucial that at the first meeting you agree on and fully understand the sort of practical document the agency expects from you.

What You Want and What Your Agency Needs

At your meeting with your agency mentor, you may well find that there is a very definite writing project that he or she would like you to take on, and that getting this project done is the primary reason your mentor has agreed to participate in your service-learning program. If this is the case, although you may not have had an opportunity to select your project, your mentor will probably welcome your ideas about how the project might be carried out. You may also find that some of your classmates whose projects are considerably less structured than yours envy the clarity and direction provided to you by your mentor. Remember that if your mentor has a specific project in mind, the agency needs it badly, and needs it now. Your project is a priority.

You may find, on the other hand, that your mentor has several possible projects in mind from which you will be asked to choose. Perhaps all of these projects are of equal importance at the moment, or perhaps your mentor believes that you will do a better job with a project if you have some choice about what project you will undertake. If your mentor offers several projects from which to choose, it might be a good idea for you to ask if one project is more urgent than the others. Your mentor will appreciate that you understand that his or her agency has priorities. If none of the projects that your mentor offers is more pressing than the others, select the project that appeals most to your interests or toward which you can apply your special skills, talents, knowledge, or experience.

An agency mentor who agrees to work with a group of students will likely either have more than one possible project in mind or a large or complex project on which she or he hopes a group of students will collaborate. If there is a selection of individual projects, you and the other students in your group will have to decide who will take which project. Generally, this is not as difficult as it might sound, since particular projects will appeal to different students for different reasons. Usually, the mentor will expect you to choose a project during the initial meeting, so be prepared to make a decision then and there.

If the project is collaborative, the initial meeting offers an important opportunity to discuss the content, audience, and purpose of the project and to get your mentor's suggestions about how and where to find at least some of the information you will need to complete it. However, your group should meet on its own to decide on the details of the collaboration—how to divide the research and writing among all members of the group.

Some students discover that their mentor has only vague ideas about what they might do for their practical writing project. Part of the "service" these mentors expect from service-learning students is help in brainstorming and developing projects for their agencies. If this is the case for you, other students in your class may envy your freedom in determining your work with your agency, although this freedom can make some students uneasy. When you are confronted with what may seem like an infinite number of options, on what basis do you choose? You may feel that you lack the necessary knowledge of your agency and the community it serves as well as the authority to decide what the agency needs. If you find yourself in this position, one of the best ways that you can help your mentor as well as yourself is to ask questions. Ask your mentor and perhaps even community members about the problems the agency most often encounters as it attempts to bring its services to its community. If you take a problem-based approach to identifying and defining a practical writing project, what you and your mentor come up with will be relevant and useful.

What Constitutes a Reasonable Amount and a Reasonable Kind of Work?

Some agency mentors may not have a good idea about what constitutes a reasonable amount of work for your project. Just as working in a community agency context may be unfamiliar to you, working in an academic context may be unfamiliar to your mentor. This is why providing your mentor with a copy of your course syllabus is important; your syllabus will presumably explain the academic context of service-learning and indicate the kind of work required in your course and what your course workload is likely to be. Still, you may find that your mentor is inclined to assign too little or too much work, given your course context.

Some mentors assign overly skimpy projects because they don't want to impose on you. This may be considerate on their part, but if your project does not satisfy your course requirements, no matter how useful it might be to your agency, it won't work for you. If you suspect that the project your mentor assigns you at the first meeting provides too little work to satisfy your instructor's expectations and the requirements of the course, say so, and work with your mentor on adjustments that will make the project more appropriate for your class. Some instructors have specific kinds or lengths of projects in mind. For example, in order to try to keep the amount of work students do reasonably equal, an instructor might expect every student to produce a minimum number of words or typed pages for a practical writing project. If this is the case in your class, let your mentor know at the initial meeting what your instructor's specific expectations are.

If your mentor, on the other hand, seems to be expecting too much work from you, how do you say no? If your mentor expects too much, it is probably because he or she doesn't understand the course context or the objectives of service-learning in your particular class well enough and may be relating to you as "just another volunteer." Be prepared to reiterate why you are there and what your mentor can reasonably expect of you. Again, the course syllabus that you and other students are working from can help clarify matters for your mentor.

Some mentors simply get carried away. These people are passionate about their work, and they sometimes selflessly dedicate long hours, long weeks, months, and years to it. Occasionally a mentor will assume that everyone else, including you, has—or should have—the same degree of passion, drive, dedication, and time to devote to the cause. If your agency mentor seems to expect too much from you say so—and say it early on. You can do this politely, and you can refer to the course syllabus to back you up.

Often students themselves are uncertain about whether or not what their mentors expect from them is too little or too much. If this is the case for you, seek clarification from your instructor. If necessary, ask your instructor to speak with your mentor.

Occasionally a student in a service-learning placement will be asked to do office chores—for example, answering phones or filing—that have nothing to do with the assigned project. Of course, many service-learning instructors do assign hands-on work in community agencies *instead of* or *in addition to* research and writing projects for agencies. Hands-on work might include working in the office in order to understand how the agency works. However, if your instructor has not explicitly assigned hands-on work in an agency as part of your course requirement but has specified a practical writing project only, answering the office phones is probably not the kind of work you should be doing. Ask yourself if the hands-on work you may be asked to do for your agency relates clearly to your writing project. If you think that the kind of work you are being asked to do is not directly related to your project, ask your instructor for help in resolving the situation.

Quite frequently, though, students in service-learning placements get extremely involved in the work their agencies do in the community, and these students often do volunteer additional time to their agencies, because they *want* to. Some students put in volunteer time at their agencies while their service-learning projects are underway; others continue working with their agencies in a volunteer capacity well after their projects are complete and their courses end. This kind of continued relationship between agencies and students is one of the richest and most satisfying outcomes of a service-learning experience.

> I continue to attend the monthly workdays at the AIDS Memorial Grove. On occasion I see my mentor at the Grove and our relationship remains very positive. I hope to continue to visit the Grove and participate in workdays for a long time.
>
> —Nik Reed, third-year student

The Service-Learning Contract

A contract is one of the best ways to ensure that everyone involved in the service-learning triad—the student, the agency mentor, and the instructor—is on the same page when it comes to a practical writing project. If everyone has the information they need and everyone agrees on the nature, kind, and scope of the project in advance, a whole lot of potential confusion and misunderstanding can be avoided.

Your instructor may want to use the sample contract that we provide on the following page. Or perhaps your instructor and the students in your class will want to write your own contract. The important thing is that you, your mentor, and your instructor have a structured way of agreeing on the project that you will undertake for your agency. Whatever contract you use, we recommend that you take it with you to your initial meeting and fill it out with your agency mentor after you define the project. Make sure that you leave your agency mentor with a copy of the contract. Then submit it to your instructor for approval.

Although a contract can help you define a project, it's important for everyone involved to maintain some flexibility. Your project will very likely evolve in some unexpected ways, because you—and probably your mentor and your instructor as well—will be learning as you go. If one thing doesn't work, you will want to try another; if you have a better idea, it will supercede an old one. Change is the inevitable consequence of adaptation and improvement.

COMMUNITY WRITING CONTRACT

This contract should be written and signed during the initial meeting between the student writer and the agency mentor and reviewed and approved by the instructor. All three parties should have a copy.

Organization _____

Web Address _____

Location _____   Mailing Address _____

_____   _____

_____   _____

Agency Mentor _____   Phone _____

_____   Email _____

Student Writer(s)_____   Phone_____

_____   Email _____

Instructor _____   Phone _____

_____   Email _____

Course _____

Quarter or Semester/Year _____

- Briefly describe the kind of document to be written (audience, purpose, topic, length).

- How will the document be used (printed in newsletter, distributed as a flyer, kept for agency's internal use, for example)? Who will be its primary readers? If there are secondary readers, who will they be?

- How will the writer get the information she or he needs (from the university library, the agency's library, interviews, other)?

- How often will the writer and the agency mentor confer?

Deadline for draft _____

Deadline for final copy _____

Writer's signature _____   date _____

Agency Mentor's signature _____   date _____

Instructor's signature _____   date _____

ADVANCE PLANNING AND TIME MANAGEMENT

It's best to work really far ahead instead of setting the deadline for the very end of the quarter as we did. That way you have more time to edit and discuss any additions.

—Rachel Seigel, first-year student

Don't procrastinate. If you wait until the last minute, you will learn the hard way that the real world is not sympathetic to school deadlines.

—Jenny Bernstein, first-year student

Students who have completed community-based writing projects in service-learning classes are in nearly unanimous agreement: these kinds of projects—whether they involve practical writing for your agency or academic writing directly related to your work in the community—are complicated, and they require more advance planning than most academic papers do. But what makes community-based projects so complicated and sometimes, yes, frustrating are the same things that make them so valuable, interesting, and ultimately satisfying. With some advance planning and attention to time management, you will be able to handle the complexities outlined here.

Logistics are complicated. There is a lot of footwork involved in getting a community-based writing project underway, keeping it going, and seeing it to completion. You will have to coordinate meeting times and schedules with your agency mentor and other community members, as well as with your instructor, and very likely with other students in your class. You will have to interrupt your routine and travel to unfamiliar territory when you visit your agency, probably more than once. In order to initiate good communication and keep it good, you will have to make a lot of phone calls or write emails frequently. You may be frustrated if you don't get answers to your questions when you want or need them. Remember that you are not just working on your own schedule, but in collaboration with many other people who are, like you, busy. It will simplify your life considerably and spare your nerves if you don't save any logistical task until the last minute; simply assume from the beginning that each task will be more complicated and will take more time than you think it will.

Collaboration is complicated. When you write a traditional academic paper, it is up to you—and you alone—to determine what you will write, how you will research it, when and how you will write it, and how much effort you will put into it. In a community-based collaboration, whether the project is an academic one or one for a community organization, you have to work with other people. Everyone has a say in what is written, how it is researched, when and how it's written, and how much effort it takes. By their very nature, collaborations are complicated. In a practical writing project, you will collaborate closely with your mentor, you will collaborate to some extent with your instructor, and you may well collaborate with other students. That's a lot of people with whom to coordinate not only times and meeting places, but also expectations, attitudes, ideas, and work styles. Collaborations take time and personal skills, including tolerance, flexibility, commitment, and persistence.

Research is complicated. When you read Chapter 9, "Researching," you will get a better idea of the levels and kinds of research that community-based writing projects may entail. Community-based research tends to be complicated because these projects have *consequence* and relate to real issues and real people in the community. Most students find that in their community-based projects they can no longer expect research to consist of one trip to the college library. In researching your project, you will probably rely heavily on primary, or original, research. You will likely find yourself spending more time interviewing experts, talking with people in the community, or digging through agency files and archives than you would in an academic project. This kind of research is interesting and rewarding, but it also takes time: you will have to figure out whom to talk with and arrange when and how to talk with them; you will need to find your way to files and archives, since they won't find their way to you.

Deadlines have real consequences. Deadlines for practical writing projects aren't negotiable. In community agencies, the work has to get done on time—and, one hopes, well—because someone else is counting on it. If you agree to take on a project, complete it. No excuses. If you agree to get your project draft or revision to your mentor by a certain date, do whatever you need to do to see that that happens.

One group of service-learning students we know of failed to get their finished flyer to their agency mentor on time. It was to be posted on Wednesday, announcing to homeless people which shelters would be open over the long Thanksgiving weekend. No one on the streets got the word.

> Deadlines in school are there but do not seem to carry as much weight. If you are late with an assignment in school, you might not get credit or you might get a lower grade, but in the real world, deadlines are much more important and carry different types of consequences. Working with a local nonprofit organization taught me some things about working and writing under more relevant circumstances.
>
> —*Scott Ransenberg, first-year student*

REFLECTIVE QUESTIONS
FOR JOURNAL-WRITING AND CLASS DISCUSSION

1. What, in terms of content and style, would be relevant and appropriate in a letter of introduction to your agency mentor? Compare your responses to those of other students in your class. Some mentors ask for résumés from students. Consider the differences between a résumé and a letter of introduction.

2. Do you have anxieties about meeting your agency mentor for the first time? Where do they come from? What actions might help ease them?

3. In many ways, students' relationships with their agency mentors are similar to employee/employer relationships. In what ways do you think your relationship with your mentor will or should be similar? In what ways do you think it will or should be different?

4. Some students think of certain types of hands-on work or writing projects at community agencies as being "glamorous" and others as being "ordinary." Discuss with other students in your class to what extent you make these distinctions, and on what grounds. Consider the relative advantages and disadvantages of so-called glamorous projects and so-called ordinary ones. For example, a project may seem glamorous if a student is given a lot of creative freedom in designing it, which can certainly be seen as an advantage. On the other hand, so much can be left up to the student that she or he might feel a lack of authority and guidance, which is a disadvantage. A more ordinary project might seem less creative (a disadvantage), but the fact that its structure is a known quantity might be reassuring (an advantage).

5. Procrastination is nearly universal among college writers, yet service-learning students, especially those who have produced practical documents for their agencies, agree: procrastination is not a viable approach to community writing. Meet in small groups, and help each other create a project schedule.

   - Consider the total amount of time that you have to complete the project; take into account your schedule and obligations and those of others.

   - Plan incremental deadlines. When will you complete the research? When will the draft be done? When is the final product due, and when will you submit it?

   - With collaborative projects, schedule group meetings according to the deadlines you have planned. Schedule a meeting after the research is complete to plan the draft. Schedule another meeting to review the draft and to plan formatting. Schedule a separate formatting session.

   - Establish a schedule for meetings with your mentor and with your instructor to discuss your draft. Make sure to allow enough time between draft and revision deadlines for your mentor and your instructor to provide feedback and for you to revise based on this feedback.

   Planning in advance can save you a lot of stress, and it nearly always ensures a better project.

TROUBLESHOOTING

WHAT IF...

> *you don't have transportation, or travel to your agency requires a three-hour commute?*

TRY TO...

> *anticipate these sorts of problems before you commit to working with an agency.* If distances are too great or transportation challenges seem insurmountable, then you should reject the idea of working with that agency—but do it *before,* not after, you make a commitment. If you are excited enough about working with a particular organization to tolerate significant personal inconvenience, great. But stick to your commitment.

WHAT IF...

> *you can't attend the initial meeting of your group at your agency?*

TRY TO...

> *do everything that you possibly can to schedule a time when everyone in your group can attend a first meeting.* If an emergency prevents you from attending, and rescheduling the meeting is not feasible, arrange a debriefing with your group members, and make a separate arrangement with your agency mentor to meet him or her and to visit the agency.

WHAT IF...

> *you call your agency mentor to arrange an initial meeting and leave a message, but you don't hear back?*

TRY TO...

> *not take it personally.* A lack of immediate response doesn't mean your mentor isn't looking forward to working with you or doesn't appreciate your contribution to the agency. Your mentor could be delayed in returning your call for any number of reasons. Nonprofit agencies are notoriously understaffed. Your mentor is responsible for many different kinds of work under the umbrella of one job. Your mentor may just be working his or her way down the list; your turn will come. Try asking someone else who works at the agency if there is a better number or a better email address by which to reach your mentor. Find out if your mentor might be out of town and if so when she or he is expected to return.

> *be politely persistent.* Call your mentor every day for two or three days, and send an email as well. Make sure that all of your messages are *specific.* Remind your mentor who you are and what your service-learning affiliation is, that you are calling to set up a meeting, and when you are available to meet. Leave your name, your telephone number, times when you can best be reached, and

your email address. Your mentor won't think you are being a pest if your persistence is polite and clearly related to enthusiasm about working with the organization and getting your project underway.

ask your instructor for help. If you know that your mentor is in town and your persistent attempts to establish contact have gone unanswered for more than four or five days, a gentle inquiry from your instructor can get things moving.

WHAT IF…

your agency mentor asks you to do too much work and you feel guilty about saying no?

TRY TO…

get over the guilt! It is reasonable to decline excessive work in a service-learning context, and you can be perfectly polite in saying no. Remember that giving a copy of your course syllabus to your mentor at your first meeting can help him or her understand your agency work within the context of the rest of your course work. Still, in some situations, especially if the agency mentor is new to service-learning, he or she may not know how to gauge what is and is not reasonable. If you feel that you have been assigned a project that is unreasonable in its scope, ask to meet with your mentor, and discuss the problem openly. If your concerns persist, ask your instructor for help.

WHAT IF…

you need an extension on your practical writing project for your agency?

TRY TO…

come to terms early on with the fact that requesting an extension on a community project is just not acceptable. If your agency has asked you to complete and submit your project by a certain date, your agency needs your project *then*, no later. For example, agency newsletters must be published at specific intervals, and the articles included in them must be edited before the issue is laid out and sent to the printer; many people need your work before they can do their own. Also, foundation deadlines for submission of grant proposals are non-negotiable, so your deadline for submitting your portion of the proposal to your agency is non-negotiable as well. If an agency deadline conflicts with a deadline for another assignment in your class, ask your instructor if she or he is willing to adjust that deadline, but don't ask your agency mentor.

CHAPTER 7

Work Styles and Writing Assignments in the Community

In academic writing, the audience reads your paper because they have to or are deeply interested in the topic. This is not necessarily the case with writing for the community where your aim may be to attract the person's attention or persuade someone once you do have the precious few minutes of his attention. In non-academic writing, I personally see a different purpose: Be persuasive. Be succinct.

—ANH BUI, FOURTH-YEAR STUDENT

When one of your assignments in an academic course with a service-learning component is to write material for the use of a community organization, you find yourself in an entirely different *rhetorical situation* than you do as an academic writer. The adjective *rhetorical* and its root noun *rhetoric* carry with them some perhaps unfortunate connotations. For example, when someone poses a question that she or he does not really want answered, we call it "a rhetorical question." When an argument is merely form, lacking content or sincerity, we call it "empty rhetoric." Although rhetoric has popularly come to connote a devious or otherwise suspect manipulation of language, its literal meaning is simply *the art and the product of spoken or written expression,* whatever the speaker's or writer's motives might be. There is such a thing, of course, as constructive rhetoric, in which speakers and writers craft their language to achieve a positive effect on an audience. A rhetorical situation, therefore, arises from any communication scenario in which a thoughtful speaker or writer must decide how most effectively to style his or her expression so that it accomplishes its *rhetorical purpose.* Rhetorical purpose depends very much on whom the speaker or writer wants to reach.

When you write practical documents in a community context, your primary readers are no longer your instructor and a few of your peers, and your immediate purpose in writing is no longer to receive a good grade. Readers of practical documents comprise new, unfamiliar, and larger audiences than most academic writers are used to. Depending on the kind of document you write and its purpose, your readers may include the public, agency staff, or others associated with carrying out the agency's work. Your purpose—whether to provide these readers with information or explanation, or to persuade them—arises from real necessity.

When you write a brochure that will be mailed by the fire department to every household within the city limits explaining a new local ordinance banning wood-burning fireplaces, your readers are the general public, and your purpose is to inform. When you write educational materials explaining tidepool ecology to visitors to a coastal park, your readers are members of the public of all ages with a demonstrated, if not well-informed, interest in the natural environment. Your purpose is to explain to them the complexity and fragility of the ecosystem they are witnessing and perhaps to persuade them, ultimately, that tidepools are not an appropriate source of souvenirs. If you write a flyer distributed to homeless people publicizing free AIDS testing, you are targeting a very specific, disenfranchised group of people in an attempt to persuade them to come into a local clinic to be tested and perhaps to receive further, much-needed medical care in the process.

Some writing targets agency insiders or professional readers, and its purpose is to promote or sustain the work of the organization itself. When you write an orientation manual for volunteers at a domestic violence hotline, your purpose in informing them is to help train them effectively to field calls from a vulnerable segment of the public. When you collaborate with agency staff in writing a grant proposal for an inner-city after-school program that is looking for a way to pay for computers for its kids to use, your readers may be members of a foundation board reviewing many grant proposals from many community nonprofits. Your purpose is to persuade these readers that your agency and its program are worth funding.

In service-learning, any writing that you do for a community agency should teach you something worthwhile; one hopes that another outcome of your hard work will be a good grade or positive evaluation. However, there are clearly more immediate objectives.

WORK STYLES IN COMMUNITY WRITING

You will find that in many respects writing in the community has much more in common with workplace writing than with most academic writing. This is understandable since private nonprofit organizations and governmental agencies are, after all, workplaces for the people who work in them, and, as businesses do, they serve a clientele. Collaborations in writing and other kinds of work in community agencies and other workplaces are quite common, whereas collaborations are less common in academic work. Working and writing in the community can help prepare you in very tangible ways for the workplace, as well as informing and enlivening your academic work.

The fact is that collaborations require both independence *and* cooperation. In order to be successful, collaborations require each member of a team to pull his or her independent weight. Student service-learners often find themselves in especially complicated collaboration scenarios because they are collaborating with so many people, in so many ways, and on so many levels. Not only are they collaborating with agency mentors in forming and revising practical writing projects, but they are also collaborating with their instructors and often with other students in completing them. Whereas working with instructors and other students may be familiar to you, collaborating with staff in community organizations may be entirely unfamiliar. It pays to understand something about the collaborative work culture in community agencies, since it differs so dramatically from academic work culture.

Understanding the Work Culture of Community Organizations

In many well-established *private nonprofit organizations,* there is a board of directors and an executive director. The board of directors generally comprises a combination of staff (including the executive director of the organization) and volunteer board members. Important decisions are generally made on the basis of a vote taken among members of the board. The job of the executive director is technically to carry out the decisions of the board, although most directors of private nonprofits have leeway in making many decisions on their own. Some private nonprofits operate by *consensus;* that is, important decisions affecting the organization are made only when all board members agree.

Not all private nonprofit organizations have boards of directors. If the organization has an executive director, generally this person has the final say on policy and procedure. If the organization operates by consensus, then all staff or project managers, and possibly even key volunteers, have equal say.

Acquiring funding is a major and ever-present concern of all private nonprofit organizations; staff and volunteers spend a huge portion of their time and energy just raising enough money to stay in business. If they don't raise funds, then they can't bring their programs and services to the community. Private nonprofits raise funds in three primary ways: (1) by applying for and receiving monetary grants or material grants (gifts in the form of computers, office supplies, or other materials) from private or corporate foundations or businesses; (2) through membership fees and monetary donations from individuals; and (3) from fundraising events. Staff of nonprofits find it frustrating that often more of their efforts go into fundraising—in the form of grant-writing, membership and donation drives, and sponsoring and hosting fundraising events—than in implementing their actual services and programs in the community.

However a private nonprofit organization is organized, staff and volunteers collaborate on a daily basis in numerous and complex tasks. They work together to conceive, articulate, and publicize their agency's mission. They educate the public through events and written materials. They devise and implement fundraising plans. They network with other groups, individuals, and policy-makers in order to gather and share information and to gain public and political support. They plan and perform outreach in the communities they serve. They conceive and carry out programs and projects that fulfill their agency's mission. Together, they keep the office organized and operational.

Depending on the size and funding of a particular agency, the number of staff and volunteers and the ratio of staff to volunteers vary. A large and long-established organization, especially if it is a national or international one, may have a number of paid staff, even in a regional office. Furthermore, because of name recognition, these organizations may have access to a fairly large number of volunteers who will likely help the agency with special tasks. A small grassroots organization will probably have a minimum of staff, often only one person who is seriously underpaid and seriously overworked. This kind of organization will rely heavily on a limited number of volunteers, dedicated but few, even in the day-to-day running of the office. No one, including staff in relatively large nonprofits, goes into this line of work because of the fat paycheck, and work in the nonprofit sector is notoriously grueling. But clearly, it is also meaningful and rewarding.

Although many, and probably most, students who work with community agencies in service-learning placements will work for private nonprofit organizations, some will work for *public nonprofit organizations,* or *governmental agencies.* Governmental agencies exist on the local (city and county), state, and federal levels. Students working with governmental agencies are most likely to work at the city or county level, with agencies ranging from fire and police departments, to parks and recreation programs, to libraries and social service programs.

Governmental agencies tend to be run differently than most private nonprofit organizations. For one thing, governmental agencies, even on the local level, are often larger operations, employing more people. There also tends to be a more distinct hierarchy in governmental agencies, often with separate departments or divisions operating within one agency. Even more so than within most private nonprofit organizations, everyone answers to someone in a governmental agency; everyone has a boss. For example, both office staff and field officers who work in the Hazardous Materials Division of a large urban fire department answer to the Head of the Hazardous Materials Division, and the Head of the Hazardous Materials Division answers to the Fire Chief. The Fire Chief, in turn, answers to the City Council.

Governmental agencies are notorious for their complicated bureaucracies, and even in efficiently run offices students' practical writing projects can evolve more slowly than in most private nonprofit agencies because there are more people involved in the collaboration. For example, one student working within the Hazardous Materials Division of a city fire department found that after his agency mentor, the Head of the Hazardous Materials Division, had approved the content of a Web page that he was writing to inform the public about household pesticides, he and his agency mentor had to submit the plan to the Fire Chief for approval. The same chain of approval had to be followed before the finished Web page could be posted to the fire department's Web site. This process took time and was occasionally frustrating for the student, but he and everyone else involved were very happy with the finished product. If you work with a governmental agency, be ready to work within a bureaucracy.

Governmental agencies are funded differently than private nonprofit organizations, but they, too, must scramble for funding. Since these agencies are funded by the government rather than by private grants and donations, they must submit budget proposals at the federal, state, county, or city level. Just because a governmental agency submits a proposal for a certain amount of money to fund operations and programs doesn't mean that it will be given this money. Many governmental agencies, therefore, are financially strapped, just as most private nonprofit agencies are. It would be relevant for you to know how the community agency you are working with is organized and funded, so ask.

Working with Agency Mentors and Staff

When you agree to work with a community agency, you may see yourself primarily as a student and as a service-learner, but staff and volunteers at your agency will see you as one of the team. They will expect you to do your job as part of that team. The emphasis on collaboration in the nonprofit sector, however, does not mean that you will not work independently. You will. Even if you are with a group of students at your agency, you will probably do quite a lot of independent work in researching and writing your project. Collaboration with agency staff will likely come into the picture most in hands-on work, and in planning and revising a practical writing project.

Once the project is reasonably well-defined and you and your mentor have agreed on its audience and purpose, you may find that you are pretty much on your own, and that your agency mentor will send you on your way, expecting you to work independently until the draft of the project is ready for review. After providing editorial feedback on the draft of a practical writing project, your agency mentor will probably send you off again with a smile and a "just do it" attitude. For students who are used to more structured and more familiar assignments, this degree of independence can be both liberating and disconcerting.

An agency mentor agrees to work with a service-learning student for one primary reason: the student will contribute something tangible to the agency's work. Since most community agencies are understaffed, having one more person to help with the work, especially with writing projects, is tremendously useful. Many of the documents that students produce have been on agency wish lists for some time, but these projects keep getting put off because staff must focus on more immediate concerns. Agency mentors are thrilled, in this respect, to work with students. One hopes, too, that agency mentors will enjoy working with students; most mentors do. They appreciate not only the work that students contribute to their agencies, but also the students' energy, their fresh ideas and perspectives.

The fact that we refer to them as *mentors*—as opposed to, say, *supervisors*—implies that mentors in community agencies do have an instructional role. Still, it is important for you to understand that an agency mentor's job differs from a teacher's job. Your teacher's exclusive job is to teach you and other students. Serving as your mentor is one of many professional tasks on your agency mentor's plate.

I think an ideal mentor is someone who is very easy to reach, gives the writer a reasonable workload, is explicit about what they are looking for in the project, and checks up on the student frequently. But there must be a balance between checking progress and giving the writer a legitimate amount of creative freedom.

—A first-year student

This student seems to be confusing the role of the mentor with the role of the teacher. Teachers *should* be easy for their students to reach. They *can* be expected to assign a reasonable workload, because they know what constitutes a reasonable workload in an academic context. Instructors *can* be expected to be explicit in their assignments, because they are teachers; likewise, instructors often *do* take the initiative in checking up on their students' progress because that is part of their job. Providing students with "creative freedom" may indeed *be* an important fundamental goal of an academic class.

Expectations that you might quite reasonably attach to your teacher cannot, however, be reasonably transferred to your agency mentor. Agency mentors can't be expected to be at students' service in the same way that teachers can, since mentors have other and different kinds of work to do. Agency mentors might not know what a reasonable workload is in a service-learning context; it is up to you to be clear and direct with your mentor if you feel that the work he or she expects from you is too much. Neither can a mentor be expected to be explicit in an assignment if he or she is expecting you to collaborate in clarifying it. It is not the mentor's responsibility to check up on student progress; rather, it is your responsibility to check in with your mentor when necessary. Ensuring that students have "creative freedom" is not the point in service-learning placements; making sure that agencies get what they need—whatever that may be—is. If your creativity can contribute to the success of a project, that's wonderful, but showcasing students' creativity is not a prerequisite for worthwhile practical writing projects.

Ideally, the mentor is someone who is patient and kind, someone who is already well established in their organization so that they can tell students exactly whom to talk to about what.

—Katie Braden, fourth-year student

The ideal agency mentor is responsive, helpful, direct, energetic. My agency mentor was a busy man, as could be expected. However, he was good about responding via email, and he left phone messages when necessary. This helped me out a lot.

—Steve Schreiner, fourth-year student

What *can* you reasonably expect from your agency mentor? Some expectations are more realistic than others. Your agency mentor should be accessible and responsive when you have important questions related to your project. But in the real world, your mentor may not be as readily available or respond to your questions as quickly as you would like. Most mentors are open to new ideas, but they also frequently have set projects in mind and a way of doing agency work that may limit your input. Because there is often a high rate of turnover among staff in community agencies, your mentor may be relatively new to the organization; although most students would prefer working with seasoned mentors, some mentors will be learning as they go, just as students are. Some will be more experienced or skilled in working with students or will enjoy it more than others: that's just a fact of life. Although of course you hope that your mentor will be kind and organized (as no doubt your mentor hopes that you will be), personality traits like these cannot be categorically expected.

Mentoring styles vary widely. One mentor may relate to you matter-of-factly, with a down-to-business attitude; another mentor may invite you over for dinner and take a more active role in providing you with guidance related to your project and beyond. There's really no telling in advance what kind of mentor yours will be. But in collaborating with your mentor, you will form an important relationship, and you will certainly have a role in shaping it.

Working with Instructors

Instructors who assign community-based practical writing projects as part of the work in their service-learning classes have a variety of individual approaches in managing these projects. Your instructor may take a hands-off approach, preferring that you collaborate primarily or exclusively with your agency mentor and, if yours is a group project, with the other students in your group. If your instructor's approach is hands-on, she or he may want to check on your progress at various stages of your project's development, as you define, research, plan, draft, and revise the project. Whether her or his approach is relatively hands-off or relatively hands-on, your instructor will be the one evaluating the finished project, since it is part of your course work. This can be confusing, especially if your instructor is providing advice and feedback on your project along the way: you may wonder, *who's the authority here, the instructor or the agency mentor?*

When you write for a community agency, the answer is *the agency mentor.* If your instructor gives you ongoing feedback as your project develops, or even just at the draft stage, he or she is trying to be helpful. Your instructor's role in helping to guide your practical writing project in the community is as an advisor; the agency mentor will have the final word on what works or does not work in a document you write for the agency's use. Your agency mentor is essentially the project boss; he or she knows much better than the instructor does what the agency wants and needs from the project.

The fact that your instructor is the one who will in the end evaluate your project involves a kind of act of faith on your part. It is your instructor's job, in collaborating with you and your agency mentor, to understand the audience and purpose of any writing that you produce for the agency; your instructor's evaluation of your project will be based on this understanding. Many instructors ask agency mentors for their assessments of students' projects before evaluating them. You need to trust that your instructor knows the specific audience and purpose of your community writing project well enough to evaluate its success on those terms rather than as a piece of academic writing.

Working with Other Students

In group projects that involve writing for a community agency, or when drafts of community writing projects undergo peer review, your collaboration process is further complicated: you are considering not only your agency mentor's and your instructor's feedback, but also feedback from other students. Of course, students with whom you are collaborating in writing a single project will have both a special understanding of and a vested interest in your work. Active collaborations with other students in a working group are most likely to occur in the formative stages of the project and in the revising and formatting stages.

After students working collaboratively have clearly defined a project with their agency mentor, they must figure how to fairly divide the work, including research. Although the research each student does may be accomplished independently, a student group needs to come back together to plan an organizational strategy for the document and to divide the work of drafting it. Although drafting the whole is very often accomplished most efficiently by each student individually drafting a part, it is essential that students collaborate in piecing these parts together. Revising and formatting the finished document should be a collaborative effort. (See "Collaborations among Peers" in Chapter 3. Also see Chapter 11, Formatting; and Chapter 13, Revising and Editing.)

Take care in a collaborative project that one student does not become the project leader. The collaborative process fails when one person or group within the larger group does more, or less, work than others. If you have had a poor experience with group work in the past, consider the possible reasons.

- *Have you shouldered the lion's share of the responsibilities in group work?*

If so, was it because your peers were lazy and you cared more about the work than they did? Or (be honest!) are you the type of person who tends to take over?

- *Have you not taken on your fair share of the responsibilities in group work?*

If so, was it because you were lazy and just didn't care? Or was it because you have a hard time speaking up?

Although simple laziness of some group members can be a factor, it is likely that the causes of most unfair collaborations run deeper than this. In your collaborations with other students, be self-aware, and pay attention to group dynamics. Early on in the collaboration, articulate an agreement among all group members that, regardless of personalities, *everyone* will contribute and *no one* will dominate.

In student collaborations, decisions that affect the whole project should be arrived at through mutual agreement so that the project is unified, coherent, and of one voice. Except in unavoidable circumstances, all students in the group should together attend meetings with the agency mentor or any other meetings or events that pertain to the whole project. Similarly, when meetings with the instructor focus on the entire project, as opposed to a student's individual part of it, all students should attend.

If your practical writing project is a collaborative one with other students, plan to serve as peer reviewers of one another's work, contributing ideas, suggestions, and editorial advice to each other. Clearly, students within collaborative groups make excellent peer reviewers since they have an in-depth understanding of the assignment, including the subject of the writing as well as its audience and purpose. However, because other students in your group are "inside" readers, they might sometimes find it difficult to read from your intended reader's perspective. A student from outside your collaborative group can also function as an excellent peer reviewer. In fact, an outside reviewer who understands the audience and purpose of your project well might be better able to read from your audience's perspective, spotting gaps in information or explanations, perhaps, or language that is unclear or not well suited for your intended reader.

Peer review is also, of course, extremely helpful if you are working on an individual project. With the suggestions and comments that you receive from your agency mentor and perhaps from your instructor as your project unfolds, you will not lack feedback. But feedback from a peer reviewer can provide you with a fresh perspective.

Collaboration in practical writing projects in the community can be both exhilarating and challenging. Working with a variety of people who are interested in and excited about your work and invested in your success can energize you and make you feel that you are contributing to something important through your writing. And you are! But intense collaboration with so many people can be confusing as well, especially if you sometimes receive contradictory feedback.

Just remember two things:

- *Make sure that you have a good grasp of the assignment, its audience and its purpose.* If you do, then you will know what you are trying to accomplish in your writing and will be better able to situate the feedback that you receive within the context of your goals in writing.

- *Remember that your agency mentor has the final word about what works and what doesn't in your practical writing project.*

DISCOURSE COMMUNITIES

> In my community-service writing project, I had to look at my writing as my audience would read it, and fit my writing to my audience's needs. At first, I discounted how difficult this task could be, and wrote my draft with an ambiguous and vague audience in mind.
>
> —*Karen Lai, first-year student*

A *discourse community* is a group of people, whether readers or writers, who not only have interests in common but also a special way of communicating within the group. These communities vary widely from coast to coast, region to region, neighborhood to neighborhood, even family to family; they vary radically with age, culture, religion, education, ethnicity, native language, and many, many other factors. Adolescents, for example, may form a vast discourse community, with a language and communication style that sets them apart from other age groups. Within this enormous community are countless subgroups—jocks, stoners, skaters, gamers, and the list goes on and on—smaller, more specifically identified discourse communities.

Discourse communities exist everywhere, and understanding them equates to understanding your audience when you are writing in the community. Members of discourse communities have common interests, both in the sense of being interested in the same things and having the same needs and concerns. They also quite often practice particular language and communication styles in expressing or sharing these interests.

Several basic characteristics can help you begin to identify discourse communities in order to understand your audience:

- *Age.* How old are your readers? If they are children, what is their age group? Elementary school age? Younger adolescents, in middle school? Older adolescents or high school students? Young adults? Older adults? Elderly people? Each of these age categories can be seen as comprising a broad discourse community.
- ***Education or literacy.*** Level of education is often related to age, and literacy is often related to level of education—but not always, and not exclusively. At what level of complexity is your audience able to read? Don't assume that all adult readers are sophisticated readers; many aren't, for a variety of reasons. On the other hand, an adult reader whose first language is not English may be a sophisticated reader in Cantonese, but not in English.

Readers with various levels of education and literacy can be seen as distinct discourse communities.

- ***Recipients or providers of services.*** Does your reader *receive* services from the organization? Or does your reader *provide* services to people in need of them? This is a fundamental distinction. Recipients of services comprise a discourse community quite different from that of those who provide services.

Of course, much more specifically identified communities exist within each of these very broad categories. A crucial part of your job in developing your particular assignment in writing for a community agency will be to identify the particular discourse community to which your reader belongs and to learn as much as possible about it.

In order to write for a particular set of readers, student writers need to become part of their discourse community. In some assignments this is easier to accomplish than in others. The more closely you identify with your reader's discourse community, the better you will understand your reader, his or her needs, and his or her language and communication style. If, for example, you are an eighteen-year-old college student writing a brochure about safe sex to be read by high school students, you are close enough in age and experience to have an intuitive understanding of your readers' experiences, needs, and attitudes as well as a good sense of how to—and how *not* to—communicate with them. In fact, as someone who has recently endured adolescence yourself, you are probably much *better* qualified and prepared to write for this particular discourse community than are the older people at the community organization you are working with.

If, on the other hand, you are an eighteen-year-old writing for an audience comprising elderly people, you have a more challenging task, since this discourse community has experience, needs, attitudes, and language and communication styles that are relatively unfamiliar to you. Let's imagine that your particular assignment is to write a simple and accessible how-to guide for elders who are interested in learning enough computer skills to access email and the Internet. You are considering a computer science major, so the subject is inherently interesting to you, and you certainly know the skills well enough to instruct others in them. What you need now in order to accomplish your task is the ability to put yourself in your reader's position and to understand what the world looks like from his or her point of view.

In order to write your elder's how-to guide to email and Internet access, you will have to understand your reader as specifically and completely as possible. You will need to take care not to project assumptions based on your own experience onto a reader whose experience is quite different from yours. The best way to learn about your reader and his or her discourse community is firsthand. Visit a retirement home.

- **Observe.** What is the daily routine? What resources exist? What are people's limitations?

- **Ask questions.** Talk to residents and staff. What do residents need? Seek advice and suggestions.
- **Listen** to people's stories; pay attention to their attitudes and their complaints.

In speaking to elderly people in a retirement community, what in retrospect may seem obvious begins to occur to you. Even among those residents who are interested in learning about new technology (and for them, computers *are* new technology), there is hesitancy, even fear. Computers are complicated and intimidating, many residents tell you. "What if I break something?" more than one person asks. For many people in this community, personal computers—whose use was common well before you were born—are utterly foreign. Most have no inherent understanding, as you do (because the cultural and educational climate you grew up in more or less demanded it), of how these machines work or what the Internet is. Whereas using a mouse was a fine motor skill you learned at the age of three, most of your potential readers don't know what a "mouse" is, much less how to use one. This discourse community has no technical language related to computers.

You realize that in order to write your how-to guide for this discourse community, you will have to explain in very clear and basic terms how computers and the Internet work before you can explain how to use them. You will have to avoid computer jargon, keeping technical language to an absolute minimum. When you do have to use terms like "window" or "desktop" or "mouse," you will need to explain clearly and simply what these terms mean. Moreover, it is crucial that you accomplish all this respectfully, without condescension; if your tone is patronizing, your reader will probably be rightfully offended and will simply stop reading, which of course will defeat your purpose. You also realize that you will have to print your guide in a larger than usual font, since poor eyesight is a fact of life for many of your readers.

---

em•pa•thy n. Intellectual or imaginative apprehension of another's condition or state of mind.
Funk and Wagnall's Standard Dictionary

ster•e•o•type n. A biased, generalized image of the characteristics of an ethnic or social group.
Funk and Wagnall's Standard Dictionary

Empathizing with your reader does not mean stereotyping him or her. A *stereotype* is derived from an automatic, overgeneralized, unexamined, and often erroneous assumption about what characterizes a large group of people. *Empathy* requires a deep and particular understanding of your reader's position in the world, what his or her life is like, what special needs he or she might have, what his or her attitudes and assumptions might be, and what language and communication style he or she might most readily understand and respond to. Writing for a relatively unfamiliar discourse community requires both research and *heart*. It requires that you become an honorary member of your reader's discourse community.

WRITING PURPOSES, GENRES, AND ASSIGNMENTS IN THE COMMUNITY

Exigence is a piece of writing's reason for being; it is the occasion of and the necessity for a piece of writing; it is the most essential connection that exists between the reader and what she or he is reading. Writers generally have to work harder in academic writing than they do in writing for the community to establish the exigence of a piece of writing, to convince the reader that what she or he is reading is important and relevant. The fact that your instructor is obligated to read what you have written does not mean that he or she will necessarily find it interesting or important. Because writing for the community is more inherently or more obviously purposeful than academic writing and targets a more specific reader who often has an inherent interest in what you are writing about, exigence is often easier to establish. For example, if you write an article about this year's upcoming programs for your agency newsletter, and that newsletter is mailed to the membership of the organization, you can assume that most of your readers will have an inherent interest in what you have to tell them; their interest is demonstrated through their membership.

However, just because your reader in the community has an inherent interest in the content of your writing does not mean that he or she will find that the writing is interesting. Your instructor *has* to read everything that you write, no matter how well or poorly it may be written, because it is his or her job to do so and to help you improve your ability to express yourself. Your reader in the community, on the other hand, has no obligation whatsoever to read what you have written; he or she will simply stop reading something that is poorly written or does not sustain his or her interest. Clearly, this would defeat your purpose in writing. In a practical writing project, your project boss might be your agency mentor, but very often your reader is someone else entirely, and whatever the specific kind or purpose of the document you write, it must *work* for that reader.

If you have had a job that has called upon you to write, you know something about the importance and functions of practical writing in the workplace. If you are like most students, however, you have not done much structured writing other than in school, and although you may not always feel entirely comfortable as an academic writer, you are likely to be more familiar with writing in academic genres than in practical ones.

As readers, though, we encounter practical writing genres constantly. When we read the newspaper, we read articles and advertisements, both practical genres. When we read flyers handed out on the street or posted on telephone poles and bulletin boards, we are reading practical genres. When we attempt to decipher the instructions to program our DVD, we are reading a practical genre. As readers of practical writing genres, we know what works and what doesn't in capturing our attention and giving us the kind of information we need. If a flyer handed to you on the street isn't personally relevant, you chuck it into the first available trash or recycling bin. Even with your inherent interest in learning to program your DVD, if the instructions are too technical, too complicated, or unclearly written, you will probably give up in frustration and get somebody else to do it or try to figure it out on your own. Understanding your assignment in terms of your reader's needs, and understanding how this translates into *rhetorical purpose,* is even more important in writing in the community—where writers and readers often do not belong to the same discourse community—than it is in academic writing.

It is likely that the writing that you do for your community agency will have a primary—or predominant, or ultimate—rhetorical purpose, just as it has a primary reader. Ask yourself:

- Is the primary purpose of the document *to inform?* Is it *to explain?* Is it *to persuade?*
- To what extent do these rhetorical purposes overlap? To what extent will they build on one another in the document?

Practical Genres That Inform

Because of its practical nature, most writing in community contexts serves *to inform* readers, providing them with specific information that they want or need. This information often pertains to the agency itself, to its activities and programs, or to subjects that are related to the agency's work. Some of the common practical genres that inform in community writing are press releases, reports, instructional manuals, brochures and pamphlets, flyers, fact sheets, newsletter articles, and Web pages.

If the exclusive purpose of the writing you do for your agency is to inform, then you must take special care in two respects:

1. Your information must be relevant, accurate, and complete, according to your reader's needs.
2. You must be careful not to editorialize.

There are many instances in practical writing scenarios in which injecting your opinion, or even the position that your agency might take in another rhetorical situation, is not appropriate. For example, the volunteer coordinator at a major metropolitan zoo surprised one student in a service-learning placement when she emphatically instructed him to stick exclusively to the cold, hard facts in writing his fact sheets about animals at the zoo. The student's job was to inform teenage volunteers about the birds of prey that they handled in demonstrations; the volunteers, in turn, used what they learned in reading these fact sheets to educate younger visitors. The coordinator did not want the student writer to inject emotion into his writing or personify these animals in any way in describing their natural habits and habitats. It was her view that if children appreciated these animals because they were interesting and remarkable in their own right, rather than because they were cute, they were more likely to grow into adults who were willing to see to it that these species were protected simply because they had a right to exist, not because they served any human purpose.

In the Appendix, you can find another example of community writing the exclusive purpose of which is to inform: Jenny Bernstein's report, "Water Quality: Tap Water," from *Indicators for a Sustainable San Mateo County: A Yearly Report Card on Our County's Quality of Life,* published by the private nonprofit organization Sustainable San Mateo County, in California. Students from Stanford University as well as local high school students, other local citizens, and agency staff have collaborated and contributed for years to this annually published report. The publication consists of factual reviews of data related to various indicators of quality of life in the county, including employment trends, per pupil funding, air quality, and homelessness. Sustainable San Mateo County's mission is to educate the public without advocating any specific approach to remedying the county's ills. Because of the organization's reputation for providing accurate information in an unbiased fashion, city and county officials have come to rely on this annual report in order to ascertain what areas of the public welfare need most attention. Although Sustainable San Mateo County advocates the basic principle that overall quality of life must be measured holistically, taking into account the community's economic and environmental health as well as social equity issues, the organization is effective in its work precisely *because* it does not take a political stand.

Practical Genres That Explain

Very often in community writing, *explanation,* which requires some degree of analysis, accompanies information, especially when an agency wants to expose the public to a particular way of looking at the facts that is in line with its mission and that supports its work in the community. Some of the common practical genres that *explain* in community writing are fact sheets, newsletter articles, Web pages, position and policy statements, project proposals and assessments, letters to policy-makers, opinion editorials, and letters to the editor.

It is sometimes difficult to clearly distinguish explanation from overt argument, or persuasion. Very often, explanation leads quite naturally to persuasion. However, whether explaining is your ultimate purpose in a practical document or a stop along the way toward argument, your first task will be to approach your subject reasonably. In explanation and analysis in community contexts, as in academic ones, the key objectives are clarity, logic, and demonstration of fact. It is possible to explain any given subject in any number of ways, but you want your reader to accept your explanation as the most credible one.

A good example of explanation in a practical document is the voters' guide that arrived in your mailbox before the last election. In voters' guides, opponents and proponents of every proposition or ballot measure have the opportunity to make brief statements that explain their positions, offering analyses, projecting costs, benefits, and other ramifications from their differing points of view. These are position statements, and they are not so much political arguments as explanations, offered from a particular perspective. The object is to get the voter to accept the credibility and reasonableness of one analysis over the other.

Practical Genres That Persuade

Persuasion or *argument* in community writing contexts is frequently *explicit.* Although a credible piece of persuasive writing must also provide information and explanation, its final objective will be to persuade the reader of something very tangible: you want to convince your reader to adopt a specific position or to take a specific action. Persuasive documents in community writing make recommendations, appeals, and requests; they include project proposals or assessments, letters to policy-makers, opinion editorials, letters to the editor, fundraising and solicitation letters, and grant proposals. Sometimes a document that we might think of as being essentially informative or explanatory in nature—for example, a flyer or fact sheet—culminates in an explicit argument.

All arguments, including those made in practical documents, need four essential elements:

1. *A claim* to be supported.
2. *An audience* to be persuaded.
3. *Exigence*, or a reason for the argument to be made.
4. *Reasons* in support of the claim.

For example, imagine that you are writing a flyer for a free clinic in your city for distribution in a neighborhood known for its drug trafficking. Your *claim* is that intravenous (I.V.) drug users should participate in the clinic's needle exchange program. Your *audience* is I.V. drug users. Your *exigence* is the fact that the rate of HIV infection among I.V. drug users in your city is on the rise. Your *reasons* in support of your claim, succinctly stated in your flyer, are that (1) using new needles instead of shared ones will reduce the user's chances of contracting HIV/AIDS; (2) using new needles will reduce the chances of the user's loved ones and unborn children contracting HIV/AIDS; (3) widespread use of new instead of shared needles will reduce the general rate of HIV/AIDS infection; (4) these needles are free; and (5) participation is confidential.

Because of their purposeful and practical nature, arguments in the context of community action tend to be, in certain respects, easier to make than academic arguments, which tend to be more theoretical. In defining your project with your agency mentor, you will probably know in advance to what extent your writing will be an argument, and you will probably know what essential claim you will make, since that claim will be inherent in the writing's purpose. You also will know who your readers will be, and since there will be both a clearly defined audience and a clearly defined purpose, exigence will be established.

A practical argument made in a community context tends to be most successful when it meets the following criteria:

■ *The argument is specific.* Practical arguments advocate. Your reader should know exactly what he or she is being asked to do and should be given the necessary information and resources to do it.

■ *The argument is well-supported.* Your reasons must clearly support your claim and, in turn, must be well supported by credible and convincing evidence, whether that evidence is statistical (based on facts and figures), anecdotal (drawing from people's experience or testimony), or reasoned (relying on logical explanation).

■ *The argument appeals to logic.* Your claim, the reasons for it, and the evidence supporting it need to make sense.

■ *The argument appeals fairly to emotion.* Your argument may well ask your reader to sympathize or empathize, or it may call upon your reader's sense of what is right or just, but it should not play on your reader's prejudices or fears.

■ *The argument anticipates hesitancy or opposition.* Based on a clear understanding of your specific reader, you will want to anticipate and respond to the reasons your reader might not go along with your argument.

These are essentially the same qualities that are stressed in academic arguments, although some qualities that are stressed in academic writing are not as relevant or practical in community writing. For example, many practical arguments appeal to emotion more patently than do most academic arguments, partly because something very tangible is at stake and many community agencies deal with the actualities of people's lives rather than with ideas about them. There tends to be more latitude in using emotional appeals in practical arguments, although no reader, whether in an academic or community setting, enjoys feeling emotionally manipulated by an argument. Argumentation in academic writing stresses acknowledging the complexity of an argument, including opposing views, in order to provide fair coverage of a topic as well as to strengthen an argument. In practical arguments, for practical reasons, you will certainly want to anticipate and address factors that might dissuade your reader from taking the position or action you are advocating; however, providing "fair coverage" to opposing views is not a value or an obligation inherent in practical arguments. In practical arguments, the goal really *is* to win an argument, whereas in academic arguments the goal more often is to contribute to an ongoing intellectual dialogue or debate.

You will find two examples of practical arguments, presented in different genres, in the Appendix. The first is the brochure "Landmine Awareness" written by Jessica Gray for the American Red Cross. Her readers are people who have a general interest in the humanitarian activities and programs of the American Red Cross. First informing her readers about the devastating effects that abandoned landmines have on civilian populations worldwide, Jessica mounts a powerful appeal to her readers, urging them to get involved in the international movement to ban landmines by (1) learning the facts, (2) raising others' awareness, (3) pressuring political leaders, and (4) joining organizations that support the International Campaign to Ban Landmines. Jessica's argument is supported by both factual evidence and photographs that attest powerfully to the extent of the problem and to the actual damage that landmines inflict on innocent civilians. You will also find in the Appendix, as an interesting comparison, Jessica's research paper on the same topic, "Landmines: Distant Killers." This research paper is not only an example of an academic project that evolved from a community one, but it is also an example of an academic, as opposed to a practical, argument.

The second example of a practical argument is a grant letter, written by Adryon Burton on behalf of her agency, Helping After Neonatal Death, appealing to a grant foundation for funding. Adryon's claim is clear and concrete: HAND needs funding from the Foundation to purchase a laptop computer and necessary hardware and software. Her audience (the foundation board) is specific, and exigence (the organization's work is limited by the lack of these important tools) is established. Her reasons, which draw on reasoned explanations, are persuasive. In order to compose this argument, Adryon had to know her agency, its work, and its needs, as well as the potential funder. She needed to persuade her readers not only that HAND was a worthy organization, but also that the specific request for funding was reasonable and well-matched to the granting foundation's mission and values.

The truth is that most practical documents in a community context have overlapping rhetorical purposes; one purpose may be primary or explicit and others secondary or implicit. For instance, your primary rhetorical purpose in writing a simple agency brochure may be to inform the community about the agency's mission, programs, and services. But in providing this information, you may well explain the need for these programs and services in the community. Your implicit argument is clear: your agency meets an important need in the community and is worthy of community support. In an explicit argument that you articulate in a fundraising letter, your primary rhetorical purpose might be to persuade your organization's membership to ante up. But your appeal will fail unless you provide concrete information about agency goals and programs and explain why people's donations are needed and how they will be spent. In fact, any document the primary purpose of which is to explain will be built on information, and any document the primary purpose of which is to persuade will be built on both information and explanation.

In spite of the fact that practical documents tend to have multiple and overlapping purposes, both explicit and implicit, you will probably find that any document you write for your agency has a primary or ultimate rhetorical purpose—to inform, to explain, or to persuade. Understanding this purpose will provide you with important clues about the content, presentation, and tone of what you write. In understanding your practical writing assignment as a practical application of *rhetoric*, you will understand the ways in which it is similar to and different from the rhetoric that you practice in academic writing.

RHETORICAL PURPOSES OF PRACTICAL DOCUMENTS		
	To Inform	*To Explain*	*To Persuade*
Press Releases	**inform** the public through newspapers and other news media about agency services, programs, and events		
Reports	**inform** the public or agency insiders, in-depth, about subjects closely related to agency work	*sometimes...* **explain** to the public or agency insiders subjects closely related to agency work from agency perspective	
How-To or Instructional Guides	**inform** the public or agency insiders how to do something	*sometimes...* **explain** to the public or agency insiders the reasons for doing something or doing it in a certain way	
Brochures and Pamphlets	**inform** the public about • agency programs and services; • subjects and issues closely related to agency work	*sometimes...* **explain** to the public • the need for agency programs and services; • subjects and issues closely related to agency work from agency perspective	*sometimes...* **persuade** individuals • to donate time or money; • to participate in agency programs or to use agency services; • to take a stand or action on issues closely related to the agency's work
Flyers	**inform** the public and specific individuals about • agency-sponsored or supported events, programs and services; • issues closely related to agency work	*sometimes...* **explain** to the public and specific individuals • the need for agency and other programs and services; • issues closely related to agency work from agency perspective	*sometimes...* **persuade** the public and specific individuals • to participate in agency programs or to use agency and other services; • to take a stand or action on issues closely related to the agency's work
Fact Sheets	**inform** the public about issues related to agency work	*often...* **explain** to the public issues closely related to agency work from agency perspective	*often...* **persuade** the public • to get involved in agency activities; • to take a stand or action on issues closely related to agency work

RHETORICAL PURPOSES OF PRACTICAL DOCUMENTS *(continued)*

	To Inform	*To Explain*	*To Persuade*
Newsletter Articles	**inform** agency insiders and the public about • agency programs and activities; • subjects, issues, and events closely related to agency activities	**explain** to agency insiders and the public • subjects and issues closely related to agency work from agency perspective; • news from agency perspective	*often ...* **persuade** agency insiders and the public • to get involved in agency activities; • to take a stand or action on issues closely related to agency work
Web Pages	**inform** agency insiders, other nonprofit agencies, and the public about • agency activities and programs; • subjects and issues closely related to agency work; • other resources, including other organizations and Web sites	**explain** to agency insiders, other nonprofit agencies, and the public • the need for agency programs and services; • subjects and issues closely related to agency work from agency's perspective	*often ...* **persuade** • individuals to participate in agency programs or use agency services; • the public to get involved in agency activities; • the public to take a stand or action on issues closely related to agency work
Position or Policy Statements	**inform** agency insiders, policy-makers, and the public about facts and background of issues and policies closely related to the agency's work	**explain** to agency insiders, policy-makers, and the public issues and policies closely related to the agency's work from agency perspective	**persuade** policy-makers and the public to adopt the agency's position on issues and policies closely related to agency work
Project Proposals and Assessments	**inform** agency insiders about background and logistics of proposed or current agency projects	**explain** to agency insiders the relative costs and benefits of proposed or current projects	**persuade** agency insiders that • proposed projects should, or should not, be undertaken; • current projects should, or should not, be continued; • proposed or current projects should be modified in certain ways
Letters to Policy-Makers	**inform** policy-makers about issues and policies closely related to agency work	**explain** to policy-makers • specific issues and policies closely related to agency work from agency perspective; • how these issues or policies impact the agency's constituency	**persuade** policy-makers to take a particular stand or specific action on issues and policies closely related to agency work

(continued)

RHETORICAL PURPOSES OF PRACTICAL DOCUMENTS *(continued)*		
	To Inform	*To Explain*	*To Persuade*
Opinion Editorials and Letters to the Editor	**inform** the public about issues and policies related to agency work	**explain** to the public • specific issues and policies closely related to agency work from agency perspective; • how these issues or policies impact the agency's constituency	**persuade** the public to take a particular stand or specific action on issues and policies closely related to agency work
Fundraising and Solicitation Letters	**inform** potential donors about • the agency, its programs and services; • its plans for the future; • issues and policies crucial to agency work	**explain** to potential donors • the need for agency programs and services; • issues and policies related to agency work from agency perspective	**persuade** potential donors to donate their time, money, or goods to the agency and its work
Grant Proposals	**inform** the potential funder in detail about • the agency, its programs, services, record of service in the community; • subjects and issues closely related to agency work and objective of the grant; • agency plans for the future, especially related to use of grant	**explain** to the potential funder • subjects and issues closely related to agency work from agency perspective; • how the potential funder's mission relates to the agency's mission and grant request; • how the grant will be used	**persuade** the potential funder that • the agency is credible and has been effective in its work; • the grant would be well used; • the grant would produce positive and measurable results

REFLECTIVE QUESTIONS
FOR JOURNAL-WRITING AND CLASS DISCUSSION

1. What does *rhetoric* mean to you? Does it carry positive or negative connotations? Why? Provide some examples of *rhetorical situations* that you encounter on a regular basis.

2. In what ways, and to what extent, can the management of a nonprofit organization be compared to the management of a business?

3. Who is the audience for the practical document that you will produce for your community agency? Describe your audience's discourse community. What are your readers' common interests, and what characterizes their language and communication styles?

4. To what extent do you identify with the discourse community that you will address in your practical document? Is it relatively familiar or unfamiliar to you? How will you gain the authority to write within and for a discourse community to which you do not belong?

5. With your practical writing project in mind, consult the table "Rhetorical Purposes of Practical Documents" presented in this chapter. What kind of document does your project call for? To what extent will the document have multiple or overlapping rhetorical purposes? What will the primary, or ultimate, rhetorical purpose of this document be?

TROUBLESHOOTING

WHAT IF…

you think your mentor has given you too much freedom to conceptualize your project? What if you need more guidance?

TRY TO…

talk with your mentor and request a brainstorming session. If your mentor does not have a very clear idea of the specific content or form of your practical document, thinking through the possibilities together might help to clarify the project for both of you.

look at examples of the kind of document that you think you will be creating. Your agency mentor may be able to provide you with these examples.

ask your instructor for help. She or he may also be able to brainstorm your document's content and form with you and may also provide you with examples of similar projects.

WHAT IF…

the feedback that your instructor offers on your draft suggests that he or she does not entirely understand the audience and purpose of your practical document?

TRY TO…

explain your project's audience and purpose again. Sometimes, the purpose of a project evolves with the project itself. Your instructor's understanding of your project's audience and purpose may be based on an earlier description of it. Try not to look at this as challenging your instructor's authority, but rather as ensuring good communication about your project as it evolves.

WHAT IF…

the peer collaboration breaks down and you are left holding the bag?

TRY TO…

avert this disaster before it strikes. If the group members' contributions to the project are significantly uneven, explain the problem to your instructor and ask him or her to intervene. If one or more of your group members drops out of the project, try to redistribute the work among the remaining members. If this work is too much to absorb, see if your instructor can suggest another person for inclusion in your group.

do the best you can to bring the project to conclusion, given the time you have and your own limitations. In a worst-case scenario, in which a project partner or partners ceased to participate, no one, including your mentor and your instructor, will expect you to do everyone's work, although everyone, especially you, will be disappointed if the project is incomplete.

WHAT IF...

in your practical writing assignment you have trouble identifying a primary rhetorical purpose?

TRY TO...

check in with your mentor and confirm your understanding of the assignment. Do you understand clearly the subject of your writing, the kind of document you are creating, your reader's identity, and what you need to say to your reader? In order to determine the rhetorical purpose of your practical document, you will need to answer these questions first.

consider the extent to which your document may involve multiple or overlapping rhetorical purposes. Refer back to the chart "Rhetorical Purposes of Practical Documents" presented earlier in this chapter and note that most kinds of practical documents do have more than one rhetorical purpose. Try looking at rhetorical purpose in your document as a set of building blocks: it is quite likely that information will provide the foundation, explanation will provide the structure, and persuasion—whether implicit or explicit—will top it off.

CHAPTER 8

Academic Writing
in a Service-Learning Context

I wrote a six-page paper on the issue of utilizing volunteers in a nonprofit organization setting, focusing on the situation at my agency. I discussed various methods to attract, inspire and maintain volunteers. I later extended this topic into a twelve-page research paper on altruism. I discussed the various philosophical and biological explanations for altruism and extended these theories to assist nonprofit organizations in harnessing the altruism of their volunteers.

—JENNY BERNSTEIN, FIRST-YEAR STUDENT

When you are asked to write about your service-learning experience for your class, you are being asked to make the vital connection between what you learn in your community work and what you learn in the classroom. Most students find that the work they do in the community through service-learning placements—whatever kind of work that is—inspires their academic work. It lends crucial importance to academic study, bringing to life information and ideas that might otherwise remain abstract or theoretical. Community work provides students with concrete and relevant writing topics, and makes writing about them more purposeful than it would have been in a strictly academic context.

There are various ways in which you might be asked to write about your service-learning experience in an academic context. Some involve informal writing, while others focus on formal writing. The immediate purposes of and audiences for these kinds of writing are academic; that is, they are primarily intended to facilitate your learning and to demonstrate what you have learned to your instructor and perhaps to other students in your class. However, even when they have not explicitly planned to do so, many students share this academic writing with their agencies and mentors because it is so highly relevant to the work that their agencies do and the communities that they serve. Many community-based academic writing assignments, therefore, have very real secondary purposes, and extended audiences. When this happens, students open up the academic community even further to include the community at large, and vice versa.

Making connections between academic study and real-world issues is what academic writing in a service-learning context is all about, and this goal embodies the most fundamental reasons for education. Writing about the experiences and ideas that you encounter in the community completes the service-learning cycle.

THE CHALLENGES OF ACADEMIC WRITING

I have always hated academic writing because it was so distant for me. Pick a topic, debate, analyze, and then argue is not my protocol. I do feel that academic writing helps me to learn how to better express myself to a certain audience. Also, I feel that in the process I am writing in someone else's voice—the academic. When I write, I always try to be as objective as possible but there is always a bit of the personal in it; I cannot avoid this. The main challenge is to fuse a balance between objectivity and personality. I want to continue to grow as a writer in this fusion between the personal and the objective. I want to make myself better understood and accepted by the world of academia while in the process not compromising my initial vision.

—Charles Kakel, first-year student

Most students recognize the value of academic writing assignments: they are designed not only to test your knowledge and challenge you to think critically about information and subject matter, but also to help you refine your ability to communicate clearly to others what you know and think. Academic writing assignments invite your participation, as a member of the academic discourse community, in an intellectual dialogue.

Even though most students appreciate the relevance of learning the ways in which to participate in academic discourse, they are often frustrated by the writing they are asked to do in school. Many students dread writing academic papers more than other assignments that their instructors give them, including readings, problem sets, or tests. This dread comes not simply from the fact that writing is hard work, although of course it is. Often, it's the form, voice, and style of academic writing that bothers students. As an academic writer, you may sometimes feel as though you are dressing up in clothes that don't quite *fit*. The structure and the stylized expression of much academic writing may feel foreign and unnatural to you.

Student academic writers often feel like outsiders in the academic discourse community because they occupy novice positions in that community. Especially early in their college careers, students often lack experience and authority in the subjects and academic disciplines in which they are writing, even though, as part of the learning process, they are consistently asked to act like—to write as if they were—insiders. The position of a novice, compared to the more secure position of an academic professional or specialist, can be especially uncomfortable or frustrating when students don't yet fully understand the nature of the discourse community in which they are writing.

Discourse Communities within the University

Academic knowledge is furthered by *discourse*—an ongoing and evolving spoken and written conversation among people interested in sharing information and experience, analyzing problems and issues, influencing thoughts and actions, and contributing to the formation of knowledge itself. In the academic world, knowledge is understood within the contexts of specific academic disciplines, although there is a good deal of overlap between and sharing of knowledge among disciplines. Still, specialists tend to communicate most often with one another within discourse communities in specialized forms and voices.

Student academic writers in various courses in the disciplines are generally expected to model their writing after academic or professional specialists in those fields, even though the purpose of students' academic writing differs from that of professional writers. Students, by definition, write to learn; students' writing is a product by which teachers measure that learning. Readers of the writing that professionals produce are by no means uncritical, but professional writing does not exist primarily in order to be judged.

When we speak of *academic disciplines,* we mean, broadly, fields of study in three major areas: the *sciences,* the *social sciences,* and the *humanities.* Areas of study within the sciences include, perhaps most recognizably, biology, computer science, engineering, environmental science, geology, mathematics, physics, and statistics. The social sciences include anthropology, economics, political science, psychology, and sociology. Areas of study within the humanities include art and music criticism, education, history, philosophy, languages, literatures, and religion. Some schools consider the *fine arts*—the practice of visual art, creative writing, drama, and music—as existing within the humanities, and some see the fine arts as a separate area. Each discipline and subdiscipline constitutes a discourse community.

Academic discourse communities are like any other discourse communities in that language and forms of writing help members communicate efficiently about subjects of great interest and concern to the group. Because writers in academic discourse communities generally communicate among themselves rather than to *lay* (nonprofessional or nonspecialized) audiences, they take certain shortcuts in their communication. For example, in using technical terms unique to their fields and referring to, rather than explaining, fundamental concepts, discipline-specific writers assume a specialized knowledge on the part of their readers. Furthermore, some writing genres in various disciplines have become standardized. For instance, the basic form of a lab report—with its sections of Abstract, Introduction, Materials and Methods, Results, and Discussion—has not changed much in over one hundred years. Its highly structured form allows readers in the discipline to know in advance exactly in what order they will encounter information and analysis so that their reading becomes more efficient.

At their best, through their common languages, styles, and forms of communication, discourse communities help identify and support the common interests of their members; at their worst, they isolate themselves, working actively to exclude others, and consequently become stale and inbred in their thoughts and actions. The language of every discourse community, including academic ones, can be reduced in the extreme to mere *jargon,* a use of language that is pompous or inflated and purposely obscure. Jargon may be incomprehensible not only to people outside a specific discourse community who nevertheless would like to understand what is going on within it, but even sometimes to people within the discourse community. When writers take too many shortcuts and assume too much understanding on the part of their readers, their writing, when it is scrutinized, may turn out to be empty or illogical. Likewise, highly stylized forms of written communication may degenerate into mere formulas, which can too easily discourage creative or independent thought. A discourse community (including professionals and students alike) can be hobbled in these ways by jargon or formulaic expression, which limits an understanding of its relevance and how it relates to other fields of study and issues outside the academy.

Students' frequent discomfort with academic writing within specific discourse communities is understandable, given their positions, especially early in their educations. They must begin to master not only a body of knowledge within a given discipline, but also conventions of discourse in that community. The learning curve is steep, and initial attempts may be awkward. Community-based academic writing assignments can help ease this awkwardness considerably. When an academic assignment is tied directly to your experiences in the community, you are able to draw on your own authority, your earned expertise, relating it in a meaningful way to more theoretical material. Furthermore, a community-based academic writing assignment will probably allow you more personal leeway in the form, style, and voice of your writing, even within the conventions of academic discourse.

Academic Work Styles

Traditional academic work styles can aggravate any detachment, isolation, or awkwardness that you may feel in the face of academic writing assignments. In the world of work outside the university, teamwork and collaboration very often get the job done, and a crucial aspect of a person's success in the workplace is his or her ability to work well with other people. In school, however, individual achievement is generally the most important measure of success, and student performance is usually evaluated individually in the form of a grade. There is relatively little collaboration among students, in large part because in an academic context students' learning is constantly being tested and measured, and collaboration complicates this measurement. Students' individual achievement tends to be more highly valued than collaborative achievement, and to a large extent, the same is true for academic scholars and researchers.

The emphasis on individual performance has certainly applied traditionally for students in the humanities and perhaps to a slightly lesser extent for students in the social sciences. Collaboration tends not to be quite as foreign to students in the sciences, who must for practical reasons work more frequently in groups to conduct experiments and report results. It has only been relatively recently that instructors in other disciplines, including those in the humanities and social sciences, have begun to implement collaborative learning more widely. These teachers recognize not only that collaboration is an important skill, but also that collaborations, including writing collaborations, can escalate and enhance students' learning in ways that individual efforts cannot.

Consider the potential benefits of collaborative learning, even in a relatively traditional academic context, as compared to an approach that is more exclusively focused on individual research, writing, and achievement. Imagine that you are a student in a Native American cultural anthropology seminar at the University of Oklahoma. The focus of the class is on the major Southern tribes "relocated" to Oklahoma—the Cherokee, Creek, Choctaw, Chickasaw, and Seminole Nations. Every class meeting features a lecture by the instructor, based on the week's assigned reading in the textbook, followed by discussion of the material. Although you find the reading interesting, you don't particularly enjoy these discussions because students in the class seem to be merely competing to impress the instructor with their comments and observations. A mid-semester test gauges students' comprehension of the material, and a research paper is due at the end of the semester. As your topic, you choose to research and write about traditional marriage customs of the Choctaw tribe. You receive a few comments from your instructor and a B + on the paper. Your final grade for the class is a C + because you didn't do well on the midterm exam.

Now imagine what might happen with an approach that emphasizes collaborative learning. At the beginning of the semester, the instructor divides the fifteen students in the class into five groups, assigning the study of one tribe to each group. Each three-member group conducts secondary research to learn about the history and culture of the tribe it is studying as well as primary research, in the form of interviews with tribal members, to learn about issues that currently affect tribal life. After the research is complete, students in each group collaborate in writing a fifteen-page paper on the tribe they have studied, due mid-semester. The instructor gathers the papers from all five groups and distributes copies to everyone in the class. Class discussion in the weeks that follow evolves from the work of all five student groups and focuses on a comparative analysis of the five tribes, from an historical, cultural, and current issues perspective.

In this example, you can see that student collaboration occurs in many forms, at many levels, and with a variety of outcomes, enhancing learning and, no doubt, posing challenges. Students in each of the small groups must determine how to divide both the secondary and the primary research they will conduct on the tribe they have been assigned. Although perhaps this research will be conducted by students independently, they must come together when the research is complete, sharing what they have learned and deciding how the parts fit together. They must decide, as a group, how they will organize their paper and what analytical conclusions they will draw from their research. In writing the paper, each of the three students will perhaps take on a distinct section. Although these three students may draft their portions of the paper individually, they will revise and edit the paper together, making sure that the parts fit logically and smoothly and that the writing voice and style are consistent throughout. They will also work collaboratively in compiling the bibliography and formatting the paper before they submit it.

These students know that the other members of their group are relying on their participation and on the quality of their work, since all three students in each group will receive the same grade on the project. They know, too, that the instructor is not the only person who will be reading their work; every student in the class will rely on it for important information and analysis, and this paper will, along with the other groups' papers, help determine the direction of the entire course. This is *real* writing. With stakes so much higher than they would be with individual projects, students will likely be highly invested in this project, putting into it their best efforts. Furthermore, since their individual research and insights will be combined with and compounded by those of their classmates, students will probably learn more about the larger subject than they would through individual or less participatory projects.

Opportunities for collaborations in research and writing abound in service-learning classes. If you are working in a community agency with other students in your class, consider the advantages of student collaborations in researching and writing academic projects for the class. Even if you are working alone at your agency, opportunities for collaboration are inherent: in researching and writing your academic projects, you have access to people—your mentor and other people in your agency and in the community that your agency serves—who can provide information, experience, and insight that will be highly relevant to your academic work.

ACADEMIC ASSIGNMENTS IN THE DISCIPLINES

> Academic writing speaks to a particular audience, just as all writing should. How useful or meaningful a particular type of writing is depends on what audience you want to reach.
>
> —*Vanessa Callison-Burch, fourth-year student*

In traditional as well as community-based academic writing, you begin to learn how people within a particular academic discourse community communicate with one another. Learning how to communicate with others in electrical engineering, economics, or literary studies is of course especially important for majors whose work in the world will ultimately involve communication in that field. General writing courses teach fundamental, flexible skills in critical thinking, research,

and writing that students can apply to their work in more discipline-specific courses. The writing assignments that students encounter in discipline-specific classes
evolve from the values and necessities of each field of study, and these, in turn,
are driven by the practical considerations of specific audiences and purposes in
each field.

The writing genres and assignments that students in the *sciences* are most likely to encounter include:

- lab and field notebooks
- lab reports
- original research papers
- scientific review papers

The primacy of these particular writing genres in the sciences has evolved from
the essential role of the scientist as original researcher, exploring the workings
of the physical world, and the critical importance to scientists of sharing with
each other the results of new research as well as new ideas based on the analysis
and comparison of them. In this process of experimentation, analysis, and communication, the goal of progress in science is supported and furthered in very
practical ways.

Students reading and writing in the *social sciences* are most likely to encounter
writing genres and assignments that include:

- field notes
- original research materials (e.g., surveys, questionnaires, and interview
  questions)
- summaries
- reviews of social science literature
- papers based on original research
- library research papers

As is in the sciences, original research is crucial to advancing knowledge in the
social sciences and therefore features strongly in writing in the discipline in the
form of presentation of findings. The subjects of this research, however, are more
slippery than in the sciences because the social sciences focus on the perplexities
of human motivations and behaviors, whereas the sciences focus on the tangibil-
ities of physical law. Analyzing, extending, and sometimes challenging the work
of other social scientists is also crucial, contributing to a dynamic, evolving discourse in the field.

The writing genres and assignments that students in the *humanities* are most
likely to encounter include:

- journals
- summaries

- response papers
- analytical papers
- research papers

Since what is valued most highly in the humanities is individual insight—whether based on personal experience, interpretation of texts, or research—writing in the humanities provides opportunities for writers to explain and demonstrate their insights. Furthermore, more so than in the sciences or social sciences, a writer's command of language and his or her rhetorical skills are highly important, a value that is understandable because literature and languages are subdisciplines of the humanities. In fact, the writer's articulateness and the effectiveness of his or her prose style are often as important as the originality of his or her thought in distinguishing a piece of writing in the humanities.

RHETORICAL PURPOSE
AND COMMUNITY-BASED ACADEMIC WRITING

The rhetorical purposes of academic writing frequently overlap, just as they do in practical writing; within the various parts of a long piece of writing, one rhetorical purpose will predominate over others at various times. However, within each academic writing assignment there is likely to be a primary, or ultimate, rhetorical purpose. In the previous chapter, we urged you to ask yourself if the primary rhetorical purpose of your practical writing task was *to inform, to explain,* or *to persuade.* We suggest that you ask the same questions in order to gauge the rhetorical purpose of academic writing tasks. As they do with any other kind of writing, the answers to these questions depend very much on who is reading your writing, and why. The *who* and *why* of academic writing are very closely related to both the nature of education and the nature of discipline-specific discourse.

In academic writing, an additional rhetorical category emerges: writing that *records.* We did not include this rhetorical category in our discussion in the previous chapter because, in practical writing, it is unlikely that the reader of your finished document will ever see any notes or journal entries that you might have written, even though these may have served as an important basis for your practical writing. However, in an academic context, where teaching and learning are the point, there may very well be an outside reader for the various kinds of writing that you do *to record*—your instructor.

Academic Writing That Records

If the primary purpose of a piece of writing is *to record,* and the primary reader is yourself, then the writing is probably informal and process-based. Writing that records may exist in the form of lab, field, or other kinds of research notes or in the form of reflective or reading-response journals. Often, instructors will assign these forms of writing and will want to read and perhaps even evaluate them. Nevertheless, their primary reader is you, and their primary purpose is to provide you with a means by which to record information, impressions, ideas, and analytical responses. In this process, you build your knowledge and deepen your understanding of a subject, and this written record will likely provide you with a foundation for formal writing.

Field notes are especially crucial to scientists and social scientists. As fieldwork unfolds, researchers need to record detailed empirical information and observations in a highly organized, thorough, and accurate way; the ultimate credibility of their work depends on this. Especially in the social sciences, field notes might also include general and specific observations, impressions, questions, and speculations. Although field notes may be informal, their completeness and accuracy are essential, since they provide a research record on which the researcher will draw in formal writing.

In service-learning classes, particularly in the sciences and social sciences, you may be required to keep field notes that record detailed information and observations related to your work in the community. You will depend on the thoroughness and accuracy of these notes if you incorporate them into your more formal community-based academic writing. In the field notes below, one student recorded crucial details of his observations at a recreation center.

This day-care and recreational center for inner city youth is located in a middle- to working-class part of Baltimore City where small homes border within feet of each other and rowhomes line the blocks. It is housed in a big ugly brick building with boarded windows. There is a single basketball court on the outside in the parking lot. Inside, there is little light and no festive decorations. There are two big tables with chairs strewn next to them. There is an old snack bar that is no longer in use and a broken refrigerator. The only things that really work in the place are two soda machines; you can get a soda for fifty cents. Towards the back is the office, where two caregivers talk on the telephone, mostly ignoring the kids. Another is playing basketball with some of the kids outside. He is lightly bullying them. For the most part, kids sit and talk with their friends, taking care of themselves. I would not send my kids to this place, but most parents who live in this neighborhood do not have this liberty of choice.

—Field notes
Charles Kakel, first-year student

Charles observed the center and the people in it closely and recorded his observations carefully, placing them and the center itself in the context of the neighborhood in which it exists. It is clear that he doesn't particularly like what he sees. These detailed field notes will be useful later on if he decides to write an analysis and argument about the inadequacies of after-school care in this Baltimore neighborhood, perhaps suggesting ways in which the situation could be improved.

Reflective journals are also frequently assigned in service-learning classes, especially those in the humanities. Although students may use journals, as they do field notes, to record information and observations, the ultimate purpose of reflective journals is more subjective. They provide a safe place where students can raise questions, explore doubts, and reflect openly. Since the experiences that you have in your work in the community and the ideas that arise from them are likely to be less familiar to you than those in more traditional academic work, reflective journals serve an especially important purpose in a service-learning context. The specific content of reflective journals varies, depending on the purpose they serve in a particular service-learning class. You may use yours to reflect on your work in the community or your reading for class from a personal point of view. Students may draw implicitly or explicitly on these reflective records in their formal community-based writing for class.

Do people who do community service feel like they can heal the world? Do we really feel that our services matter? Or are we just doing these things to make ourselves feel good? To tell the truth, I am no longer sure. During one of my conversations with the students' caseworkers, I came to the realization that it is possible for our services to fail. In order to help one person, there must be many people involved. For example, what good is it to feed homeless people one day out of the week? What they really need is help to create and maintain a stable household.

This way of thinking made me think of the students that spend their Monday or Wednesday afternoons in Froelicher Lounge. These children have low reading levels and come to our campus in hopes of improving their skills. What help can I give a thirteen-year-old boy with a reading level of a second-grader? I wonder if this program really works. When I ask, the professional staff just says that the kids consider attending this program a privilege and that they behave the best with us. That is not my question. I want to know if their test scores rise or if their vocabulary increases at the end of the semester. I want to see numbers. Could we possibly be doing all this in vain?

I am really worried that my services are not helping anyone. These kids just escape their "real" lives for a few hours, enter a world of people who falsely believe in them (because we do not know the full story) and then return to their normal lives to cope. So what are we doing so great? I feel totally hypocritical when I say that I am making a difference in my world by tutoring kids. I should have worked with these kids before they entered the point of no return. I honestly feel that someone had the power to step in but they did not. Therefore, we all failed!

—Reflective journal entry
Sidney Saunders, first-year student

This journal entry does not express the whole range of Sidney's thoughts and feelings about the reading program with which she worked, thoughts and feelings that evolved in the course of her service-learning experience; there is, of course, a fuller picture. But this journal entry provided Sidney with a crucial opportunity to express some extremely important doubts about the effectiveness of her community work—doubts that ultimately should not, that cannot, be ignored. (For another example of reflective journal writing, see Rebecca Evans's journal in the Appendix.)

Academic Writing That Informs

Informal academic writing that is intended *to inform*—for example, a summary of something that you have read—can serve you as a test of your understanding. However, writing that informs generally has, by implication, a primary reader other than the writer, and its primary purpose is to provide this reader with information. Since information has to do with facts or with summaries of others' work or ideas, writers whose purpose is to inform must be accurate, and they must take care not to editorialize.

Students who conduct original research in both traditional and service-learning classes, especially those in the social sciences, must often design and write original research materials, including surveys, questionnaires, and interview questions. These materials must be very carefully conceived and written in order to be useful. Information gathered from surveys may be analyzed *quantitatively,* or statistically, revealing important trends. Information derived from interviews may be analyzed *qualitatively,* or individually, as in case studies, for example. Both quantitative and qualitative results of original research may be used along with other evidence to support the writer's analysis or arguments. (For more information on conducting primary research, see Chapter 9, Researching.)

In practical writing genres, the purpose of a great deal of writing is to inform readers accurately and neutrally: a brochure informs women how to perform monthly breast exams; instructions inform taxpayers about how to fill out the 1040 income tax form. In much traditional academic writing, writing that ostensibly informs often doesn't really, if the reader is the instructor and he or she is already informed. Although there are exceptions, frequently the purpose of writing that informs in a traditional academic setting is to provide *practice* for students in a kind of writing that they will encounter in contexts in which they will have more authority.

Since service-learning *is* a context in which you have more authority, community-based academic writing that informs provides more than mere practice: it actually does inform your academic reader. Since your experience in the community is unique, your instructor will not understand it until you provide him or her with essential information. For example, many instructors ask students to write community-based project or research proposals (see below), the primary purpose of which is to inform the instructor of your plans. Providing academic readers with accurate and unbiased information is an important building block, if not an end in itself, in responding to most community-based academic writing assignments.

> Upon entering the tutoring program, I thought I would be working with students who didn't know themselves or the direction they wanted to take in their lives. I expected them to be students who were "borderline" or "at risk" but still showed potential. Instead, I learned that they were in the top level in their grade. They were among the smartest students in the school and already had the best chances of going on to high school and college.
>
> They are very aware of their title as "the best." They all seem to have a support group. Although they are intelligent, I suspect that they are in "gifted" and "top" classes for a combination of reasons.
>
> I want to study the influences of tracking on middle school students. The most obvious possibility, to me, is an examination of students who have been tracked and the effect that this has had on their self-esteem and identity. This would also question the impact of tutoring programs such as this one. Are we working with the right people? Does labeling them make certain students immune to outside criticism and others immune to outside encouragement?
>
> —Research paper proposal
> *Rebecca Evans, first-year student*

In her proposal, Rebecca has informed her instructor of her community-based research paper topic idea and of the questions that will motivate her research. With this understanding, her instructor is in a position to help guide Rebecca in her research.

Academic Writing That Explains

When you write *to explain,* you are not neutral; your critical thought is engaged. It is possible to explain in informal writing, if only to oneself. For example, in a reflective or reading-response journal, explaining can be extremely useful as you begin critically to engage ideas, experiences, or the written works of others. In a formal piece of writing, however, if your primary purpose is to explain, you will probably have a specific reader in mind. In explaining a subject in writing, you must analyze it by breaking it down into components and examining each. You must ask yourself how each part functions and relates to others before reassembling these parts with a better understanding of the whole, articulating the most fundamental conclusion that you have drawn from your analysis. Clarity and logic are crucial in academic writing that analyzes and explains, as they are in practical writing contexts. The reader—whether your instructor or others—will not accept your analysis if it seems illogical. If there are gaps in your explanations, or if your language is not precise, your reader will not understand what you are trying to explain.

Most of the formal academic writing assignments that you receive in service-learning classes will require that you explain something to your reader. You will need to explain in response papers, analytical papers, and research papers (those based on original research, secondary research, or a combination). You may need to explain, for example, the way in which your community agency accomplishes its mission in the community or how your work in the community relates to concepts or readings presented in your course. As with writing that informs, the reader of your explanations in traditional academic writing (that is, your instructor) is already likely to understand very well what you are explaining. However, since your explanatory writing in service-learning contexts is likely, at least in part, to draw on your experience and the authority that you have gained through your community work, your explanations in community-based academic writing will probably be more original and more functional. Explaining something clearly and logically may be the ultimate rhetorical purpose of a community-based academic assignment, or it may serve as a crucial foundation in your development of an argument.

Response papers are common assignments in humanities courses, and they come in many forms. Often, in writing a response paper, you are responding in a personal way to a text—a book, a poem, or an essay, for example—but in other kinds of response papers you may be responding to a situation, an idea, or a belief. In a philosophy class, for example, your instructor could ask you to respond to a hypothetical situation: what would you do if you were one of four survivors in a lifeboat and there were only enough food and fresh water to keep three people alive? In a history class, you might be asked to respond to an idea or a belief: the U.S. decision to drop the atomic bomb on Hiroshima, thereby ending World War II, was widely held by U.S. and Allied citizens to be the right one. Do you agree that it was? Response papers in the humanities give you an opportunity to express personal experiences, ideas, or beliefs and to relate them to those presented in other texts and to real and hypothetical situations.

Experiential essays are akin to academic response papers, and they are very common assignments in service-learning classes. Many instructors ask their students to write essays based on their personal observations and experiences in their community work. This kind of assignment provides you with an opportunity not only to inform your instructor and other students about what happened in your service-learning, but to explain important aspects of your personal growth. In an experiential essay, you might be asked to write about a hands-on experience that you had at your agency and to reflect on what it taught you. For example, if as part of your service-learning work you helped serve the evening meal at a soup kitchen, how did the experience affect your attitudes about the homeless? If your hands-on experience with your agency included participation in a work day, building a trail with other volunteers at a county park, what did you learn about the nature of work and cooperation?

Specially bent shovels and axes had been laid out on the ground. A friendly fellow volunteer noticed my confusion as I just stood there and told me where to start digging. The Trail Center had fixed small flags on trees above the level at which the trail should be. I figured out that in order to build a trail on an incline, you have to first decide at what level the trail should be, then dig into the hill for a foot or two above that level. Afterwards, you fill in a foot or two below the designated level, using the earth you took from the top. Slowly, the line of flags turned into a trail.

The sun rose higher and it became hotter. The trees did not provide enough shade anymore. Pretty soon, my forehead dripped with sweat. My shirt clung closer and closer to my body. Nevertheless, watching the progress that we as a group made kept me going. People shared small discoveries they made, stuff they found on the ground like an especially large earthworm or bones of a small animal. We shared new skills with each other, giving advice on how to build the trail even faster. After only a half-hour of work, we had a solid ten feet of trail....

We put our tools down and walked back to the van. Amy had organized sandwiches and cold drinks for lunch, donated by several local businesses. Everybody had stories to tell. Some had to cut entire trees from the path; others had seen a rattlesnake and saved it from the axe of a nervous trail builder. I was surprised by how few first-timers were around. Almost everyone I talked to told me how Geoffrey always shows great

(continued)

(continued)

organizational skills for these trail building sessions and how much fun it is to see how quickly the work gets done when a lot of people volunteer as they had today. There were some people who complained about tool shortages and I thought some volunteers showed their egotistical sides when it came to petty issues about the level of the trail. Most people there I would classify as liberal environmentalists, but it wasn't politics that united them; it was more of a sense of appreciation for the day and nature. If someone had told me earlier that day that I would be thinking that our lunch break was too long, I would have laughed.

—Excerpt from an experimental essay
Markus Rogan, first-year student

(For another example of an experiential essay, see "Mother Hubbard's Cupboard" by Elizabeth Cole in the Appendix.)

Academic Writing That Persuades

Writing the primary purpose of which is *to persuade* is argument. Many people prefer the term *persuasion* when they are referring to rhetorical purpose, since *argument* can carry with it connotations of hostility and even irrationality. When persuasion is your goal in writing, you must draw a strong conclusion, generally from analysis and articulated through explanation; your explicit and ultimate goal is to convince your reader to adopt this conclusion as his or her own. Obviously, writing that persuades is extremely reader-focused. In effective persuasion, the writer needs to know her or his reader well, understanding the range of perspectives on the subject at hand and anticipating and addressing possible questions and objections that the reader might raise in order ultimately to strengthen his or her own argument. Many people equate argument or persuasive writing exclusively with taking positions on social or political issues or policies; in fact, arguments can evolve from an interpretation of a novel or an historical event as readily as they can from an analysis of a social policy.

As is the case in practical writing genres, it is often difficult to make a categorical distinction between academic writing that explains and that which persuades, since conclusions drawn from analysis and articulated through explanation often naturally evolve into argument. Both explanation and argument are arrived at through analysis, and argument would be weak indeed if clear explanation were not involved.

Many community-based academic assignments, including analytical papers and research papers of all kinds, call on students to articulate explicit arguments. Academic argument in service-learning courses tends to be much less theoretical than argument in many, more traditional, academic contexts. In a community-based academic argument, you may very well draw on concepts that inform the discourse in the discipline in which you are writing, and you are very likely to refer to readings that you encounter in the course and in outside research. But your point of reference is not exclusively theoretical; as a service-learner, it is informed and enhanced by practical experience. You have seen how academic subjects and issues related to them apply in the community outside the university. Your arguments are likely to be closely related to your own experience and firsthand observations, and you will have earned more authority and a higher level of credibility as you pose an academic argument.

Any argument that you write in response to a community-based academic assignment will likely have a great inherent advantage over many traditional academic arguments: it will probably have clearer *exigence* (or established relevance) because it will relate to actual, as opposed to theoretical, issues in the community. Topics and kinds of argument that arise from community-based academic assignments vary widely, depending on the class, the instructor, and the student's own interests. For example, in a critique, you might examine your agency's organizational structure to determine how its funding base or the way in which the agency is run enhances or undermines the accomplishment of its mission. In an issues-based argument, you might take a stand against a public policy that impedes your agency's work, or you might argue for (or against) your agency's position on a particular issue. In a feasibility study, you might evaluate the costs and benefits of an existing or proposed program at your agency, in the end arguing for a particular course of action.

Community-based academic arguments can be of various lengths and involve outside research to varying degrees, or not at all. In one assignment, you might be asked to write a three-page essay that articulates an argument based on your own observation and experience. In another assignment, you might be asked to write a twenty-page research paper addressing a topic of interest that has arisen from your community-based work and to formulate an argument from it.

In the Appendix, you will find an example of a relatively concise argument, "Grass or Astroturf? Environmental Groups and Corporate Sponsorship," by Rebecca Freeland. This was Rebecca's response to a community-based academic writing assignment in which the instructor asked each student to formulate an argument related to an issue faced by the community organization with which each student worked and to draw on both primary and secondary sources in doing so.

In researching and writing about the controversy over corporate funding of nonprofit organizations, and how the environmental agency with which she worked addressed and attempted to resolve this controversy, Rebecca located an important and relevant topic in which she is sincerely and personally interested. She is able to ground a more general investigation of her topic by applying it to the specific case of her agency, about which she knows a great deal. Her interest energized both her research and her thinking about her topic. She writes with authority in informing her reader, analyzing the problem, and arguing for a solution because she had access to knowledge and points of view gained from a rich variety of sources. In addition to the kinds of secondary source information that students traditionally consult in research papers, she used her firsthand experience and observations during the course of her service-learning, as well as primary sources in the form of experts she met through her community work.

Caitlin Corrigan's longer research paper, "Food Not Bombs: An Anarchist Community in Action," the final project in her service-learning class, opens with this paragraph:

> In the kitchen of a Baltimore rowhouse, several pots sit bubbling on the stove, each one emitting a savory aroma. A guy with half-formed dreadlocks and a pierced lip tends them with haphazard vigilance, adding garlic, onions or another can of organic tomato sauce to the nearest pot. Tinny punk music roars out of a paint-splattered boombox perched precariously on a milk crate, and several people sit beside it, slicing apples and almonds for a fruit salad. A round wooden tabletop behind is filling with finished pots of vegetable soup, brown rice and beans, and butternut squash flavored mashed potatoes. The tiny army carries the food out to the street, packing it away in cars along with a few cardboard boxes full of dry goods and clothing. Another box carries the reusable bowls and utensils that the hungry people who line Gay and Fayette will use to eat the fruit of this afternoon's labor. This box also contains the big white banner that announces the source of each Sunday's feast to any interested passerby: Food Not Bombs.
>
> —*Caitlin Corrigan, first-year student*

Students in service-learning, like Rebecca and Caitlin, often write more interesting papers than students in traditional academic contexts do because the topics they address are rooted in concrete community issues, issues with which they have gained personal experience and in which they have developed a personal interest. Furthermore, because their experience in the community has extended their network of resources, they usually find that their repertoire of source material expands: service-learners tend to consult not only key secondary sources, but also a rich variety of primary sources. (For an example of an extended community-based research paper, see "Landmines: Distant Killers" by Jessica Gray in the Appendix.)

Perhaps we should understand all community-based learning—whether it happens in the classroom or in the community—as collaborative. Even academic writing that is independently composed in a service-learning context is collaborative in that it is born from communal endeavor. It arises from your interactions with your agency mentor, with others at your agency, and with people in the community. In the classroom, with your peers and instructor, your community experiences find a context, and your ideas coalesce.

What is the point, ultimately, in accumulating knowledge in any field unless we apply it to practical concerns?

REFLECTIVE QUESTIONS
FOR JOURNAL-WRITING AND CLASS DISCUSSION

1. Recall an academic writing assignment that you think was unique and engaging. What made this assignment different from others that were tedious and unexciting? Was this assignment more difficult? If so, what made it challenging? What made it enjoyable in spite of its difficulty?

2. What kinds of academic writing assignments are you most comfortable with? Do you prefer open-ended assignments that allow you to include personal experience and perspective and to incorporate personal voice, or do you prefer more structured assignments that you can approach more objectively? Explain the reasons for your preferences.

3. In her book *Gender Trouble: Feminism and the Subversion of Identity,* Judith Butler writes, "The binary regulation of sexuality suppresses the subversive multiplicity of a sexuality that disrupts heterosexual, reproductive, and medicojuridical hegemonies." What does Butler mean? If you encountered this passage in your reading in a Feminist Studies class, how would you respond to it?

4. Consider the differences between technical language and jargon. Assemble a list of technical terms related to a particular academic discipline or profession. Try to locate an example of writing that is laden with jargon in that same discipline or profession. Who is the audience for the example you chose? What do you think makes it jargon?

TROUBLESHOOTING

WHAT IF...

> *you are planning to write an academic paper in which you will analyze your community agency's effectiveness in fulfilling its mission in the community and your agency mentor has asked to have a copy when you are done?*

TRY TO...

> *consider carefully, and in advance, the relative advantages and disadvantages of letting your mentor and others at your agency know of such a project before you have*

completed it. Especially if you plan to ask people at your agency to serve as sources of information in your study, you will need to be clear and straightforward about your project from the beginning. Let them know that there is an evaluative purpose to your project and that you will be analyzing both strengths and weaknesses. Most agencies will welcome the opportunity to read your analysis, conclusions, and suggestions. On the other hand, don't let a promise to share what you will write with agency staff compromise your objectivity and honesty. Since you obviously don't want to censor yourself, you might want to wait until your assessment is complete before deciding whether or not to share what you have written with your agency.

WHAT IF…

your instructor asks you to write an essay about your agency and your feelings about working there, but you are hesitant to share your thoughts and experiences with your instructor because they are negative?

TRY TO…

understand that your instructor expects the truth. Although your instructor no doubt hopes that your placement will work out beautifully, she or he knows that not every placement will. That's not what happens in the real world. Your instructor will not be shocked or offended at your negative response in the same way that a community audience might be. An honest assessment is part of what your instructor will be looking for in your community-based academic writing.

WHAT IF…

you feel that your work at your agency is pointless, that you aren't really helping anybody?

TRY TO…

find a way to express your feelings and to work them through. Write about them in your reflective journal. Talk to your instructor and your classmates about them. Hearing about other people's experiences in the community and their feelings about community work, whether they are similar to or different from yours, will help you put your feelings in perspective.

focus on constructive action. Ask yourself what you can do in very small ways to make your contribution to your agency and to the people it serves more meaningful and more effective. You may not be able to change everything, but you can change small things.

learn more about the larger problem. Consider turning what might feel like a bleak or pointless experience into a larger research topic. If you think that the work your community agency does is seriously compromised is some way, ask yourself why. Ask yourself how the situation might be improved. Research these questions. Write about them. Who knows? Perhaps in the future you will be the one to make these changes happen.

PART III

Construction Zones: Fulfilling Your Service-Learning Assignment

CHAPTER 9

Researching

Research is the systematic study and investigation of a topic outside your own experience and knowledge. When you do research, you move from what you know about a topic to what you do not know. Doing research means more than just reading about other people's ideas; when you undertake a research project, you become involved in a process that requires you to think critically.
—LAURIE KIRSZNER AND STEPHEN MANDELL, *THE BRIEF HOLT HANDBOOK*

Although a practical document written for your agency and an academic paper based on your community experience may seem to have little in common, both will require you to conduct research outside your experience and knowledge. Research is crucial to your full understanding of your agency and its work in the community as well as to your understanding of how community issues relate to what you are studying in class. Many students find that the compelling and complex experiences they have with service-learning motivate deep and innovative research.

Researching community-based assignments, whether for practical or academic projects, calls on students to draw from a rich variety of sources. Rather than relying heavily, or exclusively, on library research, service-learners generally take on more primary research, drawing on the authority not only of academic experts but of experts in the community as well. Your academic research skills will no doubt help you in researching your community project, but your community-based research will also suggest intriguing possibilities and valuable strategies for your academic work.

RESEARCHING WITH ATTENTION TO AUDIENCE AND PURPOSE

It would be ridiculous if one were to write based on concepts that exist within a small academic community when attempting to write for everyone and anyone.
—*Nik Reed, third-year student*

139

Just as language and communication styles vary uniquely from one community to another, so do ways of knowing. Communities value different kinds of knowledge and express knowledge differently. What is essential to know in one community may not be nearly as important in another. Whereas literary scholars interested in the work of Herman Melville might be fascinated by biblical references in *Moby Dick* and might avidly read anything other scholars publish on the subject, most of the rest of the world won't care much, if at all. Someone who is passionate about skateboarding is likely to confront a blank stare when he or she tries to explain to someone with no inherent interest the technicalities of a revolutionary new skateboard design featured in a Web site for skateboarding enthusiasts. A community environmental group, up in arms about developers' plans to bulldoze a marsh to make way for shoreline housing, faces an uphill battle in its "Save the Saltwater Harvest Mouse" campaign because neither the fate of the mouse nor details of marsh ecology may be of interest to most citizens. Different communities care about different things, and their concerns are informed by different kinds of information and different kinds of knowledge.

Whatever the specific topic might be and whatever kinds of research may be involved, built-in assumptions about audience and purpose are inherent in most academic writing. Your audience is generally limited to an academic reader; your purpose is to deepen your knowledge of a particular subject. Some of the information that you include in an academic paper might be considered common knowledge, but it is common knowledge only in the contexts of the academic community and the specific discipline to which your study belongs. Let's say that in a cultural anthropology course, you interview several Ozark Mountain families and use these interviews in combination with secondary research as the basis of a paper about the social organization of families who have lived in the Ozark Mountains for four generations or longer. If you share your paper with one of the families that you interviewed in the Ozarks, you will probably come to a quick understanding of the limited purposes and the specialized audience of your paper. The very subjects of your study might have a difficult time understanding or relating to what you have written about them and how you chose to examine your subject.

This is not to say that cross-community research can't be used to create a strong community-based research project. It can, and it very likely will in your project. For example, even if you conduct much of your research in the field (that is, in the community at large), you may need to supplement your community-based research with trips to your college or public library. Of course, if your assignment is to write an academic paper based on your service-learning experience, you will also find that library research is enhanced and reinforced in essential ways by community research. For example, if your academic paper about socialization among preschool-age children for your class in early childhood development focuses exclusively on library research and leaves out your observations as a service-learner in a community day-care center, you would be missing the point of service-learning.

In a service-learning context, your research will be driven as much by audience and purpose as your writing will be, but often—especially in practical research and writing projects—by audiences and purposes that differ quite dramatically from those you are accustomed to in an academic setting. For agency documents, research needs to be focused and practical; it must be relevant to purpose, providing readers with the information that they need. Because you are probably more familiar with purely academic research, it may take some reconceptualization on your part to ensure that you approach your research from practical rather than academic necessity.

To figure out how to research any community-based project, whether practical or academic, put yourself in your reader's shoes.

- Who is your reader?
- What does he or she need to know?
- Why does he or she need to know it? What's at stake?
- How much detail does your reader need, and what kind of demonstration and support?
- What do you hope your reader will do in response to the information that you provide?

Your answers to these questions will help direct your research.

> Our community writing project was not about finding answers to questions, but rather about generating questions in people's minds. Academic research facts can be stated with an air of indifference, and community writing facts could not (at least for the purposes of our project). In including certain things like historical information, for us there was always this element of trying to evoke a certain response, a certain interest, a concern, from the audience.
>
> —*Terence Chia, second-year student*

The facts that Terence and his peers found in doing library research for their nonprofit agency are ones that we could all find if we looked for them. However, it is *how they used these facts* that made this project different from most academic research projects they had undertaken. Terence and his group were not researching statistics about the lives of Native American children in urban areas simply because they had an academic interest in the subject and had chosen it as an academic research topic; rather, they used their research to provide information and to bring about a proactive response from their audience, mostly Native American readers.

Students need to conduct different kinds of research for practical writing projects and to use that research in different ways, depending on the document their agency needs and the targeted audience for that document. If you and two other students write a grant proposal for an agency that distributes food to homeless shelters in the community, you will have a full range of reference, primary, and secondary research to do. One of you might find out which foundations and grants are appropriate sources of funding for your agency and its program. This research would entail consulting reference sources. Another student in your group might conduct research on how much food your agency distributes to the shelters it serves, which might involve setting up primary source interviews with coordinators at each of the shelters. The third member of your group might gather statistical evidence related to the increase in numbers of homeless people in the community, in order to back up the claim that there is a need to expand your agency's programs and services. This secondary research might entail a trip to city hall to look up this data.

There might be substantial differences in research and presentation of evidence even within the same practical genre, depending on audience and purpose. The following excerpts are from newsletter articles written for the same agency, but they are from two different newsletters with two different audiences and purposes.

On April 7, 1999, the University of Missouri at Columbia and the American Red Cross entered the <u>Guinness Book of World Records</u> by sponsoring the world's largest blood drive. A tremendous amount of determination and organization gathered 3,539 donors and 3,155 units of blood.... Who says a little friendly competition wouldn't be a good idea? It could generate some good, old-fashioned rivalry, as well as enough blood to potentially save 16,000 lives. With all of the resources available to us here at our university, an effort to create the world's largest blood drive does not seem too far-fetched.

—From a newsletter article written for the Stanford Blood Center
by Serena Blodger, first-year student

Since blood is intrinsically unique to an individual, a platelet recipient may have a mild transfusion reaction. Such a reaction occurs due to a difference in antigens (which vary tremendously) between a donor and recipient's blood.... Therefore, platelets are often irradiated to prevent this type of response in patients with impaired immune systems. For nearly 25 years, cesium has been used to safely irradiate blood. According to Vince Yalon, director of the Blood Center, while cesium is continued to be used, "modern microprocessors have allowed us to become much more refined in radiation dosage." Blood donated by family members is always irradiated. This is a standard practice performed to reduce conflicts between antibodies and antigens.

—From a newsletter article written for the Stanford Blood Center
by Andrew Goldfarb, first-year student

In the first example, the student was asked to write an article that would inspire people to donate blood at the Stanford Blood Center at Stanford University. This was an article for the center's general newsletter, which is distributed to thousands of people at the university (including all students) and in the surrounding community. Since the purpose of this newsletter is to encourage people to donate blood, and the audience is predominantly members of the community familiar with the Center, Serena decided to focus her research on other colleges' and universities' successful blood drives in order to issue a challenge to her community. The agency mentor pointed her in the direction of the Internet and local newspapers for the majority of her research; she relied mainly on nonspecialized secondary sources. She used her findings to help create a competitive tone for the article because she wanted her university to break the University of Missouri's blood donor record. Her blood donor research statistics sound almost like a rival team's football scores.

The second example comes from a student who was asked to research and write an informative article that would appear in a different newsletter that the Stanford Blood Center publishes, one that targets readers who have not only already donated blood but who, even more specifically, are considering participating in apheresis (or platelet) donation. The purpose of this newsletter is to provide these specialized readers with specific information about apheresis donation. For this article, Andrew needed to examine specialized secondary sources rather than the more popular ones that Serena used. Although many of the sources that he found were very dense and difficult to understand, he knew that he needed to make the information accessible to an audience that was only generally informed, even though they had a specialized interest. Andrew does not explain why people should give blood because that is not his purpose. A general appeal to his readers to donate blood would be pointless because they already *do* donate blood; platelet donors donate their blood as often as every two weeks. Andrew's readers are a specialized group who would like to know more of the technical details about what happens when their platelets are transfused into a patient.

Andrew's research was more complicated and detailed than Serena's because that is what the audience and purpose demanded of him as the author. Both service-learning projects were considered equally successful, however, because both served their audiences and purposes well.

I found working for the Stanford Blood Center to be a valuable experience. I was captivated by the technical knowledge I acquired during my work with the organization and was intrigued by the inner-workings of the Blood Center. Between meeting with my project coordinator, doing research on my own, crafting interview questions, conducting an interview with the Blood Center's head administrator, and finally composing an article for their quarterly newsletter for apheresis donors, I put much time into my service-learning project. Needless to say, I found that my work was both practical and rewarding; knowing that what I was writing would be presented to an audience of several thousand people often provided me with the extra motivation I needed to offer my best work.

—Andrew Goldfarb, first-year student

In completing your community-based writing project, you are likely to investigate sources in some combination of three research settings: in a library, online, and in the community at large. The kinds of information that you encounter in each setting will have different uses in what you write, depending on your audience and purpose.

LIBRARY RESEARCH

Most students equate library research to academic research, and although other and often underutilized kinds of research are available to academic writers, developing library research skills is essential in both service-learning and traditional course contexts. Through library research, academic writers gain a more in-depth knowledge about topics than they would in merely cramming for a test and spitting out memorized information, since the research process involves *active* rather than *passive* learning. Engaging the information, ideas, and perspectives that you encounter in library research makes you accountable as a critical thinker; examining the work of authorities in the field helps you develop your own ideas and formulate your own arguments. Whether you conduct your research in a school or public library, you will encounter sources in various forms—most essentially in the form of *reference sources, primary sources,* and *secondary sources.*

Reference Sources

Reference sources serve two purposes. They provide you with fundamental background information on your topic, and they tell you where to go to find information in depth.

- To gather fundamental background and to help focus your topic, consult *general knowledge sources,* including *encyclopedias* and *dictionaries.*
- To help you locate more specific information pertaining to your topic, consult *library catalogues* and *periodical indexes.*
- Ask your *reference librarian* for help.

General Knowledge Sources

In the reference area of your library you will find a variety of sources for acquiring general information about a topic. These sources may include compilations of statistics, maps and atlases, encyclopedias, and dictionaries. Since many people rely on these sources for general research, you probably won't be able to check them out of the library, so be prepared to review them on the spot or to photocopy especially relevant material.

Encyclopedias and *dictionaries* are among the most useful general knowledge sources. Some exist in print form, while others are available online or on CD-ROM. Ask your reference librarian which general knowledge sources are available in your library and in what form.

General encyclopedias such as the *Encyclopedia Britannica* will be available in the reference area of your library, where you might also find more specialized encyclopedias pertaining to your topic. Specialized encyclopedias break down large topics into narrower divisions and applications and feature relatively specific articles about these more focused subjects. The *Encyclopedia of Anthropology,* the *Encyclopedia of American Religion,* and the *Encyclopedia of Associations,* for example, will provide more specific overviews of subjects within these particular areas of interest than the *Encyclopedia Britannica* will. Some articles in specialized encyclopedias include useful bibliographies listing books and recent magazine and journal articles on specific topics.

Similarly, specialized dictionaries—for example, the *McGraw-Hill Dictionary of Scientific and Technical Terms,* the *Dictionary of Symbols* by J. E. Carlot, or the *Grove Dictionary of Art*—provide more than simple definitions of words. They explain fundamental processes and concepts that may relate specifically to your topic.

Library Catalogues

A library catalogue consists of a complete listing of a library's collection, including all the books, films, audiotapes, and reference materials it owns as well as all the newspapers and magazines to which it subscribes. Some public and college libraries still use old-fashioned card catalog systems—cards filed in drawers (and cross-referenced) by subject, author, and title. Now, most libraries catalogue their collections electronically, although the basic idea is the same as with the old card catalogues. If your library's collection is electronically catalogued, you will search the collection (by subject, key word, author, or title) from a computer terminal.

Many students have been frustrated in their research because they harbor a fundamental misconception: they search a library's catalogue expecting to find, along with books, specific articles published in magazines and newspapers, and when they do not find them, they wonder why. Remember: a library's catalogue will tell you which newspapers or magazines are included in the library's collection, but it will *not* tell you what articles you will find in them. To discover this, you need to consult a *periodical index.*

Periodical Indexes

A periodical is a serial publication—that is, a publication that is published in a series, at regular intervals—including newspapers, magazines, and specialized journals. Indexes list articles that have been published in periodicals, and they may be searched by subject, key word, author, and title. You are probably familiar with general periodical indexes such as the *Reader's Guide to Periodical Literature,* which can be of great use in locating articles in a broad range of general subject areas. However, as with encyclopedias and dictionaries, many specialized indexes exist to help you locate periodical literature within specific subject areas.

For instance, if you were searching for information about Parkinson's Disease, you could look in the *Reader's Guide* to find articles in *Newsweek* and *Scientific American,* magazines that are geared to general readers looking for basic or moderately in-depth information. If, however, you were looking for articles that go into much more technical depth and detail, you would probably want to search the specialized *Index Medicus* or *Medline* (an online index), which will reference articles in scientific and medical journals such as the *New England Journal of Medicine* and the *Journal of Neurology, Neurosurgery, and Psychiatry.* Other indexes, specialized in other areas of study and research, include the *African Studies Database, Agricultural and Environmental Biotechnology Abstracts,* the *Family Studies Database, Historical Abstracts,* the *International Index to Music Periodicals,* the *Population Index, SciSearch, Sociological Abstracts, Toxnet,* and many, many more.

Consulting specialized indexes to locate periodical source material can help you focus your research according to a specific discipline or topic. Bear in mind, though, that the more specialized the index is, the more specialized the publications included in it will be; and the more specialized the publications are, the more technical the articles that they include will be. Highly technical articles published in professional journals can be extremely challenging for lay readers, including students, to understand. If you don't understand what you're reading and exactly how it pertains to your research topic, you're not going to be able to digest and explain the information to your reader.

You will discover that relatively few indexes exist in print form only. Many indexes exist only online or on CD-ROM. Your reference librarian can help you learn how to access these reference sources, whether they are printed or electronically stored.

People

Don't forget that living, breathing people—especially reference librarians—can serve as invaluable reference sources: *they can tell you where to go to find out what you need to know.* Two important aspects of any reference librarian's job are to help you discover ways in which you might approach and explore your topic, and to help you locate relevant source material in the library. There's no such thing as a stupid question. Don't be shy about asking reference librarians for help.

In community-based research, be sure to include librarians at local public libraries among your reference sources. They may be as useful as, and in some cases even more useful than, academic librarians in advising you on community-based research. It's quite possible that a librarian at a public library will be better informed on local issues and resources than academic librarians will be, since the general public comes through his or her workplace every day.

Primary Sources

The term *primary research* can mean two different things. It can mean that the researcher is conducting original research (including experiments, field observations, or interviews and surveys of the researcher's own design), or it can mean that the researcher is studying primary texts or similar original work. In the "Research in the Community" section of this chapter, we will discuss original research in the form of interviewing and surveying. Here, however, in the context of library research, we are concerned with *primary texts.*

When you write an analysis of a poem or a novel that you read for class, the poem or novel you are working with is the primary text. If the topic of your research paper is the Bill of Rights, the text of that document will serve as primary text. Primary texts of many and various kinds—depending on the subject of your study—will be available at your college or public library.

Primary texts also exist in the form of original documents held in libraries' special collections. Some college libraries house special collections or *archives.* These collections of original materials might include unpublished writings, letters, and mementos from someone famous or from a specific period in history. In some cases, these original materials will not be available in any other form. For example, the Lyndon Baines Johnson Library in Austin, Texas, houses President Johnson's papers, diaries, photographs, and other personal items. In going through some of the contents of this archive, a researcher would get a sense of Johnson the man as well as Johnson the president. Although access to some special collections and archives may be limited to some degree, most do grant access to researchers, including students.

An investigation of original archival material can enhance research immeasurably, since archival research is so immediate and participatory. Examination of original materials brings research subjects to life and allows the researcher to interpret them in truly original ways. Imagine the difference that the opportunity to conduct archival research could make if you were working on a paper about the Japanese internment camps in the United States during World War II and were actually able to hold the fragile, yellowed pages of a handwritten journal that a woman in the camps kept during her two years there. This one person's account might convey the experience of the internment camps in a way that no secondary source could.

Ask your reference librarian what special collections and archives are available in your area—not only at your college or university, but at other institutions and other libraries as well. Perhaps these collections will relate in a relevant way to a topic that you are interested in researching.

Secondary Sources

Simply *knowing* and *understanding* in depth a topic like energy deregulation is incredibly satisfying. I read, read, read, then read some more. When I probably should have been writing, I was reading the entire Hearing before the Subcommittee on Energy and Power. I know that in three years, when I find my paper on deregulation and read it over, I'll get so much more satisfaction out of it than if I had done a half-hearted job at research.

—*Noah Cates, first-year student*

Secondary source material is anything that has been written (or recorded in any other form) by someone else *about* your topic. When you fill in the gaps or extend your understanding of a topic by consulting a source other than a primary one, you are probably using secondary source material.

Someone else's primary research can serve as a secondary source for you. Whether a source is considered primary or secondary depends on how you use it. For instance, nineteenth-century author Elizabeth Gaskell's biography *The Life of Charlotte Brontë* is a secondary source if you are researching Brontë, but it is a primary source if you are researching and writing about the works of Gaskell. The Supreme Court transcript of *Roe v. Wade* is a primary source if the subject of your research and your paper is *Roe v. Wade,* but the editorial in the *Washington Post* that provided commentary the morning after the Court's historic decision is a secondary source.

Secondary sources exist in many forms. Several of the most commonly used forms are described below. Strong academic research strives to include a variety of sources, since each kind of secondary source has its special advantages and drawbacks.

Books

Books that serve as secondary sources may include critical studies, histories, and biographies, to name a few. Book sources provide both context and depth in research of specific topics.

Newspaper, Magazine, and Journal Articles

Periodical literature consists of news articles in international, national, or local newspapers (for example, the *London Times,* the *New York Times,* or the *Daily Oklahoman*), articles in popular magazines and journals (for example, *Time, Fortune,* or *Sports Illustrated*), and essays and reports in professional or scholarly journals (for example, *New Left Review, American Quarterly,* or *Publications of the Modern Language Association of America*). Articles, because they are more particularly focused than books, may apply more specifically to your topic. Recent periodical publications also tend to be more current—more cutting-edge—than many book sources, although they often lack the kind of background and context that books provide.

Media

Media sources may include documentary films, transcripts of television broadcasts, or audio recordings. Even popular documentary sources may offer specific information and in-depth analysis. If they focus on personal example or testimony, they can also provide the human touch that interviews can, serving to balance sources that may be drier or more detached in their analysis.

Government Documents

Official documents published by governmental agencies on the federal, state, and local levels include a variety of material, ranging from compilations of statistics (for example, the 2000 Census), to records of congressional hearings and congressional committee reports, to transcripts of city council meetings.

SOME CRUCIAL NOTES ON NOTE-TAKING

In consulting reference, primary, or secondary sources in library research, take care! Make sure that you take careful notes.

- *Record factual information accurately,* including bibliographic information. When you work with many sources, it is very easy to lose track of what came from where if you have not been keeping track all along.

- *Try to summarize and paraphrase information and ideas from sources instead of just transcribing quotations.* Good research involves more than simply consuming facts, information, ideas, and examples gathered from outside sources and regurgitating them undigested into your writing. Summarizing and paraphrasing in notes is one way to ensure that you really understand information and have thoroughly digested the ideas that you gather from sources.

- If the author has expressed an idea particularly well, *record the quotation accurately,* word-for-word, complete with original punctuation.

- Because learning about your subject through a study of library sources requires careful analysis of this material, *record your own questions and analysis* in your notes as well.

- Remember that *sloppy note-taking can lead to plagiarism*—presentation of someone's else's ideas, writings, or spoken words as one's own—and it is plagiarism *whether it is intentional or not.* (For more on plagiarism, see Chapter 12, Documenting.)

Evaluating Library Sources

It is crucial to the credibility of your own research that you critically evaluate the reliability of any source that you consult, whether it is reference, primary, or secondary. Here are some worthwhile questions to ask in evaluating sources that you locate through library research.

Is the source credible? Is the author well qualified? Just because someone writes about a subject doesn't mean that she or he is qualified in any special way to do so. Don't take the author's qualifications at face value. For example, the fact that the author is a medical doctor (a title most people view with respect) doesn't necessarily qualify her or him to comment with any particular authority on education policy.

Is the publication reputable? A self-published book undergoes no editorial scrutiny. Even some well-established periodical publications don't have a stellar reputation for credibility, and some very popular general publications—for example, *Time* and *Newsweek*—don't carry as much authority as more specialized publications do.

Does the source display a detectable bias? Authors and publishers may harbor biases, including political agendas. For example, articles on the same subject in *Mother Jones* (a politically progressive magazine) and in *New Republic* (a politically conservative magazine) will provide very different perspectives on "the facts." Remember, though, that the existence of a bias in a source doesn't automatically disqualify that source. In fact, every argument is, by definition, biased. But it is important for any researcher to be aware of bias and what constitutes it in any given source and to balance one perspective with another in comprehensive research.

Can factual information be corroborated? A statement of fact in print does not necessarily make it a *valid* fact. Especially if there is any reason to suspect a lack of credibility or the existence of a bias in a source, make sure that facts offered there can be corroborated by a variety of other sources.

Is the source current? An outdated source, especially if you are researching a topic in which new developments occur at a fast rate (for example, in genetic research, computer technology, or current political debates), may well constitute flawed research. Although an outdated source can provide background and historical context, it is worthless in providing up-to-date information.

INTERNET RESEARCH

Here's my take on the whole Internet sources issue: the Web/Internet is the most valuable *and* the least valuable source of information. Its value lies in its ubiquity and its quantity of information. Its problem, however, is just that. First, the reliability of its sources is questionable at best. Second, the vast quantity of information can sidetrack you if you are not careful.

—*Terence Chia, second-year student*

The advent of the Internet has given us an alternative to library research. Internet research can indeed be helpful in almost any research project: a plethora of Web sites and electronic databases are available to you at the click of a mouse. But researchers who rely exclusively or predominantly on Internet research are probably cutting their research possibilities very short and may be opening themselves up to flawed research.

As Terence points out, one of the Internet's greatest assets is that it offers such abundance and variety of information; you can research subjects ranging from the Civil Rights Movement to genetic engineering to the history of suburban shopping malls to alpine wildflowers. But therein also lies one of the problems. Because the Internet reflects popular culture, what you will find there is unpredictable and often haphazard. Most printed material by reasonably reputable publishers undergoes some editorial scrutiny before it appears in print. There is at least *some* degree of quality assurance in print publishing. Most material published on the Internet, on the other hand, does not undergo any editorial scrutiny. On the Internet, anything goes. What you turn up in an Internet search of your topic might be a museum's archives, a city's information pages, or online text of a fine article originally published in a reputable newspaper, magazine, or journal—or it might be an individual's irresponsible "mouthing off" or a fringe political group's propaganda.

Students involved in community-based research will probably find that Internet research is more generally—and genuinely—valuable to them than it is to students conducting traditional academic research. The reason for this is that the Internet serves "the community," in a vast, democratic sense. Private nonprofit and governmental organizations have found the Internet to be as valuable to them as it is to advertisers and retailers in reaching the public. Whether you are conducting research to write a practical document for your agency or an academic paper in a service-learning class or any other, by all means, check out the Internet. But develop a strong, healthy skepticism about what you find there.

Using the Internet as a Reference Tool

The Internet can serve as a terrific reference tool. In fact, many of the reference sources, including general knowledge sources and indexes, that you can access electronically at your library, or through your library's Web site, come to you via the Internet. Libraries pay a lot of money to subscribe to these databases, and one of the things that they are paying for is a degree of quality assurance. If you access a database through your library, you may not like the material that you ultimately locate (for example, you may disagree with the point of view expressed in an article that you find through an online database search), but you can be reasonably certain that the sources listed are fundamentally credible.

Quality assurance is by no means guaranteed when you search the Internet using popular search engines, such as Yahoo.com and Google.com, among many. Although these general searches can yield links to some interesting and credible sources, they will also provide you with links to commercial sites (some in disguise as educational sites), rabid political sites, and individuals' home pages. So enter at your own risk, with your critical lenses firmly in place.

Web pages themselves—whether they are government sites, nonprofit organizations' sites, or sites sponsored by educational institutions—can provide you with the next level of Internet reference sources: hyperlinks. Remember that these links can lead you anywhere, although generally speaking, the more credible the Web site is that provides the link, the more credible the source will be at the other end of the link.

Using the Internet for Secondary Research

Many Web sites are maintained by museums and archives, universities, government agencies, and other credible institutions and can serve researchers as invaluable sources of information. These sites often provide fascinating and abundant information that is particularly useful to students at smaller or more isolated schools where libraries may not have as many resources to choose from. Furthermore, many newspapers and magazines are published online as well as in print, so students don't have to rely on their libraries' limited subscriptions to periodicals in order to access these kinds of sources. Web sites maintained by nonprofit organizations—although they may have a distinct social or political bias—are also important sources, particularly to students in service-learning placements.

Remember, however, that many Web sites are not sponsored by particularly reliable sources. Anyone can post virtually anything on the Internet, and just because material is published there doesn't mean that it's credible. Web sites may feature information from individuals who aren't qualified in any particular way. They may promote the political, religious, or other agendas of groups that exhibit a patent bias. Some Web sites are underwritten by entrepreneurs who, in the guise of providing neutral information, are trying to sell you something.

Evaluating Internet Sources

Here are some important points to consider as you strive to weed out the junk and propaganda that thrive on the Internet, so that the valuable and credible sources that you find there will become more apparent. (Thanks to the Stanford University Libraries for providing the template for these points.)

Purpose

- What is the purpose of the Web site? Is it to inform, persuade, present opinions, report research, or sell a product?
- Does the site contain advertising? If so, can you easily discern the difference between the advertising and the informational content?
- Who is the audience?

Source

- Who is the author of the site? What are his or her qualifications and experience? Is his or her institutional affiliation given? Is contact information given? Is the site without an author?
- Who is the sponsor of this site? Is it part of a larger site? Is there a link to information about the sponsor?
- If you are having problems locating the author or sponsor, look at the domain abbreviations (edu, org, gov, com, net) and the URL (the Web address). Remember that the "~" in the URL could point to someone's individual home page that has no official sanction. Be especially careful with this on *edu* domain pages, since many of these are actually student pages.
- To find out about a sponsoring organization or author, you can run the names through any major online search engine, including Yahoo.com, Google.com, and Deja.com.
- Another way to find out who is responsible for the site is to back up through the URL to get to a higher level. Play around on the site and figure out where you are.

Reliability

- Do you find documented facts or personal opinion on the site?
- Be sure to look for the point of view and the tone of the language the author or sponsor uses. Be aware of evidence of bias.
- Remember what you know. How accurately are the facts and ideas presented? Are they sensationalized? Are they exaggerated?
- Are sources of information cited? Can you verify them in another resource? Watch out for numbers without an identifiable source, and beware of facts that cannot be verified from other sources.
- Are there a lot of spelling errors or typos? If the finished product is a mess, it may indicate that the content is also a mess.
- Did you find your way to this site via a link from a trustworthy site?
- What kinds of links are provided? Are they relevant and appropriate?

Timeliness

- If you are in Netscape, you might try looking under "View" or "Page Info" to see when the page was created and revised. Is the date of creation shown? Is it revised and up to date?
- How current are the links? Have some expired or moved? If you are looking at a page that has been kept up to date, this could mean that it is more reliable than one that is not well maintained.

Using the Internet for Primary Research

For better and for worse, the Internet has opened up a world of almost immediate accessibility. People who work in the nonprofit sector have found that the Internet has had a dramatic, positive effect on *networking*—their ability to exchange information with one another and to coordinate strategies that help promote their missions and work on local, national, and even international levels. As a service-learner associated with a private nonprofit or governmental agency, you can use the Internet to network, too. Your community-based research can be enhanced considerably by checking out the Web sites of agencies that do work similar to that of your agency, in communities both near and far away. Via the email links commonly provided in these sites, you can contact people at these agencies in order to request information or to ask them questions crucial to your research.

Before the advent of the Internet, researchers who wished to conduct primary research in the form of interviews with experts often had to have physical access to them. If an expert were not available on campus or in a community nearby, students were out of luck. Telephone interviews were a possibility, but students usually discounted them because the effort seemed extraordinary, or calling a stranger's office or home felt like the invasion of privacy that, in fact, it was. Email has changed things. An email inquiry is much less awkward (for everyone) than a cold call. If you can locate an email address for someone you would love to talk to about your project, it is entirely conceivable to contact that potential source via email and request—*very politely*—an email interview. You may get a negative response or none at all, but then again, you may get your interview. An advantage of an email interview over in-person and telephone interviews is having a written transcript of your questions and the interviewee's responses.

If you choose to be bold in your research by networking or exploring the possibilities that the Internet offers of conducting e-interviews, *be respectful.* Unsolicited email can be an invasion of privacy. If someone whom you contact via email does not respond, don't write again. If someone says no to your request for an interview or declines to answer your questions, respect that answer. (See more on interviewing in the next section.)

RESEARCH IN THE COMMUNITY

In community-based research, as compared to academic research, the notion of what constitutes expertise shifts. An academic authority may have credentials and expertise that are expressed and confirmed through research and publishing in an area of specialty. Experts in the community at large are often qualified in different ways, and for different reasons, having earned their authority in nonacademic professions or through practical or personal experience. As a service-learner conducting research for community-based projects, you have access to both academic and nonacademic authorities. Making use of both types of sources will enhance your research and writing.

Reference Sources in the Community

In your search for community sources and resources, *people* will be your most valuable reference source. By all means ask your instructor for advice about where to begin, but be aware that she or he might not be able to help you as directly with community-based research as with academic research. The most productive reference sources for research in the community will be community members themselves, people who live and work every day with the issues that you are researching.

Agency Mentors and Community Members

Perhaps the most obvious reference source for your community-based research is your agency mentor. She or he will probably have a good idea of where to find primary and secondary sources that will aid your research, especially when you are working on a practical writing project for your agency or if your academic project relates directly to your agency's work. Of course, this does not mean that your agency mentor will simply hand you all of the research material that you will need, even in a practical writing project.

Your mentor will be able to direct you in a search of agency files. In most cases, the agency will have collections of data, newspaper and magazine articles, archived material, and other resources related to agency work and community issues. You might start by exploring sources in your agency's files and then move on from there to research outside the agency. Your mentor, since she or he is directly involved with the community, can also be helpful in referring you to others in the community, people who qualify as experts in one way or another and whom you might want to interview or survey as part of your community-based research.

Many other people in the community can serve as important reference sources. Think creatively about who, given your research topic, these people might be. Depending on the nature and subject of your community-based project, you might ask city officials, educators, clergy, business people, local activists, or neighborhood residents for advice on *where to go to find out what you need to know.*

Networking with Other Agencies

Other nonprofit agencies that work on issues similar to those with which your agency is involved can serve as important reference sources. For instance, if you are working on a project for a domestic violence prevention program, contact other agencies that work with domestic violence and women's issues for ideas about sources of information relevant to your project. Your agency mentor can probably refer you to other organizations in your area and beyond, but to supplement your mentor's suggestions, try searching the Internet as well. If your school has a volunteer clearinghouse, look through its files to see what community agencies in the area work on similar issues.

Primary and Secondary Research in the Community

In many community-based research and writing projects, secondary research actually takes something of a backseat to primary research, whereas in traditional academic research, the reverse is generally true. In community-based projects, an important aspect of most students' work is to examine how issues (which might be relatively theoretical in a strictly academic context) play themselves out in the community and apply to the lives of people who live there.

Primary Research

Whether your community-based project is academic or practical, primary research could be essential to your research. Except for firsthand observations in the form of field notes (see Chapter 8, Academic Writing in a Service-Learning Context), interviews or surveys are the forms of primary research most commonly used by service-learners in their community-based projects.

People whom you consult as primary sources might be those with a specific expertise in the subject that you are researching. These people might include providers of community services. You might interview, for example, a priest who runs a neighborhood midnight basketball program intended to keep young people off the streets and out of trouble. Community experts might also include people with other kinds of professional or hands-on experience. For instance, if you were researching the effectiveness of a city's campaign to educate the public about safe alternatives to household pesticides, you might survey owners of local hardware and garden supply stores to see if residents' purchasing patterns had changed.

On the other hand, your primary sources might be people whose general or more personal experience you are interested in ascertaining. You might survey or interview people who receive services in the community—the midnight basketball players, for example—to find out what they gain from these services. In other situations, your primary research might target people who do not participate in or benefit from agency or other community services in order to try to discover why they don't.

Ultimately, whether your service-learning project is practical or academic, community-based primary research helps to bring your subject to life and demonstrates how important community issues apply in the lives of the people whom these issues impact most directly.

Secondary Research

> I looked into the history and context of the cement plant issue. I also looked up some of the references the mayor made that were not directly related to the cement plant, because I wanted to make sure I understood the arguments he was making and the meanings his speech had to community members.
>
> —*Louise Auerhahn, fourth-year student*

Often, secondary sources serve to ground and contextualize the primary research that service-learners do, their necessity arising from rather than leading to primary research. Louise's case is typical of the ways in which secondary research is used in many community-based projects. For her community-based project, Louise chose to work with a grassroots environmental organization that focuses primarily on issues of environmental justice and environmental racism. The organization is located in a poor and working-class town with a predominantly African American and Latino population. This town is encircled by others that are predominantly white and affluent. The town's mayor delivered a speech at a city council meeting in support of a commercial cement batch plant's proposal to begin operations in town. His main argument was that the plant would bring in tax revenue and create new jobs. Various neighborhood and community nonprofit organizations thought that the cement batch plant was a bad idea, however, because of the carcinogenic dust that might be produced. Why, they wondered, don't we hear about cement batch plants moving into more affluent communities?

Louise was asked by her agency to listen to the mayor's speech and write a piece about it for the agency's newsletter, which would be mailed out to several thousand residents. Louise could have simply listened to the speech and reported its content; however, she wanted to make sure that she understood all of the issues behind the mayor's proposal. Her secondary research entailed trips to the college library, to read about cement dust and its effects on health, and to the public library, to track down news articles and editorials from local papers. The secondary information that Louise included in her newsletter article provided technical and historical background on the cement plant issue for readers who might not be familiar with all of the aspects of the controversy.

Especially where access to secondary research materials is concerned, your agency mentor and others in the community may see you as someone with *connections*—connections in the form of your access to the information contained in your campus library. Most college and university libraries are accessible to the public, but in some cases, people in the broader community may not know this, or they may not feel comfortable conducting research on campus. Even if a college's relationship with the community is good, there may still exist a sense of a closed community on campus.

Interviewing

I enjoyed interviewing community members and organization heads in San Mateo County for the Sustainable San Mateo newsletter article. It was a wonderful opportunity to hear what members of the community thought about the controversial issues of teenage pregnancy and childcare and how different organizations were striving to achieve unique goals to help the situation. As an out-of-state student, it gave me an opportunity to learn more about the community and the unique challenges faced by the community.

—Cindy Yuchin Lin, third-year student

Hearing my interviewee's tone of voice was so important because I wanted to express that tone of voice in my article.

—Allison Campbell, first-year student

Interviews help to provide the convincing particulars of experience and expertise, as well as voice, to both practical and academic writing. Interviewing involves more than just sitting down for a chat with someone. There are a number of steps involved and important details to consider in planning and executing a successful interview.

Arranging an Interview

In arranging an interview, be knowledgeable, be polite, and be confident. Although it is possible that you will contact potential interview subjects by email, a phone call is generally a better way of getting in touch, since personal contact is, after all, the point. Calling also improves your chances of finding out immediately whether or not you have been granted an interview.

You may be nervous about making this initial call to a person you would like to interview, especially if you have never met. So before you pick up the phone, take a couple of breaths and try to relax. The worst thing that can happen is that your interview request will be denied. However, most people are flattered that interviewers choose them to question on subjects about which they care deeply, and they usually respond positively to interview requests.

When you call your potential interviewee, clearly and unambiguously state your name, your affiliation, and your reason for calling:

> Hello, this is Todd Johnson from the University of Massachussetts. As part of a community service component of my environmental studies class, I'm writing up a fact sheet that will be included in the electric bill next month. The topic I'm writing about is which trees and shrubs are safe to plant under or near power lines and which ones are not. I was wondering if you might have a half an hour some time this week to sit down with me and answer a few specific questions I have.

This monologue would be fine in a voice-mail message. If you reach the person directly, of course, your information would be sprinkled with conversation on both sides. If you do get a voice-mail recording, remember to leave your contact information, including your phone number and email address, if you have one.

If your interviewee responds positively, make arrangements for the interview right then and there. Since this person is doing you a favor, be flexible and prepared to conduct the interview on the interviewee's terms as much as possible. Before you hang up, confirm the date, time, and place of the meeting, get directions, and remember to thank your interviewee.

Preparing for Your Interview

> I was really intimidated because I had never done a personal interview before. Since I was the one in control—the decisions were mine—I was worried about doing the interview the right way.
>
> —*Allison Campbell, first-year student*

You will want to know enough about your subject and your interviewee in advance to know what questions you want to ask. Whether your interviewee is a professional expert or a person whose personal experience is relevant to your research, you should not ask the kinds of basic questions that constitute background information for the subject of the interview. Rather, your questions should relate to your interviewee's specific expertise or experience.

Conduct Background Research

Let's say that you are writing a feature article for the *Naval Home Newsletter*. Its primary readers are veterans who live at the Naval Home and the staff who work there, although the newsletter is also mailed to families of residents. You have chosen to focus your article on one of the residents, a woman who was a Navy WAVE during World War II and one of the first African American WAVES. When you call her, she agrees to be interviewed.

Before your interview, conduct some background research on World War II in general and more specifically on both women's and African Americans' contributions to the war effort. Not only will this secondary research provide important context for your article, but it will also prepare you well for your interview, helping you to formulate meaningful and relevant questions. Because your background research will provide you with general knowledge, you will not need to waste precious time with your interviewee going over the basics; rather, you can use your precious interview time to get at the unique information and perspective that only your interviewee can provide.

Formulate Your Questions

Before the interview, think carefully about the specific questions you would like to ask. You might want to run your questions by your agency mentor, your peers, and your instructor, since they might be able to spot inappropriate questions, help you rephrase others, or identify important questions that you might not have considered. Write down your questions and bring them with you to the interview so that you can refer to them directly. By the time the interview rolls around, however, you should be so familiar with them that you need only glance at them.

You may realize in the course of an interview, or following it, that some questions that you thought would be relevant or appropriate might not be. Allison Campbell, a first-year writing student, worked up a set of questions to ask four different doctors who help families cope with the deaths of infants shortly after birth. Based on these interviews, she would write an article for the monthly newsletter of her agency, Helping After Neonatal Death (HAND). HAND provides weekly support groups for grieving parents and other family members, but the newsletter is the organization's main project. Here are Allison's original questions:

1. Tell me your professional experience with neonatal death.
2. How does the death of a patient affect you?
3. How do you handle the parents in this situation?
4. How often do you feel that the death could have been prevented by caution on the parents' part or on other people's parts?
5. How big of a problem is neonatal death? In other words, how often does it happen?
6. What's the major cause of deaths in the infants you have seen?
7. Do you have anything you would like to say to the community or the parents about this problem?

Given what you know about the audience for the newsletter, you will probably note that the fourth question is certainly the most awkward of the bunch; it is a question that an interviewer would never ask grieving parents if they were the interview subjects. Most parents, having lost an infant, feel incredibly guilty even when they know that there was nothing they could have done to prevent their baby's death. It only took Allison her first interview with a doctor, who was himself uncomfortable with the question, to realize that her readers—grieving parents—would find doctors' answers to this question as disturbing as the question itself. Allison writes, "I ended up putting much more emphasis on questions 1,

2, 3, and 7. I did this because I realized that the parents do not want to hear about the diseases and the medical aspect of it (they've probably already heard so much about it from their own experiences) and they would much prefer to hear about the human aspect of being a doctor."

Conducting Your Interview

Show up, appropriately dressed, a few minutes early for your interview, if possible, so that you will be relaxed and focused when you begin. "Appropriate dress" will depend on whom you are interviewing and where the interview is taking place. If you are interviewing volunteers during the lunch break at a tree-planting work day sponsored by your agency, wear work clothes that you don't mind getting dirty; you will probably be expected to pitch in. If you are interviewing elementary school children (who run the gamut of being total hams or extremely shy), you will want to dress nicely, but not so formally as to intimidate them. If you are interviewing men and women who work at city hall, you will probably want to dress more professionally. Just use common sense.

Tape recording your interview is an excellent idea, for a couple of reasons. First, if the material covered in the interview is at all complex, you will welcome the opportunity to review it later. Second, if you plan to quote your interviewee, a tape recording will ensure the accuracy of these quotations. If you plan to tape the interview, make sure to ask your interviewee's permission before you start.

One possible disadvantage of taping is that it may make some subjects nervous. It will aid both your interviewee's and your confidence if you take the time to familiarize yourself with the equipment in advance in order to avoid fumbling or running into technical problems. Usually, after a few minutes, neither you nor your interviewee will remember that a recording is being made. Even if you do record your interview, it is a good idea to take written notes as well, since some technical problems might not become apparent until *after* the interview has taken place. If you do not use a tape recorder and rely solely on your notes, remember to confirm quotes by letting your interviewee check them if your writing will be published.

You will probably want to begin the interview by getting additional information about your interviewee and confirming the information that you already have, including the spelling of your subject's name, his or her position and job title, and any degrees, licenses, or personal experience that qualify him or her as an expert on the subject of the interview. Also make a note of the date, time, and location of the interview; this information will be relevant in your writing when you acknowledge and cite your source. You might also note any details about the location if you are interviewing the person on his or her home turf. Details about setting and perhaps even about your interviewee's appearance and personality may be relevant in some kinds of writing, including feature articles and some academic papers, in which conveying mood and tone is important.

You will also want to make sure that you have your interviewee's permission to use his or her name in what you write; there is a possibility that your interviewee will prefer to remain anonymous or would like you to use a fictitious name. It is important to respect your interviewee's wishes where anonymity is concerned.

During the course of the interview, if the interviewee says something that is not quite clear to you, or that you would like to have confirmed or rephrased, ask for clarification. A phrase like "So, you're saying that ..." should produce the desired result. If your interviewee goes off on a tangent, look for an opportunity to bring him or her back to the subject by asking one of your prepared questions. On the other hand, tangents can sometimes be productive, especially if you know enough about the subject to help guide them by asking relevant spontaneous questions. If the opportunity arises to learn something new and unexpected, be prepared to seize it.

Limit your interview to the length of time you agreed on in advance. No doubt your interviewee has other business to attend to as well, whether it is to get back to the courtroom to argue another case or to join classmates for recess. When you are finished, thank your interviewee for the time and the help, shake hands, and leave. It is a good idea to follow up the interview with a thank-you note. Your interviewee will also appreciate your sending a copy of any writing in which the interview is featured.

Transcribing Your Interview

Review your notes immediately following the interview when it is still fresh in your mind. Many writers who do a lot of interviewing transcribe their handwritten notes immediately following an interview, either on their computers or on note cards that can be easily coordinated with other note cards from other primary or secondary research. If you have tape recorded the interview, it is a good idea to transcribe the tape—or at least the most relevant parts—and then make note cards from your transcription.

Long-Distance Interviews

If you locate a good interview subject who lives too far away for you to arrange a personal meeting, you may have to conduct your interview by phone, mail, fax, or email. Most of the basic guidelines for successful interviewing above will apply to interviews conducted in these other forms as well, but with some additions. If you are interviewing over the telephone, you will want, in your initial call, to set up with your interviewee a convenient date and time (specifying length of time) to call back, when both you and your interviewee will be prepared to talk at length. If you would like to tape record your phone interview, it is essential to ask permission, since your taping will not be obvious to your interviewee. Because your interviewee is doing you a favor in giving you his or her time, you should plan to pay any long-distance charges.

If you are conducting your interview by mail, fax, or email, you will need to write out a list of questions, keeping them as well focused and as brief as possible. Be careful to phrase your questions clearly, and make sure that they are neatly typed. In a cover letter, provide any relevant information about your project, along with the date by which you need your interviewee's answers, allowing him or her a reasonable length of time to respond. Be prepared to follow up with a telephone or written inquiry if you have not received your interviewee's response within the time promised. When you interview by mail, always enclose with your questions a self-addressed stamped envelope so that your interviewee can simply drop his or her response into the nearest mailbox.

Follow-Up Questions

Sometimes, as you proceed with your research, you will realize that you would like to ask your interviewee a few follow-up questions. Discovering that you have follow-up questions is not a sign that you have failed in your investigation in any way; it simply indicates that, as your own understanding of your subject grows, you are recognizing what specific gaps need to be filled so that you can better answer the questions that have motivated your research. Usually, since you have established a relationship with your interviewee, asking and getting answers to follow-up questions can be accomplished over the phone. Give your interviewee a call and ask if you can pose your questions then and there or at a future time that would be more convenient for him or her.

> My experience with my community-service project has been educational in that I have gained invaluable interviewing skills. My project for my organization really gave me a foundation for research interviews that I have used many times since. In no other setting would I have had the motivation and guidance to gain such competence in interviewing. I am certain that this skill will be useful in many of my future endeavors, whether it be for an honors thesis or a newspaper article.
>
> —*Jenny Chen, first-year student*

Surveying

When you need to gather specific information from a number of people so that you can ascertain and compare their behavior, attitudes, values, or beliefs, conducting a survey can provide you with the kind of information that you need. Whether you conduct research on behalf of your agency or as part of your community-based academic work, the results of a survey can be extremely revealing and very useful.

Suppose you are working with a nonprofit organization that is promoting construction of an extensive system of bike paths in your town. There are a few existing bike paths, mostly around the university, but they are not linked and they do not extend from one end of town to the other. Your agency has asked you to write, distribute, and analyze the results of a survey in order to learn about citizens' bicycling habits and their attitudes about biking as opposed to driving, as well as to gauge their response to the proposed extended bike-path network. The results of this survey will be included in an information packet that your agency plans to distribute at the next city council meeting in hopes of persuading city officials to support the project. Survey results will also be made available to the public to encourage community support.

What Kind of Survey Is Appropriate?

Some surveys are *random.* The goal of a random survey is to seek responses from a cross-section of the population, selected randomly. For a random survey, you might give yourself a week to conduct the survey. During this period, you might position yourself at various locations in town and at various times of the day and evening, asking people at random if they would respond to the questions for your survey.

Other surveys are *targeted,* soliciting responses from people identified with particular groups. For example, if you wanted to know, specifically, about the cycling habits and attitudes of students at your school, you would station yourself at various locations on campus, over several days, at different times of the day and night, and distribute your survey to students only. However, within your sampling, you would select your subjects randomly. You would not, in other words, distribute your survey only to people who happened to be riding bicycles.

Ask yourself which kind of survey would be appropriate to the kind of information you are gathering, and from whom.

Designing and Writing Your Survey

In designing your survey questionnaire, consider carefully what, if any, background information you need. Is it important that respondents give their names, or is anonymity better? Do you need to know where your respondents live, and if so how precisely? Is information about gender, race, or ethnicity relevant? Do you need to know anything about your respondents' professions or academic majors, their hobbies, or their political affiliations? Don't ask more questions than are absolutely necessary; necessity is determined, of course, by the direct relevance the questions and answers have to your subject.

There are several kinds of questions that you might ask in your questionnaire. *Two-way questions* ask the respondent to choose one of two answers:

> *Do you bicycle?*
> _____ yes _____ no
> *Do you ever bike to work?*
> _____ yes _____ no
> *If you do bike to work, do you bike to work most of the time?*
> _____ yes _____ no
> *If you use existing bike paths mostly for recreational biking, would you begin to bike to work if a network of bike paths made it easy and safe to get from your home to work?*
>
> _____ yes _____ no

If your survey consists of brief two-way questions, you could ask them orally and tally your respondents' answers on the spot. Generally, however, a written questionnaire is more reliable, and through it you can gather more information. Whether the questions or the answers to them are oral or written, you must pose the same questions to everyone, and you must consider carefully what these questions will be and how to phrase them neutrally. The answers to two-way questions can be useful, and they are easy to analyze, but since they limit the range of answers, their usefulness can be limited.

Complex questions are better answered with a range of possible answers. *Multiple-choice questions* provide for this range while at the same time directing responses into categories that lend themselves to relatively simple analysis:

> *On average, how often would you say that you use existing bike paths?*
> _____ less than once a month
> _____ more than once a month but less than every week
> _____ at least once a week
> _____ several days throughout the week
>
> *Why do you cycle?*
> _____ for recreational purposes
> _____ for physical training
> _____ as an occasional means of transportation
> _____ as a primary means of transportation
> _____ other (please specify) _____
>
> *If there was an extensive bike-path network throughout town, how much more often would you bike to work as opposed to driving?*
> _____ there would be no change in frequency
> _____ on nice days, I would definitely bike to work
> _____ I would almost always bike to work
> _____ other (please specify) _____

A third kind of question, the *open-ended question*, provides the widest leeway in individual responses as well as the greatest challenge in analyzing and categorizing answers:

> *Why do you, or do you not, use a bicycle to get around town?*
>
> *Where do you think the money should come from to pay for a new, extensive system of bike paths?*
>
> *If you think that your city* should not *provide an extensive system of bicycle paths, what are your reasons?*
>
> *If you think that your city* should *provide an extensive system of bicycle paths, what are your reasons?*

Such questions are complicated, and the answers to them are highly subjective. But in some cases, you might not want to limit your respondents' answers in any way, especially if you are looking for their own ideas rather than a confirmation of your own. Answers to open-ended questions are obviously difficult to report statistically, but they may offer information and ideas that are hard to come by through more limited kinds of questioning.

Analyzing Interview Material and Survey Results

Quantitative analysis is statistical. Responses to two-way and multiple-choice questions in surveys lend themselves to quantitative analysis of data. And quantitative analysis of data, almost by definition, lends itself to generalized conclusions. Be careful, though, not to generalize too broadly from the results of a survey in which your sampling is limited.

Qualitative analysis, on the other hand, requires the researcher to consider the content of responses on an individual basis. The analysis of responses to open-ended survey questions, as well as the analysis of what a subject has to say in an interview, must be considered in individual, not categorical, terms. Certainly, you can group responses of various individuals in like categories, but take care in qualitative analysis not to generalize too broadly. Generally speaking, the higher the level of expertise of the person who is providing a qualitative response, the higher the level of generalization you can draw from it. Still, even if a survey respondent or interviewee is very knowledgeable on the subject, one response is simply that: one response.

KNOWLEDGE IS POWER

Who has the right to define knowledge? How does the control of knowledge affect power relations? What is the relation of "popular" knowledge to "official" knowledge? How do relatively powerless groups empower themselves through research and information?

—John Gaventa, "The Powerful, the Powerless, and the Experts: Knowledge Struggles in an Information Age," Voices of Change

Have you seen the movie *Erin Brockovich,* the story of a low-wage employee at a law firm who is compelled on her own to research the high incidence of cancer in a community located near a power plant? This film is based on actual events in which a citizen wanting answers brought about significant change in the community and in society as a whole. In the end, her findings led to the largest lawsuit ever against Pacific Gas and Electric Company.

Your research for a community-based project may not bring about changes nearly as dramatic as this, but your research *will* make change. You will, with your agency and the people who work there, help to bring knowledge, and through that knowledge, power to the community. Take a look at Jenny Bernstein's piece, "Water Quality: Tap Water," in the Appendix. Obviously, Jenny used her research findings to craft this report. But this example of a practical writing project does not exist in a vacuum; this research *does* something. Officials and agencies in local government depend on this report and others published in *Indicators for a Sustainable San Mateo County: A Yearly Report Card on Our County's Quality of Life* to let them know what is going right and what is going wrong in their community, and to help them determine how quality of life and environmental safety can be maintained and improved.

Changing the world may not be the first possibility that comes to mind as you contemplate the value of the research that you do in school. But when you conduct cross-community research, you are, through the very process of sharing information and exchanging knowledge, helping to bring about change. Knowledge empowers everyone.

A Case in Point: Stanford University Hospital and Medical Waste Burning in East Oakland

In the spring of 1999, a student who was a member of a campus group, Students for Environmental Action at Stanford (SEAS), began work with another local environmental group, Greenaction, as part of a service-learning internship. She was asked to gather information on Stanford University Hospital's medical waste disposal program. There had been reports of poor air quality and respiratory problems from East Oakland, a neighborhood comprised of mainly working-class Latino, African American, and immigrant Vietnamese and Laotian people. Some residents suspected that the source of these problems was the last commercial medical waste incinerator in California, operated by Integrated Environmental Systems and located in their neighborhood. Greenaction knew that Stanford University Hospital sent its medical waste to this incinerator and was a major customer of IES.

The intern went to East Oakland and began canvassing the neighborhood for interviews. Many residents, although some were hesitant at first to speak with a student from Stanford, agreed to be interviewed. In story after story, she found that people said the same things: they were having noticeable health problems that ranged from burning eyes and headaches to increased asthma on burn days; they could see emissions coming from the incinerator. None of the neighborhood residents believed that what they were seeing was steam or some other nontoxic emission.

She began her Stanford research by working her way down a list of phone numbers of people who dealt with medical waste at the hospital. Eventually, she found someone in the Waste Disposal Department who confirmed that, yes, Stanford University Hospital did send its medical waste to the plant in East Oakland. She was assured that IES was a responsible company and that both the type of waste burned and the incineration methods were within state environmental regulations. Her source at the hospital offered to give her a hospital waste tour. Although the tour was impressive, many of her questions went unanswered, especially those concerning the exact content of the waste being burned.

At this point, the intern was joined by four first-year writing students enrolled in an environmentally themed course with a community-based writing component. Together, the five students divided the research, with one group concentrating on East Oakland and the other on Stanford University Hospital.

In East Oakland, more community members came forward with complaints of respiratory problems and headaches, and the issue began to arouse concerns among a broad coalition of community groups as well as in local government. Local media began to pick up the story, reporting that since 1996 IES had racked up more than one hundred violations of its air permit, according to air district records. It was also reported that an entire wall at the incinerator plant had been eaten away by hydrochloric acid, one of the many toxins burned there.

Meanwhile, the group focusing its research on Stanford University Hospital discovered that much of the waste being sent for incineration in East Oakland— including plastic biohazard boxes containing used syringes, bloody gauze, and latex gloves—was made of polyvinyl chloride (PVC) plastic, which, when burned, releases toxic chemicals. Of these toxic emissions, dioxin was the most worrisome. The students discovered in their library and online research that a recently released U.S. Environmental Protection Agency study had found dioxin to be even more toxic than previously thought, linked to cancer, birth defects, and developmental, immunological, and other health problems even at very low levels of exposure.

On November 1, 2000, after many months of investigation and pressure exerted by students, East Oakland residents, and a coalition of community and environmental groups, Stanford University Hospital announced its plans to begin moving away from incinerating its medical waste at the IES facility in East Oakland. Hospital officials pledged to (1) immediately remove 60 to 70 percent of the PVC from the waste stream currently incinerated, (2) recycle PVC containers instead of incinerating them, (3) move to on-site steam sterilization of wastes by January 2002, and (4) phase out PVC plastics wherever feasible. Debate in East Oakland over the IES incineration facility continues. Many people believe that this plant will inevitably be shut down or convert to safer technologies in disposing of medical waste.

This campaign has been an enormous cross-community collaboration. What began as one student's community-based research project grew to compel the research of other service-learners and community members. Their work culminated in major and widely publicized community action involving a powerful coalition of concerned residents and other citizens, community nonprofit organizations, students, and city, local, and state governmental agencies and officials. Crucial exchanges of knowledge in this case led not only to better informed communities, but also to more empowered ones—communities in which change can, and does, occur.

REFLECTIVE QUESTIONS
FOR JOURNAL-WRITING AND CLASS DISCUSSION

1. In small groups in class, analyze the following sources. Which seem reliable and which do not? On what do you base your answers?

   - A history of poverty in the United States published by Columbia University Press

- A newspaper, *Street Sheet,* published by a coalition of homeless people
- A Web site analyzing the results of a survey conducted by the Environmental Protection Agency
- A pamphlet about abortion distributed by the Promise Keepers
- A Web site from the University of Michigan discussing public health policy
- An article about factory farming published in a PETA (People for the Ethical Treatment of Animals) newsletter
- An essay on the ethics of animal testing written by an economist
- An article in the *National Enquirer* with the headline "Aliens Come to Earth as People's Pets!"
- A chapter on service-learning from a doctoral dissertation in progress

2. What is a *fact*?
3. What do you think makes a community issue controversial?
4. John Gaventa refers to "popular" knowledge and "official" knowledge. What does he mean by these terms? In your experience, what are some of the sources of each kind of knowledge? What power dynamics do you see at play between them?

TROUBLESHOOTING

WHAT IF…

you can't find anything at the library on your topic?

TRY TO…

ask the librarian for help. It is much more likely that you need to find the correct subject or key words to use in your search than it is that nothing exists on your topic. The reference librarian can help you.

WHAT IF…

you are asked to research or write something in a highly specialized language and you don't understand it fully?

TRY TO…

look up the terms. Most community-based practical writing projects target a general audience, but if you do find yourself researching and writing for a specialized one, you might have trouble understanding the lingo. Ask your agency mentor to help clarify certain words and phrases for you. If you are conducting an interview with someone like a medical professional, ask your interviewee for an explanation of the terms. If all of this seems too daunting, you can always approach your mentor to see if there is a different type of project you can do—one with a different audience and purpose.

WHAT IF...

a practical writing topic is too controversial and you want to step back and find a safer one?

TRY TO...

speak to your agency mentor and level with her or him about your discomfort with the topic. A good agency mentor will understand and not pressure you to continue with a project that is problematic for you. Ask your mentor if there is another project that you could take on, one that you do not find upsetting.

WHAT IF...

your agency asks you to investigate covertly and you don't feel comfortable in this role?

TRY TO...

explain the reasons for your discomfort to your mentor. If, for example, your agency asks you to represent yourself only as a student and not mention your affiliation with the agency when you talk to a source, you might not feel comfortable about telling half-truths. Your discomfort would be entirely understandable, and you should not feel pressured to proceed. Once you explain your feelings to your mentor, the pressure should ease.

WHAT IF...

an interviewee asks to remain anonymous and you are concerned that anonymity will weaken the credibility of your writing?

TRY TO...

remember that if someone asks to remain anonymous, he or she has a good reason for doing so. Generally, the reason is personal. In rare instances, the source may be worried about losing her or his job. In either case, respect a request for anonymity. Professional journalists have to deal with this all of the time. If they did not respect the anonymity of their sources, no one would ever tell them anything.

CHAPTER 10

Mapping, Organizing, and Drafting

*Each time I sit down and stare at a blank piece of paper, or a white computer screen,
I am embarking on an adventure...not only for myself, but for the reader as well.*
—ALLISON O'SULLIVAN, SECOND-YEAR STUDENT

When you begin a new writing project, you may, like Allison, feel that you are "embarking on an adventure." For many students, though, beginning a writing task feels stressful and frightening more than anything else. If, however, you follow a writing progression—moving gradually from setting down your initial thoughts, to establishing an organizational strategy, to drafting your work—instead of attempting to write a first and final version in one sitting, you will find the task of writing to be much more manageable. The process of mapping, organizing, and drafting an academic or a practical piece of writing will allow you to move from relative chaos to relative order.

Both academic and practical community-based writing call for mapping, organizing, and drafting, but the approaches that you take to each kind of writing task differ in significant ways. Mapping an academic project is about invention. In mapping, you allow your ideas on a topic to pop up willy-nilly and collide with one another. The value of mapping in academic writing is that it gives you the freedom to explore ideas without having to commit to any one particular approach. Once you've mapped the possibilities of a project and selected one approach, then you can develop it, employing the more logical and rigid constructs of organization. In organizing, you will select key ideas and establish key points and evidence, arranging them in patterns that make sense to you and might make the most sense to your reader. In drafting, you build upon the skeletal structure that organizing provides, taking your first stab at articulating the whole. You flesh out information, explanation, and argument; you begin to work with your individual writing voice and style.

Mapping a practical writing project, on the other hand, generally has more to do with achieving an unambiguous understanding of your assignment (its topic, audience, purpose, and genre) than with invention. Organizing a practical project will have as much to do with form and format in the genre in which you are working as it does with selection and arrangement of content. In drafting a practical project, you will be attempting the first full articulation of your text, but you will also be tailoring that text to concrete format specifications and conforming the tone and style of your writing to a specific audience and purpose.

COMMUNITY-BASED ACADEMIC PROJECTS

I was asked to turn in a rough draft of my research paper on the media portrayal of breast cancer, which I had become interested in through my work with Breast Cancer Action. But I felt that writing a draft would not be the best way to begin. Instead, I did a collage of quotes from my sources and organized them in the order in which they would appear in my paper. Then I wrote topic sentences and major themes that would relate the various quotes. After I organized it in this abstract manner, my paper was easy for me to draft.

—*Megan Vanneman, second-year student*

The strategies that writers use in mapping, organizing, and drafting are highly individual to each writer. Whatever strategies you use at various stages of your academic project's development, we urge you to consider, in sequence, the following goals:

1. **Invention:** Explore freely the various ideas that you have about your topic, perhaps in answer to a question or questions that are driving your individual response to the assignment and to your research. From invention, the seed of your thesis is likely to germinate.

2. **Content Development:** From invention, begin to identify a central idea as well as the most crucial points that relate to it, points that arise both from your research and from your original thinking about your topic.

3. **Arrangement:** Consider how to arrange specific ideas and points relative to a tentative thesis that has grown from your central idea, and begin to consider how your arrangement of content will accommodate the format conventions of the academic genre in which you are writing.

4. **Articulation:** Express yourself fully and clearly in a way that your reader will understand. In informing, explaining, and persuading, experiment with voice and style in your writing: (a) consider the needs and expectations of your academic reader and (b) communicate your unique identity as an academic thinker and writer.

Mapping Your Academic Project: Invention and Content Development

If you have a complete and accurate understanding of your assignment and you have gathered the information that you need through research, you are ready to begin mapping your project. Mapping can take various forms, and every writer has a unique way of approaching this stage of writing in which *invention* and the beginnings of *content development* are so important. One of the most useful methods of mapping many kinds of academic writing, however, is *freewriting*.

Freewriting

How often have you sat in front of your empty computer screen just watching the cursor blink at you? How many times, with your pad and pencil in front of you, have you written and rewritten that first sentence, over and over? Freewriting can jump-start your thinking and writing process, helping you generate material, especially when you feel stuck.

Especially if you haven't done freewriting before, you might warm up with a freewrite that is unrelated to the writing assignment that you have been given. Set a timer or an alarm clock to go off in ten minutes. Choose a random word or phrase. Then begin to write. Don't let your fingers leave the keyboard or your pencil leave the paper. Write whatever comes into your mind. Don't censor yourself, and don't worry about grammatical details or whether your writing is making sense. The main idea is to write everything and anything that comes into your mind, beginning with the word or phrase that you have chosen. When the timer or alarm goes off, stop writing and take a look at what you've got. Perhaps you will notice a progression of thought in what you have written about the word or phrase that you chose.

After this warm-up, set the timer again, this time for fifteen to twenty minutes. Begin by articulating your topic in a single word or phrase, then write down everything that comes into your mind about it. Put down other words and phrases, apparently random associations, questions, ideas, arguments, dialogue, word pictures—anything that comes into your mind. If you are writing about your agency and the work that it does, try describing the agency office or a site in which agency work takes place, or describe someone whom the agency serves. Record how things look, feel, smell, sound, taste. Keep your writing immediate; try not to overanalyze. Don't think, "This is my topic, so I have to sound smart"; this exercise is for you and no one else. There is no room here for the critical editor within us all who likes to butt in and censor our ideas before we have even had a chance to explore them. Lock that editor out of the process; there will be a time and place for editing later. When the alarm goes off and you read what you have written, chances are good that you will see some of the seeds for both central and secondary ideas that will ultimately appear in your paper.

Students often wind up using parts (much revised) of early freewriting in drafts and finished versions of their academic writing. For instance, you might suddenly see your introduction within the jumble of freewritten words, or you might find there some of the important questions that you think your paper should address. You will probably also hear a particular tone in your freewrite. Recognizing this tone is especially important if you have not already consciously acknowledged your feelings about or your stance on your topic; it was there all along, but you had not been in touch with it until now.

Not all ideas gleaned from freewriting will be particularly relevant. Freewriting can also help you identify and eliminate false starts and tangents, ideas that you don't want to write about and approaches that, ultimately, you don't want to take. These are also important realizations.

Caitlin Corrigan did the following freewrite to begin her community-based academic writing project for her service-learning class.

The smell of the rice and beans mingles with the bubbling tomato sauce and simmering vegetable soup as I stir the contents of all three pots. An occasional bug will dart out from one of the rickety burners, and when it comes time to drain the pasta, a guy with ratty dreads and a pierced lip will use someone's shirt as a potholder over the tiny kitchen sink. This is the staging ground for Food Not Bombs—a tiny kitchen in a cluttered apartment filled with a dozen hungover guys and a couple of dogs. You will find no agency director here. The food is ready by 2:30 and we pack up all the aforementioned dishes, along with a fruit salad and some more pasta. We end up taking three cars to city hall. "Jim," who's sort of the driving force behind FNB, told me that at one point he was the only person cooking and serving. Today we're arriving at the park with close to a dozen people. According to Jim, the numbers tend to vary depending on how many people crashed at the cooking house the night before. Everything is set up quickly including the FNB banner that's set up on the corner to attract passersby. Within seconds, people arrive and begin helping themselves to the hot tea

(continued)

(continued)

and food, as well as the cardboard boxes full of nonperishables, candles, and other assorted goods.

I cannot begin to describe the difference between providing food outside on a street corner and "serving" food inside a shelter. There was a tangible feeling of exchange going on—people didn't just humbly accept food, they met my eyes, thanked us, and hung around for conversation. I wasn't really able to determine if there were many "regulars" but more than a few people were aware that what we were doing could "get us into some trouble" and I think that made things a little more equal somehow....Food Not Bombs is so refreshing because it is like the anti-organization. It's just a bunch of people (mostly men actually, which I found interesting) who take a few hours every week to actually do something they believe in. There is no hierarchy, no personal mobilization. Simply action for action's sake, which I found really easy to jump into. I'm really glad to be doing FNB as it seems to be the complete opposite of the sort of selfishly motivated volunteerism I was sketchy about being associated with.

—Caitlin Corrigan, first-year student

Caitlin knew that she wanted to write about her agency, Food Not Bombs, and its practice of anarchy. Notice that Caitlin's freewrite begins with sensory impressions of her agency—the smell of the food, the guy with the pierced lip, the cluttered apartment, the dogs. Details of scene and setting are a great way to begin a freewrite, since they are vivid and relatively easy to record. They provide a springboard for ideas and analysis that evolve from them—in Caitlin's case, exploring the difference between serving food outside as opposed to inside a shelter, the lack of a hierarchy at Food Not Bombs, and finally, the kinds of volunteers that Food Not Bombs attracts.

In the subsections that follow in this chapter, you will see how the development of Caitlin's project progresses from this freewrite to clustering to outlining.

As you encounter her project in these various stages of development, notice that Caitlin hangs on to some ideas from this freewriting exercise, expanding and extending them in her cluster and in her outline. In fact, Caitlin mined this early freewrite for the introduction to her final paper. You can read this opening paragraph in Chapter 8, Academic Writing in a Service-Learning Context.

Through freewriting, you may not yet have pinpointed the central idea of your paper, but perhaps you have articulated an important question or two that will motivate your thinking and writing from this point forward. You may have identified the approach that you will take to your topic or perhaps some key points that you know you want to cover. There is still a long way to go, but the important thing is that you have begun to write your paper.

Organizing Your Academic Project: Content Development and Arrangement

Freewriting can help you map your project at a point in the writing process in which you are most concerned with invention and development of content. At whatever point *content development* begins to call for a coherent strategy of *arrangement*, organization will be your main task. Two quite different but potentially equally effective ways in which you might begin to organize your material for an academic writing project are *clustering* and *outlining*.

Clustering

Clustering can function as an effective bridge between the mapping and organizing stages of writing, since it allows your ideas to flow relatively freely but at the same time helps you envision a definite shape and direction for your paper. In clustering, your main argument and the supporting points will probably become clearer to you, which will allow you to move more confidently toward outlining.

To begin a cluster, write in the middle of a blank sheet of paper a word or phrase that suggests the subject you want to explore. Circle it. As you begin to think of words, phrases, ideas, and images that you associate in any way with your central thought, write each down and circle it as well, drawing a line to connect it to the word, phrase, idea, or image that engendered it. Draw additional lines as well to illustrate its relationship to other bubbles in your cluster. Don't stop to edit yourself; as in freewriting, there is no right or wrong way to go about clustering. If you get stuck, draw more circles to fill.

Clustering can be particularly effective when it is used in combination with freewriting. When your cluster seems complete, try freewriting for five or ten minutes, weaving the images, ideas, and associations of your cluster into a sequence that makes sense to you and leaving out what seems irrelevant. Clustering, and the freewriting that may grow out of it, should help you focus your topic and see how it might be organized and further developed.

For her Food Not Bombs paper, Caitlin Corrigan created three separate clusters, each of which expanded on a particular point that she wanted to address in her paper. Here is her cluster starting with the word "anarchy":

Several points appear in this cluster that serve as the basis for key sections of Caitlin's finished paper: anarchy's ties to activism; popular misunderstandings about anarchy being anti-community; and the model that anarchy provides of a reverse power structure in which all members of a community can thrive. The cluster begins to articulate an argument in support of Food Not Bombs and its anarchistic goal to empower all members in the community.

Like Caitlin, when you cluster, you will still be inventing content, but you will also be in the early stages of applying an organizational structure to that content. As you read the outline of Caitlin's paper, you will see how relevant and useful many of the ideas included in her cluster prove to be. You will probably have a similar experience as you move from clustering to outlining.

Outlining

Of all the various strategies for mapping and organizing a piece of academic writing, you are probably most familiar with outlining. Many teachers in your past have probably required you to turn in outlines of essays, both short and long, before submitting your draft or final work. Outlines—at least detailed outlines—are unnecessary for some kinds of writing, but they are extremely useful when your job is to plot an organizational strategy for a long or complex paper. Outlines make it easier to spot gaps in information or coverage that you still might need to fill. Here, as an example of a full outline for a long and complex paper, is Caitlin's outline for "Food Not Bombs: An Anarchist Community in Action."

> **Thesis**: Educating people about the symbiosis of anarchy and community is one of the underlying goals of Food Not Bombs.
>
> I. Introduction
>   A. Set the scene
>   1. Describe the kitchen at the Baltimore row house
>   2. Describe loading the cars with the food, dry goods, and clothing
>   3. Finish setting the scene with the large banner we hang up at our location outside of city hall: Food Not Bombs
> II. "Food Not What?"
>   A. Historical background on the twenty-year old organization being founded in Boston
>   1. The "Clamshell Alliance"
>   2. FNB's connection to the antinuclear nonviolent protests
>   3. Mass arrests leading to seminars and workshops—creative resistance was put into practice
>   B. Protests against First National Bank of Boston
>   1. Bank's funding nuclear arms industry
>   2. Redlining Boston ghettoes
>   3. Homeless people encouraged to participate in protests and street theatre
>   C. History of FNB = connection to activism, community, anarchism
>   1. Nonviolence
>   2. Vegetarianism
> III. Anarchy: A Brief Definition and Myth Debunker
>   A. Definition of anarchy
>   1. Political theory based on nonhierarchical society
>   2. Emma Goldman

B. History of anarchism

    1. Ancient democracies of Athens, European assemblies and American West in the 19th Century

    2. Catholic Worker Movement in the U.S. establishing houses of need—Dorothy Day

C. Anarchism is not the antonym for community

    1. Anarchism is not a state of chaos

    2. Anarchism = order from the bottom up

D. Anarchists looking toward state of natural equality

    1. WTO protests in Seattle

    2. Analyzing parts of modern life we overlook

IV. Community: Why It's Necessary

A. Definitions of community as related to anarchy

    1. Michael Taylor's *Community, Anarchy and Liberty*

    2. What kinds of relationships do people have in a community?

B. Need for a decentralization of power in communities

    1. Everyone is accessible and receptive to everyone else

    2. Community as an approach to anarchistic living

V. Food Not Bombs: Building an Anarchist Community

A. How FNB is a real manifestation of the ideas about the relationship between anarchy and community

    1. FNB avoids hierarchy typical of traditional voluntary associations

    2. Practice anarchist alternatives to organizing and activism

B. Nonviolence (another anarchist principle) at the heart of FNB

    1. Nonviolence as it relates to vegetarianism

    2. How FNB brings together all members of the community each week on the sidewalk in front of city hall

VI. Conclusion

A. Emma Goldman's ideas about "real wealth"

    1. Community participation backed by anarchist ideology as good way of achieving this sort of wealth

    2. Strengthening community from the inside out

B. FNB's role in the anarchist movement

    1. Furthering nonviolent ideologies

    2. Not wanting to see people go hungry due to misdirected government policies

    3. FNB serves food weekly, even though they are under constant threat of getting arrested

C. Community's role in FNB

    1. Community interaction with FNB—understanding differences

    2. Community's role in FNB's efforts

This outline—the skeletal structure of Caitlin's paper—is clear and quite thorough. Your outline may look similar to this one, or it might be more sketchy. Outlines do not need to be perfect in order to be useful. In fact, one of the ways in which they serve writers best is by providing them with the confidence that they need to take worthwhile risks in drafting.

Drafting Your Academic Project: Arrangement and Articulation

Usually, a draft provides the first occasion in which you attempt to articulate the whole, fully, from beginning to end. Especially if your paper is long or at all complex (as most community-based academic papers are), the prospect of writing a coherent draft can be overwhelming unless you have an outline to work from. However, sticking to your outline *at all costs* can actually be a constraint in drafting. Don't be afraid to stray from your outline; a productive outline should give you the confidence to explore promising tangents in your draft. In fact, none of the strategies for mapping ideas and organizing material should restrict you, but rather each should open up new possibilities.

In writing a community-based or traditional academic paper, you generally have considerable freedom to come up with an original argument and to establish your position on your topic. In fact, this is the most essential point of most academic writing. Through earlier mapping and organizing strategies, your primary argument (that is, your thesis) should have become clear to you, and you will have discovered and arranged key points and evidence in support of it. The main challenge of the draft is to begin to articulate your argument in the clearest and most effective way for the person or people who will be reading your paper. The best advice for drafting—assuming that you are clear about whom you are writing to and what you want to accomplish—is to *just do it*.

Your draft will also offer you the first opportunity to experiment with voice and style in your writing. *Voice* conveys the writer's unique personality or attitude, while *style* is the way in which voice is expressed in writing. Voice and style aren't only about the writer, however; they have to do with the relationship between the writer and the reader. In other words, as much as your writing voice and style reflect who you are and your relationship to your topic, they also must accommodate the needs and expectations of your reader. Maintaining this kind of reader awareness while expressing yourself as a writer can, at times, be a delicate balancing act.

Refer back to Chapter 8, Academic Writing in a Service-Learning Context, and read the opening paragraph of Caitlin Corrigan's paper. How would you characterize her writing voice? How would you describe her style? This first paragraph sets the tone for the rest of the paper, and it invites the reader into a world that may be entirely unfamiliar. Caitlin conveys warmth, both literal and metaphorical, in describing the kitchen at Food Not Bombs. She brings the reader into the agency to experience firsthand this agency's mission and goals. She sits the reader down in a warm kitchen, a comfortable place. This is voice and style at work. Consider what a different tone would have been conveyed had she opened by defining anarchy, for example, or by explaining the organization's missions and goals in abstract rather than concrete terms.

In a draft, nothing is set in stone. Drafting offers opportunities for experimentation, especially in organization and style. The best way to check the clarity and effectiveness of a draft is to ask readers to respond to it. Based on readers' responses, you can revise and edit with the reader more firmly in mind. (See Chapter 13, Revising and Editing.)

PRACTICAL WRITING PROJECTS

The most influential difference between mapping and organizing academic writing projects and practical ones has to do with the fact that practical writing arises from more explicit assignments than academic writing does. You will generally have a great deal of freedom in responding to an academic assignment: you select the topic; you establish your approach to it; you arrive at your own conclusions; you choose an individualized voice and style in communicating them. As a writer for your agency, you will probably have considerably less freedom (although more potential impact) in responding to your assignment:

- Your topic will probably be assigned to you.
- Your approach will be determined by your document's audience and purpose as well as by its format.
- Although your own conclusions are important, you will probably articulate a collective, not a personal, perspective.
- The voice and style of your writing will speak for your agency, not for you.

In academic writing, whether community-based or not, you write in order to express yourself to your reader; in community writing, you write to express your agency.

Mapping, organizing, and drafting academic projects emphasizes a highly individualized approach to thinking and writing, which is a fundamental value of academic culture. We have to understand mapping, organizing, and drafting in different terms in order to apply them productively to writing in the community. Your goals in mapping, organizing, and drafting a practical writing project and an academic one might be similar in some respects, but there are crucial differences:

1. **Assignment:** Understand all aspects of the assignment, including the topic; your document's audience, purpose, and genre; and the setting and circumstance in which the reader will encounter your document.

2. **Content Development:** From an understanding of your assignment, begin to identify the most crucial point that your document should make, distinguishing it from supporting points and other relevant information from your

research. Keep content directly relevant to audience and purpose, and be ready to adapt it to the genre and specific format of your document.

3. **Arrangement:** Relative to your document's central point, consider how to arrange supporting points and relevant information. Begin to consider how arrangement of content will accommodate the format of your finished document.

4. **Articulation:** Express yourself clearly and succinctly in a way that your specific reader will understand and be able to absorb in the setting and circumstance of his or her reading. In informing, explaining, and persuading, keep voice and style consistent and appropriate to audience and purpose. Remember that you are expressing your agency, not yourself.

Compare these goals with the goals for mapping, organizing, and drafting academic projects on page 171 and note the differences.

> The writing I was required to do was not meant to impress with stellar ideas or difficult vocabulary. It had to be clear, concise, specific, and useful. It had to be understandable to the general public—simple and informative, but not patronizing.
>
> —*Irina Nedeltcheva, first-year student*

Brainstorming, freewriting, clustering, and outlining are specific mapping and organizing strategies that can help you materialize your practical writing project, but these strategies will be helpful to varying degrees, depending on the type of project it is. Furthermore, the ways in which you might apply these strategies in creating a practical document differ, often substantially, from the ways in which you might apply them to an academic paper.

Mapping Your Practical Project: Assignment and Content Development

You will not use mapping to invent a writing topic for a practical project because you have already been assigned one. Instead, mapping will help you understand your assignment better. *Brainstorming* and *freewriting* can be especially useful tools in accomplishing this understanding.

Brainstorming

> Brainstorming is a goal-directed search for ideas. This is what makes it different from either freewriting or writing a first draft.
>
> —*Linda Flower, Problem-Solving Strategies for Writing in College and Community*

Brainstorming can be even more useful in community-based practical writing than in academic writing. In the collaborative work culture of a community agency, people are usually quite accustomed to brainstorming together in order to clarify projects and goals. Although the assignment that you have been given for your community writing project may be clear from the beginning, you might discover that your agency mentor has an initially sketchy understanding of your assignment. In this case, you should brainstorm with your mentor—and perhaps include other people at the agency in your session, if they have a direct relationship to your project—in order to clarify your assignment. A brainstorming session should produce ideas about the topic, audience, purpose, and form of your finished document, to whatever extent that any of these elements is missing from your and your mentor's understanding of your project. By the end of the session, you should have decided, together, which specific goals to pursue in these categories.

Occasionally, a mentor will leave it up to you—or to your group, if your project is collaborative—to envision the particulars of a practical writing assignment, which is fine. But to whatever extent your assignment is explicit or open, the important thing is that before you begin to develop and organize content, or to draft, you *must* know what you are working toward.

You can certainly brainstorm alone, if your mentor has left the particulars of the assignment up to you, but since the idea in brainstorming is to generate as many possibilities as you can before settling on one, brainstorming works best when more than one person is involved. If you are working alone, use your instructor as a brainstorming partner; together you can map a concrete direction for your project.

If your project is a collaborative one with other students, you will want to brainstorm with your group, especially if the details of your practical assignment are at all unclear. Together, you can brainstorm with your mentor or, if your mentor has left the particulars of the assignment up to your group, independently.

A brainstorming session with your mentor is likely to be guided by him or her. If you are brainstorming with a peer group, however, it might be helpful to refer to these general guidelines for brainstorming:

- Before your session begins, assign one person to record the ideas that arise during the session.

- Address one aspect of the task at a time and in a sequence that makes sense: for example, brainstorm the topic first, then the audience, then the purpose, then the format of your project.

- Encourage everyone to participate.

- Generate as many ideas as possible in the form of words and phrases, images, associations, questions, memories, experiences—whatever!

- Don't censor yourself or others; don't judge anyone's contributions in brainstorming.

When your brainstorm is complete, discuss the possibilities in a more structured way. Consider all ideas fairly, and don't dismiss or discount any idea automatically. After this discussion, make decisions—by consensus—about the topic, audience, purpose, and format of your project.

Freewriting

Freewriting to explore the nuances of your thoughts about your topic will probably not be as directly useful in practical writing as it is in academic writing. But freewriting can definitely help you in other ways: to achieve a more concrete understanding of your reader, the situation in which he or she is most likely to read what you've written, and the effect that you hope your document will have on him or her.

Consider doing several separate, but related, freewrites. Try responding to these prompts, in sequence:

1. Reader: who are you?
2. Where and how will you encounter what I have written?
3. How will you react to what I've written? What will you think and do?

The results of these freewrites can bring the concrete realities of your task to the forefront, helping you to solidify your goals and to establish empathy with your reader. Through freewriting, you may be able to envision more clearly the steps that you will take in developing and organizing the content of your document and adapting it to format.

Organizing Your Practical Project: Content Development and Arrangement

Clustering may be a valuable strategy in developing and organizing a wide variety of practical writing projects. The extent to which *outlining* might be useful in developing and organizing your project depends very much on the kind of project it is.

Clustering

Clustering a practical document can help you generate points that you might want to include, and it can help you select among these points. Most practical documents must be concise; some—brochures, for example—must be *extremely* concise. Clusters are visually oriented, as are many practical documents. Therefore, a cluster may work especially well in that it allows you to visualize both the content and the potential arrangement of a practical document.

Imagine that you are asked to write a brochure for a new weekend program at the local community center aimed at keeping high school students from driving after they have been drinking. The program will be staffed by parent volunteers, although the designated drivers will be teen volunteers. You have been asked to write a brochure that will recruit the parent volunteers. Your clustering of the brochure might look something like this:

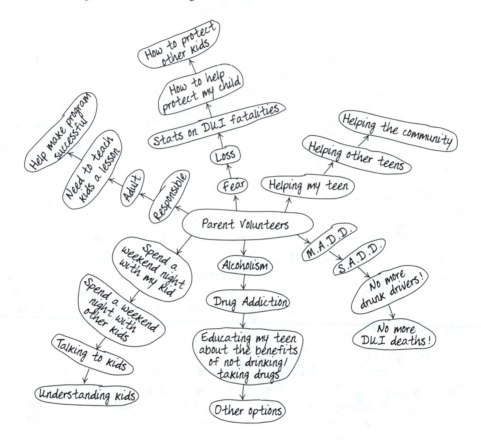

This cluster, with the brochure's audience at the center, reflects parents' many and various concerns about the effects of alcohol and drugs on their children. These concerns range from fears about alcoholism and the consequences of drunk driving to desires to help MADD (Mothers Against Drunk Driving) and to understand kids. The purpose of the cluster is to help you explore the brochure's subject *from its reader's point of view* and, in doing this, to develop content that is relevant to the specific reader. From the material generated in this cluster, you can begin to establish some of the key goals of the brochure, and you can begin to imagine in what sequence you might want to present them:

1. Inform parents about the statistics on teen DUI fatalities.
2. Persuade parents that they can make a difference by volunteering for the weekend safe-ride program.

3. Empower parents with the assurance that they can help educate their own children and other teens about the benefits of not drinking and/or taking drugs.

4. Convince parents that if they volunteer with the program, they will not only be helping their own families, but the community as a whole.

Through clustering, you can also begin to identify a tone that would be effective in writing your document. The key emotion driving the cluster above is concern, and this emotion will also drive the tone in the finished brochure, influencing the style in which it is written and even the way it looks on the page.

Outlining

If your practical document is short and relatively straightforward, outlining will probably be of limited use. Creating a formal outline for a flyer, for example, would probably be a waste of time. However, if your project is long and relatively complex, outlining might be a very good idea indeed. In length and complexity, some practical writing projects—for example, reports, project assessments, grant proposals, as well as some newsletter articles and Web pages—resemble academic writing, and in these kinds of projects in particular, outlining can be extremely useful, if not essential. If you have been assigned this type of project by your agency, review the section on outlining academic projects beginning on page 177 in this chapter.

Because most practical writing projects arise from explicit assignments, you may be provided with at least a rough outline for yours, since your agency mentor might want to make sure that you cover certain essential points. Or there might be specific content guidelines imposed on your project by another source, especially if you are writing a grant proposal.

Grant proposal guidelines are very often issued by granting foundations. These guidelines, in fact, will provide you with the beginnings of an outline for your specific proposal. A typical set of guidelines for a grant proposal might look like this:

I. Need

   A. What specific community need does your agency address?

   B. Why is your agency's work important?

II. Objectives

   A. What does your agency wish to accomplish if the grant is awarded? (Be as specific as possible about your agency's goals.)

   B. If the grant is requesting special equipment rather than an award, how will that equipment be used?

   C. Generally, how will your agency benefit the community it serves?

   D. More specifically, who will benefit from the agency's work? (A group of people who are somehow underrepresented?)

   E. Will your agency increase public awareness about specific issues?

   F. Why is the work that your agency does unique?

III. Methodology
   A. Describe how your agency will use the grant money to implement the changes in the community.
   B. Will the agency involve staff, volunteers, and other community members?

IV. Are there other organizations that your agency hopes to collaborate with on this project?
   A. Who are they?
   B. How will they work with your agency?
   C. How will the combined work better benefit the community?

V. Evaluation
   A. What short- and long-term changes do you expect your agency to be able to make if awarded the grant?
   B. How will these changes be measured?

If you are writing a grant proposal to submit to a specific funding source, make sure that you develop and organize your proposal according to the specific guidelines provided by that source. If you are writing a *template* grant proposal—that is, a proposal that your agency can later adapt and submit to a variety of funding sources—you might want to work from the guidelines above.

Drafting Your Practical Project: Arrangement and Articulation

Assuming that you are well prepared—that you know the assignment well, that you have all the information that you need, and that you have an organizational strategy—the fundamental advice about drafting a piece of academic writing applies as well to drafting a practical document: *just do it*. However, being well prepared to draft a practical document, even an apparently simple one, is more complicated than being prepared to draft an academic one. This is because most practical documents require an acute audience awareness and a clear understanding of your document's practical purpose and format. Audience, purpose, and format will affect all of your drafting decisions in fundamental ways, including the arrangement of your document on the page and the tone and style in which you write.

We suggest, as a final check, that you complete the Community Writer's Inventory provided here. That will help you complete the accompanying Community Writer's Statement of Audience and Purpose. Your response to these exercises can also serve to guide a peer reviewer or your instructor in reading your draft before you begin to revise and edit it. (See Chapter 13, Revising and Editing.) We also suggest that you read Chapter 11, Formatting, in which we discuss visual communication and practical document design, before you draft your practical document.

COMMUNITY WRITER'S INVENTORY

1. *What kind of document are you producing?* A brochure or pamphlet; booklet; fact sheet; flyer; Web site or Web page; article (for newspaper or newsletter?); in-house report, proposal, or assessment; opinion editorial piece; letter to the editor; promotional letter; letter to public official; grant proposal; other?

2. *What are the primary and secondary rhetorical purposes of the document?* To *inform*; to *explain*; to *persuade*? More specifically, to investigate and report; to inquire or interrogate; to entertain; to inspire; to challenge; to sensitize; to incite or excite; to promote; to challenge; other?

3. *Who is the primary reader of the document? Is there a secondary audience?* Young children, young adolescents, older adolescents, adults? Specialized or general readers? Providers or recipients of services? Other?

4. *Further characterize your primary readers, according to any of the following categories that you believe are relevant, or others that you can think of:* age, more precisely; education or literacy level; socioeconomic position; native language; cultural background; ethnicity; physical ability; profession; level of sympathy, hostility, or neutrality; other.

5. *Characterize any secondary readers in the same way, and note any differences between primary and secondary readers.*

6. *Describe the situation in which your reader is most likely to encounter what you have written in its finished form.* Quick read or on-the-run; slow read, time to read carefully; arrives in the mail; handed out on the street; posted (where?); in the newspaper; in a newsletter; in a brochure picked up at the agency (or elsewhere?); in a book; accessed online (through random search or directed search?); available to anyone; available to select readers; other.

7. *Where did you get the information you need, or where will you get it?* Primary sources: interviews with experts; interviews with people in the community; surveys; archives; agency files? Secondary sources: in agency libraries, school libraries, or public libraries; government documents; audio or visual media? Which sources are most important?

8. *What modes of development are necessary in your document? Where and why?* Description; narration; process analysis; definition; classification; illustration and example; comparison and contrast; cause and effect analysis; argument/persuasion?

9. *Describe the writing voice that works best for your document.* Formal, academic; casual, easily accessible; stylistically vivid (for example, humorous, satiric); neutral or bland; other.

(continued)

(continued)

10. *Describe the general form of the finished document.* One-sided page; front and back of one page; double-fold brochure. Full-width text; columns; other. Headings; subheadings. Introduction and conclusion. Complete sentences and paragraphs or short lines of text.

11. *Describe the particulars of format.* Large print, standard print, small print; various fonts in various places; questions and answers; bullet points; Web page links. Graphical elements, enhancements: document design, layout; print in color, black and white, gray scale; photos or graphic images; drawings; tables or graphs; other.

COMMUNITY WRITER'S STATEMENT
OF AUDIENCE AND PURPOSE

Try articulating your community writing task using the pattern of information that emerged from the Community Writer's Inventory.

I am writing a/an _____ (kind of document) for _____ (agency), whose mission is to _____ . My primary purpose in the document is to _____ (rhetorical purpose), and my secondary purpose is to _____ my readers, who are _____ (audience and their specific characteristics). Since my purpose and my audience will be encountering my writing in _____ _____ (situation), my writing voice must be _____ . The form and format of the document (_____) will also help make my points effectively. I need to research _____ (kinds of sources) to get the information I need to produce a credible and effective document, and I expect to develop and articulate my points using the following modes of development: _____ _____ .

REFLECTIVE QUESTIONS
FOR JOURNAL-WRITING AND CLASS DISCUSSION

1. Freewrite for twenty minutes about the writing topic that you are currently developing. For example, if you are preparing to write an academic paper related to your work with your agency, you might try focusing your freewrite on the way in which your agency's work relates to your paper topic. Or choose an important aspect of your topic, and freewrite about that. If you are preparing to write a practical document for your agency, try

focusing your freewrite on characterizing a typical reader of your document. Or try describing the situation and circumstances in which your reader is likely to encounter your document and the effect that you hope it has on the reader. If one freewrite seems promising, you might want to try a series of several on your topic.

2. At the early stages of mapping a community-based academic project, create a cluster around what seems to be the central idea of your paper. Bring your cluster to class. Pair up with one of your peers and exchange clusters. Don't criticize; just tell each other what you notice about ideas, patterns of relationship, and progressions. Then brainstorm together other ideas for each cluster.

3. Take a look at the cluster on page 184. This cluster helped the writer to develop a sense of audience for her brochure to recruit parent volunteers in a weekend safe-ride program. Create a cluster that might help you develop a sense of audience for a partner brochure—one to recruit teenage volunteer drivers for the same program. When you are done with your cluster, compare the two. What aspects of the clusters are similar? How do the clusters differ?

4. In the following examples, in what ways and to what extent do you think audience and purpose might affect the writer's approach in the early stages of planning and writing?

   - an ad campaign for a client
   - a brochure for a nonprofit agency
   - a term paper for an instructor

In each instance, how much control over content or form might the writer have? How much room might there be for the writer's individual voice? Which writing tasks appeal to you? Which don't? Why?

TROUBLESHOOTING

WHAT IF...

you go through all of the stages of mapping and organizing and you still cannot get a handle on the audience and tone of your practical document?

TRY TO...

clarify the audience with your agency mentor. If your audience seems too broad, brainstorm with your mentor to identify it more specifically.

spend time with your reader. If you understand who your audience is, but do not understand enough about it, try spending time with the people for whom you will be writing. For example, if your audience will be elementary school kids, see if you can arrange to observe a class in a local elementary school. Just observe and listen. Contact with people who are like your readers will help you clarify audience and tone.

WHAT IF…

you have too much information for the size of the document that you need to create?

TRY TO…

categorize the information. Look for redundant information and opportunities to combine points. Locate the best example, or two comparative examples, instead of many. Choose the most profound statistic. If you use quotations, use only the most relevant and poignant ones.

discuss the information with your mentor. If all of your information is unique and essential, then reevaluate the scope of the project. Ask your mentor if other agency publications have covered some of the territory that you are attempting to cover in your document. Determine whether some of the material can be dropped.

WHAT IF…

your mentor has asked you to create a document for an audience that is too vague or too large?

TRY TO…

share your concerns with your mentor. Through your initial work on this project, you may have anticipated problems related to audience and purpose that your mentor may not have considered. For example, if your assignment was to write a document for readers who range in age from adolescent to elderly, you may have come to realize that the agency needs to produce three separate documents—one for teenagers, one for adults, and one for seniors. Your perspective and advice, which come from knowing your project well, will probably be much appreciated by your mentor.

CHAPTER 11

Formatting

It is ... important to keep in mind that in graphic design, problem-solving and creativity occur simultaneously. If graphic design does not solve a problem, then it is simply self-indulgence—a kind of pointless talking to one's self.

—MARTIN HOLLOWAY, GRAPHIC DESIGNER, IN *THINKING CREATIVELY:
NEW WAYS TO UNLOCK YOUR VISUAL IMAGINATION* BY ROBIN LANDA

Form is function. The format of a document—the way it looks on the page—communicates in and of itself a great deal about its audience, its writer or sponsor, and its purpose even before the reader begins to absorb the text. The *denotative* message, or literal meaning, of written text is furthered by the *connotative* message, or the secondary message that is conveyed through a document's design.

Most academic writers are not accustomed to thinking very deeply about what motivates format conventions and what drives formatting decisions. A lot tends to be taken for granted about formatting in academic writing (*it's just the way things are done*), and academic writers often think of formatting as merely applying the finishing touches to a piece of writing after the text is written, in the final editing stages. If part of your work in a service-learning class is to create a practical document for your agency, however, you will find that formatting occupies a front-and-center position. Very little is taken for granted in practical writing and document design. Practical writers need to consider principles of *visual communication* from the beginning, because very often what a document says is inseparable from how it looks.

AUDIENCE AND PURPOSE: THE FOUNDATION OF FORMATTING DECISIONS

In order to be effective, visual communication, like written communication, requires the writer-designer to have a clear understanding of the audience and purpose of the document that she or he is producing. In academic writing, achievement of this understanding is relatively straightforward. If you can answer the following questions unambiguously, you probably have a sound foundation for making appropriate decisions about formatting, as well as content and style, in academic writing:

1. *Do you understand the assignment?* Do you understand specifically what you are being asked to do and what material you are being asked to present?

2. *Do you understand your reader?* Do you understand his or her individual needs and expectations? If there is a secondary reader (for example, your peers or your agency mentor), is he or she just along for the ride, or should you consider his or her needs and expectations as well?

3. *Do you understand the purpose of your writing?* Do you understand its general and specific goals? Do you understand the effect that you want to have on your reader?

4. *Do you understand the accepted format conventions of the discipline or genre* in which you are writing?

In practical writing in the community, however, understanding assignment, audience, purpose, and genre conventions is considerably more complex. Your assignment might be to work in a practical genre with which you have no previous experience. Your reader might be virtually anyone, and your purpose, too, will be widely variable. It is quite possible that all four components—assignment, audience, purpose, and genre—will be much less familiar to you in a community context than in a strictly academic one. Answering the basic audience-and-purpose questions above is still essential to making effective decisions about formatting a practical document, but you will probably have to break down these general questions in different and more specific ways, and you will probably have to dig deeper, and wider, for the answers.

Because a practical writing assignment will probably involve more unknowns than an academic one, understanding exactly what your agency mentor is asking for is *crucial.* A minor misunderstanding of an academic assignment might produce relatively minor consequences in the finished product; what might seem to be a minor misunderstanding of a practical writing assignment could render the finished product useless. Check—and recheck!—your understanding of the assignment with your agency mentor. Specifically, make sure that you understand the following aspects of your practical writing assignment:

- **Practical genre.** What kind of document does your mentor want you to produce? A brochure? A flyer? A fact sheet? A newsletter article? A Web page? A grant proposal? All of these documents could deal with the same subject matter, but clearly they would do so in very different formats. A brochure about agency programs would provide only the most essential information and highlight only the most essential points, using headings, brief paragraphs and bullet points, probably supported by lots of graphical elements. A description of agency programs in a grant proposal, on the other hand, would involve much more detailed information and explanation, articulated in full sentences and thoroughly developed paragraphs, without a lot of graphical bells and whistles, which would probably serve only to distract your reader.

- ***Specific audience.*** Who will your primary reader be? Any of the practical genres above might target readers of various ages or backgrounds. Even if it covers the same information, a flyer or fact sheet written for children will differ in style and format from one for adults. An interactive game format such as the one that Jennifer Washington uses in her "Scavenger Hunt" (included in the Appendix) might be fun for kids, but it certainly wouldn't work for adult readers. Ask your mentor to give you as complete a picture as possible of your reader. You might even ask her or him to write a profile of the typical reader.

- ***Specific purpose.*** Ask your mentor to explain to you as concretely as she or he can what purpose your document should serve. This will include the document's rhetorical purpose (to inform, to explain, or to persuade), but ask your mentor, too, exactly what she or he hopes that the reader will *think* or *do* after reading this document. The better you understand purpose in concrete terms, the better you will be able to employ visual communication to help you accomplish this purpose.

- ***Reading occasion.*** Related to both audience and purpose, make sure that you understand the setting and circumstances in which your reader is most likely to encounter your document. This understanding will aid you in making effective formatting decisions. If your reader is most likely to encounter what you have written when he or she is on the move—for example, if your flyer will be handed out at a career fair or posted on a phone pole— bullet points will be much more effective than long paragraphs in presenting what you have to say.

> Our genre was a newsletter. We wanted to make it readable. When I say "readable," I mean such things as putting pictures where they are needed, and not putting articles in odd places that people would find inconvenient. Format is extremely important. I have seen newsletters (including the one that preceded ours from our agency) that had terrible layout. Quite frankly, I would get extremely bored reading them. The amount of time we spent on formatting was pretty equivalent to the amount of time we spent on writing.
>
> *—Jimmy Wu, first-year student*

TEXT FORMATTING

Formatting decisions occur on a number of levels in practical document design. You will have to consider how text is presented, and even how to integrate graphics and text. Decisions about the presentation of text may be governed by fundamental considerations, including the *length* of the document, the *dimensions* of the piece, and elements such as *type formatting* and *featured text*. These basic considerations usually relate explicitly to the practical genre in which you are working.

Length

The content and visual style of any written document is affected—in conception, writing, revising, editing, and formatting—by the length of that document. Many practical documents are considerably briefer than most academic papers, and this fact calls on students to be highly selective about content as well as highly efficient in presentation of text in practical documents. The length of some practical documents will be *specified,* or limited, explicitly. For example, if your agency mentor asks you to produce a one-page fact sheet on a particular subject, your text will have to conform to that 8½″ by 11″ page.

Length in other documents may not be specified, but you will have to consider very carefully what would be a *reasonable* length as opposed to an unreasonable one. Some practical documents—such as grant proposals and in-house reports and assessments—may allow you more space in which to develop points and arguments in detail, but succinctness is nonetheless essential to effectiveness in these practical genres as well. For example, just because there may not be a set page limit for a grant proposal does not mean that you have an unlimited amount of space in which to provide information and explanation and to make your argument. If you are not clear, direct, and succinct, your reader will lose interest, to the detriment of the proposal.

Dimensions

The length of your practical document is not the only spatial consideration that you will have to take into account. Document layout also affects the presentation of text in many ways, most of which are genre specific. As with document length, you may need to accommodate specified dimensions. For example, in the overall layout of an agency newsletter, you might be allotted a certain number of column inches. Or in a double-fold brochure with three exterior and three interior panels, your text may have to accommodate a one-half-inch margin for each panel:

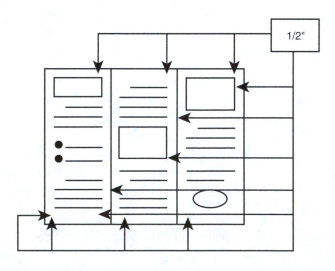

Decisions about adapting text to interior dimensions, too, may be related to *reasonable* specifications rather than to *explicit* ones, and what might be considered reasonable often has to do with your audience's reading environment. For example, if you were writing text for a Web page, you would probably want to present that text in relatively short paragraphs and bullet points, since reading large blocks of text—or long documents, for that matter—in a Web environment is uncomfortable for most readers. Similarly, in a newspaper or newsletter article, you will probably want to keep your paragraphs short in relation to the whole article, since large blocks of text can be off-putting when presented in columns.

Type Formatting

Your choice of font style and font size is in part a decision about presentation of text and in part a decision about graphic presentation. On the most fundamental level, when you consider what font style and font size to use in a given document, you must take into account your document's readability. Again, readability will depend on reading occasion—the setting and circumstances in which your reader will encounter what you have written.

If you are producing a flyer, it will probably have to capture your reader's eye when that reader is on the move. Therefore, the style and size of the font that you use to hook your reader will have to be both compelling and readable at a glance. The heading of a flyer might be presented in a stylized and very large font in order to grab your reader's attention. For example, in a flyer in which your job is to publicize the opening of a homeless shelter, your heading might read:

WHERE WILL YOU SLEEP TONIGHT?

Once your reader is hooked, the font for the rest of the flyer may be plainer and smaller, but its style and size will still have to maintain appeal and readability for a reader who is pausing only briefly to read what you have written.

Fonts may be more or less plain or more or less stylized; either way, they have character. If you are considering a highly stylized font, make sure that it is appropriate for the message that your document conveys, in synch with its audience and purpose. Look back to Chapter 2, Writing in College and Writing in the Community, and note the various choices of font style and size that Terri Iwata and Nicole Louie made for their brochure for the Mid-Peninsula YWCA Rape Crisis Center (page 19). The primary purpose of the brochure is to encourage friends and family of survivors of sexual assault in a difficult task: to provide help and support to loved ones who are recovering from this trauma. One of Terri and Nicole's challenges in formatting was to find a way to visually convey a sense of hope. You can see how their typographical choices help them convey the connotative message:

They WILL live.

If, on the other hand, you are writing a report for staff at your agency or a grant proposal to a potential funder, choice of a highly stylized font would not be appropriate. Readers of these sorts of documents are professionals who read a lot in the course of any workday, so you will want to select a plain and professional font style of reasonable size (not too large and not too small) for your document. The font should not distract or challenge your reader in any way; it should allow her or him to focus exclusively on your document's content, and it should be easy on the eye. The plainer and more professional fonts will probably be familiar to you, since they tend to be the ones that you use in formatting academic writing.

Featured Text

Text can be graphically featured in various ways. Whether featured text appears in the form of a *headline,* a *bulleted list,* or *boxed text,* the fundamental intent is the same: it is meant to draw the reader's attention to that item first, before he or she reads the main text. Therefore, obviously, text that is graphically featured, whether by font style or size, or by bullets or boxes, should warrant the reader's focused attention.

Headings

Headings—including titles, headlines, and subheadings—are one way of graphically featuring text in a document. A title (of a report, for example) or headline (of an article, for example) captures the overall content of an entire document, probably in a literal way.

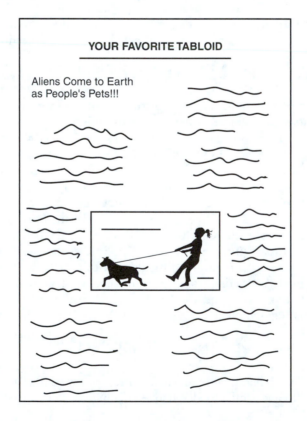

On the other hand, a heading for a flyer may not convey the literal content of a document so much as to suggest it, peaking the reader's interest. (See the example in "Type Formatting" above of the heading for a flyer publicizing the opening of a homeless shelter.)

Headings and subheadings within the body of a document communicate how it is organized and direct the audience's reading. In longer documents (such as this book), headings and subheadings help to clarify especially complex organization. In long and short documents alike, headings and subheadings also serve to draw the reader's attention to parts of the whole that he or she might be particularly interested in, while allowing the reader to overlook portions that might not be as personally relevant. Several documents included in the Appendix demonstrate the use of subheadings, including Jenny Bernstein's report, "Water Quality: Tap Water," and Andrew Goldfarb's newsletter article, "An Inside Look at Platelet Donation."

Bullets

Bullets provide a means of accentuating and clarifying items in a list. These items are generally stated succinctly—in words, phrases, clauses, or single sentences— and in parallel syntax. Bullets focus your reader's attention on the items in the list, so if you use bullets to highlight text, make sure that the items relate clearly and logically to one another. For example, if you bullet a *list of facts,* make sure that these facts pertain directly to the same subject. If you bullet a series of *steps in a process,* make sure that you leave no step out, that all of the steps are crucial, and that you present them in logical sequence. Check the logical order of a bulleted series of *points,* as well; for example, ask yourself if one would need to consider one point *in order* to consider the next one. Furthermore, in a bulleted list, make sure that items or points are of approximately equal importance.

Most word processing programs include bullets in their formatting features, and you will probably have more than simple dots to choose from. For example, in Microsoft Word, you can choose among the following:

•	Dots	❏	Open squares
➤	Arrows	❖	Four-point design
■	Small squares	✓	Check marks

Several practical documents included in the Appendix employ bullets, including "An Inside Look at Platelet Donation," in which Andrew Goldfarb uses bullets to present a list of facts; the grant proposal that Adryon Burton wrote on behalf of HAND, in which she uses bullets to summarize her agency's mission; and Jordi Feliu's "Home Safety Plan," a Web page for the Palo Alto Fire Department, in which bullets highlight each question on the "Home Safety Test" at the bottom of the Web page.

> It was a good exercise for me to write for a Web site, where ideas have to be distilled down to the bulleted essences—no fluffy cushioning allowed.
>
> *—Rebecca Freeland, first-year student*

Boxed Text

Boxes are another way to highlight specific text, often in the form of a quotation from the full text. Boxed text is frequently used in newsletter and magazine articles as a method of pulling out and emphasizing an important point of content. In documents that are heavily interview-based, as this book is, boxed quotes may feature the spoken words of an interviewee, conveying not only an important point of content, but also a sense of the character and voice of the person or people interviewed.

Most word processing software provides a variety of styles for framing text, from simple lines to fancy borders and background shading. You might even choose to use no border at all. For an example of text that is featured in this way, see "Mother Hubbard's Cupboard," an essay by Elizabeth Cole, in the Appendix.

> We used short nuggets to educate quickly, text boxes—no argument, just information, but thoughtful, illustrative and poignant at times.
>
> *—Anamaria Nino-Murcia, second-year student*

GRAPHICS

The graphic design elements of a practical document range from general design features, such as color of paper and print, to more specific elements, such as clip art; tables, charts, graphs, and maps; and photographs and other artwork.

General Design Features

> In my report for *Indicators for a Sustainable San Mateo County,* I am seeking consistency in the format, organization, and style used in *Indicators* from year to year.
>
> *—Jenny Bernstein, first-year student*

Some general design features of practical documents produced for agencies may be predetermined. You might be asked to print what you have written on agency stationery or adapt it to a pre-existing template. For example, Jessica Gray was asked to adapt her brochure, "Landmine Awareness" (see the Appendix), to an overall design used for all brochures produced by this local chapter of the American Red Cross. These pre-existing design features include the logo of the American Red Cross at the bottom of the brochure's leading panel, the black bar at the bottom of the final panel, the black and red diamonds that help to visually separate the various panels of the brochure, and the Red Cross maxim, "Help Can't Wait," printed across the base of the three consecutive interior panels. These common design features help to create continuity among individual publications that the agency produces.

Students who write Web pages for their organizations also often accommodate their work to existing Web-page templates. Jordi Feliu's Web page on home safety (see the Appendix) was posted on the Palo Alto Fire Department's Web site. The heading bar, with its graphics and logo, as well as the navigation bar to the left are common features among all of the individual pages within this Web site.

In the document that you write for your agency, many general design features will be left up to you. Decisions about fundamental design elements such as the use of borders and banners or choice of paper and print color might be yours. Have fun making these decisions and trying them out in your drafts, but make sure to ask your agency mentor to approve them before they go to press. Remember, your mentor has the final say on what works and what doesn't in format, just as he or she does in content.

Clip Art

A variety of copyright-free clip art is included with most word processing programs. You can access an even wider variety of clip art in other graphics software programs. There are books, as well, that contain a plethora of copyright-free artwork and designs. Any of these sources can provide you with graphical images and design features that may prove useful to you in formatting and planning the layout of a practical document. If you don't have and cannot afford to buy the clip art that you need, investigate what resources might be available at your school. Most campuses have computer labs or academic technology centers that own site licenses to graphics software. This software will not only help you locate clip art that you might consider using in your document, but may also help you plan and execute document layout.

Tables, Charts, Graphs, and Maps

Representative images such as tables, charts, graphs, and maps are extremely useful sources of visual information. You may have used tables, charts, or graphs in your academic writing. These graphics render numerical data in a form that is much simpler and more direct than explanatory prose. Furthermore, in being able to visualize statistics in relative terms through a table or graph, readers can analyze data on their own. Each of the three bar graphs that Jenny Bernstein includes in her "Water Quality" report (see the Appendix) illustrates levels of one of three contaminants—lead, copper, and trihalomethanes (THMs)—found in San Mateo County's tap water in 1998 and 1999. Each of the three graphs contains three measurements, the first indicating the maximum contaminant level that is considered safe by state and federal governments and the second and third indicating levels of the contaminant detected in samples of tap water from each of the two major water providers in the county. If you found this written explanation of the information included in Jenny's graphs confusing, consider how complicated a written *analysis* of this information might be. Then return to Jenny's graphs to appreciate their visual simplicity.

Another type of graph—a pie graph—is included in Andrew Goldfarb's article, "An Inside Look at Platelet Donation" (see the Appendix). Andrew is making the point that apheresis (or platelet) blood donors are far too rare. The visual depiction of this statistic in the form of his pie graph brings this point home with an impact that numbers embedded in text could not.

Maps are also frequently included in agency documents, especially in brochures and Web sites. Maps are, of course, useful in providing directions, perhaps to the agency's office, or as a way of locating the agency or the territory that it serves within a broader geographical area. If it is appropriate in your document, you may want to use a simple hand-drawn map that you or someone else at your agency has created. If you would like to use a map—or any other graphic image, including tables, charts, and graphs—that someone outside your agency has created, you will need to acquire permission to use it. (See "Step Six: Select Photos and Artwork, and Acquire Permissions" at the end of this chapter for more on the subjects of copyright and permissions.)

Photographs and Original Artwork

Photographs and original artwork can add beauty, poignancy, clarity, and personality to practical documents. Photographs, in particular, are widely used in agency brochures, pamphlets, and Web sites, since digital technology makes reproduction of high-quality images a relatively simple matter for desktop publishers. In fact, easy access to photographic reproduction may tempt you to overuse pictures; photographs will not serve your document well if crucial text must compete for space and battle for the reader's attention. If you do use photographs or other artwork, be highly selective in the images that you choose. Use these images sparingly; if you use more than one image, spread them in a balanced way throughout the document. One image is not as good as another; make sure that the artistic and technical quality of images that you use is high.

Jessica Gray's use of photographs in her Red Cross "Landmine Awareness" brochure (see the Appendix) demonstrates the powerfully persuasive impact that a few well-chosen photographs can have in reinforcing a written argument. Jessica had to ask herself what, visually, would convey her point that landmines are a global problem. What images would move readers in the United States, where landmines do not threaten our own lives, to action? From the cover photo of prostheses lined up in a cabinet to the picture of the person with a hole blasted in her leg, it only takes the reader a moment to be persuaded that landmines are devastating. Jessica's choice of the three photographs by Paul Hansen personalizes the landmines issue, knocking down national borders. In these photographs, we can imagine ourselves or the people we love dying in landmine explosions—or living without limbs and with permanently scarred faces.

> Creating brochures for the Red Cross was a great experience for me. Planning and refining exactly what I wanted to say as well as coming up with creative and eye-catching wording and layout always took more time than I expected. However, I think that the finished product was worth the extra time.
>
> —Jessica Gray, first-year student

SEVEN STEPS IN PRACTICAL DOCUMENT DESIGN

Students who research, write, and produce practical documents for their agencies must be much more aware of document design than academic writers need to be, since design tends to be such an important aspect of the overall effectiveness—or lack of effectiveness—of writing in the community. Your document's format should be on your mind from the moment that you receive your assignment, as you conduct research, as you plan and organize content, as you draft, and as you revise and edit your work. At this point, it should be clear to you that design in practical writing is not simply a product; it is a *process* that affects the development of your project at all stages.

Breaking the most explicit aspects of document design into steps may help you coordinate these tasks more successfully, although depending on the specific nature of your practical writing project, some steps may be more relevant than others.

Step One: Clarify the Assignment

Clarifying the assignment means understanding the following:

1. What practical writing genre you will be writing in and what the conventions of that genre are.
2. Who will be reading your document.
3. What setting or circumstances that reading is most likely to occur in.
4. What general purpose the document will serve.
5. What specific effect it should have on its reader.

The best way to confirm or to develop your understanding of your community writing assignment is to discuss it in detail with your agency mentor. Refer back to the section "Audience and Purpose: The Foundation of Formatting Decisions" at the beginning of this chapter for more on understanding practical writing assignments, and refer to Chapter 10, Mapping, Organizing, and Drafting, for advice on brainstorming in order to clarify assignments.

Also clarify with your mentor whether or not final formatting of your document will be your job. Most agencies are delighted when students offer not only to write document text but to format documents as well. Some agencies, though, especially with certain projects, will already have someone else lined up—possibly a professional graphic designer—to format the document that you write.

Step Two: Determine the Format Basics

Once you understand the assignment, including the practical genre with which you will be working, research the format basics in that genre. If you are writing content for a Web site, look at lots of Web sites; note what features are standard, and what format elements work and don't work for you as a Web reader. If you are writing a newsletter article, look at as many different newsletters as you can, noting format conventions in the genre. If you have been assigned to write a flyer or a fact sheet for your agency, open your eyes: you will run across a number of flyers and fact sheets in your day-to-day life. College campuses are full of them!

Start reading newspapers if you have been assigned a press release or a letter to the editor to write, and examine not only how these documents report on or argue their subjects, but also how long they tend to be and how they read in columns.

You can also make a trip to the library to locate books on graphic design or desktop publishing. Many bookstores, as well, carry books on these subjects. Many of these sources will offer practical tips on document formatting in specific practical genres. In some cases—as with grant-writing—you will find books in libraries and bookstores that provide advice about writing in a specific genre.

Step Three: Find Out about Budget Constraints

Some students have been ultimately quite disappointed when they found that their agencies did not have the funds to produce their projects in the forms in which they had produced them. It would be a shame, for example, to design a beautiful full-color brochure for your agency only to discover that it could only afford to print the brochure in gray scale. Find out in advance about your agency's production budget in order to avoid this kind of disappointment. Furthermore, redesigning your project because you hadn't understood budget constraints would mean that a lot of time and effort on your part had been lost, and if someone else at the agency undertook this task, the project would feel much less like your own in the end.

Step Four: Locate Specific Samples

Once you know the general format conventions of the genre that you are working in and understand your agency's budget constraints, locate as many specific samples as you can of practical documents that most closely resemble yours. These samples should be similar to your document not only in genre, but also, if at all possible, in subject and content. Analyze these samples critically to determine how other writers have approached subjects similar to yours and which design elements you would like to incorporate in your project, and which you would like to avoid.

Make sure to ask your agency mentor for specific samples of documents that the agency has produced in the past. Ask your mentor what he or she finds effective and ineffective about these materials. If you are writing a Web page, familiarize yourself thoroughly with the content and design of your agency's site. If you are writing a grant proposal, ask your agency mentor if the agency has copies of past grants that can serve as models for you. You will also find that looking at grant guidelines published by various foundations (often on their Web sites) will give you insight into the content, organization, and format of grant proposals. (See the grant guidelines sample on pages 185-186 in Chapter 10, Mapping, Organizing, and Drafting.)

Step Five: Sketch Your Layout

Although sketching a preliminary layout is not necessary in some practical genres (grants, for example), it will be indispensable in others. Genres in which layout is particularly important include brochures and pamphlets, guides and booklets, flyers and fact sheets, newsletters and newsletter articles, and Web pages.

You can sketch the layout for your document by hand or within a word processing or graphic design software program—or both. However you do it, you will need to know your project's dimensions first. For example:

- Will your *fact sheet* be printed on one side of an 8½″ by 11″ page, or will you have both front and back of the page to work with? How much space will you leave for the margins?

- Will your *brochure* be printed front and back on 8½″ by 11″ or 8½″ by 14″ paper? Will it feature six panels or eight? How much space will you allow for margins within each panel? Will you need to leave space on the back panel for a mailing label and postage?

- How many columns are you allowed for your *newsletter article?* How wide will these columns be, and how wide will the margins be?

A small hand-drawn sketch is an excellent way to begin envisioning the format of your document. In these rough sketches, you can play with overall layout and design; this process takes very little time and encourages creativity and originality in approach and design.

8 1/2 inches

11 inches

Working with a *grid* provides a more systematic approach to sketching your document's format and design, since you can adapt grids to specific measurements. Professional graphic designers use detailed and complex grids, but you can gain a lot by using simple grids. For example, most widely available word processing programs allow you to set up columns and blocks of specific widths and depths. Grids allow you to experiment casually with text and layout.

If your document's design and format are entirely up to you, play with grids to discover what elements you would like to include and how and where you would like to place them. Fiddle around with fonts and font sizes that you might consider using. In the initial design stages, you can even print out portions of a document as you envision them, in bits and pieces, and arrange them puzzle-like on a mock-up page.

It may be that you are adapting your text to an existing format. For example, you might be writing an article for an agency newsletter. If you know the total amount of space allotted for your article, the specific dimensions of that space, and the fonts and font sizes that will be used, a simple grid can help you tailor your text very specifically to the format available to you. In experimenting with format, even before you have any draft text prepared, you can use a grid to freewrite about your formatting ideas. Then print it out and see how it looks. (See the example of such an exercise on the following page.)

More sophisticated desktop publishing software programs, such as PageMaker, make document layout, including incorporation of photographs and other graphical elements, relatively easy and allow you to produce a polished finished product, if that is part of what your agency expects from you. Whereas standard word processing programs are widely available on campus computers, you might have to search harder for access to a computer with more specialized programs, like PageMaker. But ask around; they probably exist on your campus. Your agency, too, might own these software programs, and you might be able to work on your project at your agency during off-hours.

Step Six: Select Photos and Artwork, and Acquire Permissions

If you think that you might want to use images, such as photographs or original artwork, as a feature of your document design, begin exploring the possibilities early. Consider taking photos yourself, if you have confidence in your abilities as a photographer and access to decent equipment. If you are an artist, explore your ideas in sketches.

If you locate an image in print or online that you would like to use in your document, remember that you will have to get permission to use it. Using copyrighted images and graphics without permission is a violation of copyright law; ultimately, if you violate copyright law in creating a document for your agency, the agency will be held accountable. If the image exists in print form, contact the publisher to inquire about permissions. If it is from a Web site, contact the site's creator or webmaster. If the image is original and unpublished, seek permission to use it directly from the person who created it.

MY HEADLINE
By ME!

Here is my text. Let's see. I have a total of two and a half columns, so I will have to fit what I write to that. And I'd like to use a boxed quote from one of the girls.

I need to remember to keep my paragraphs pretty short—shorter than in papers for school. If I used long paragraphs like I do in my essays for school, the reader would just see a big old mass of black print on the page. That might put them off. So, keep 'em short.

Now, let's see what graphic things I could include. If I'm trying to explain the goals of the after-school career workshops, I could present them in bullets, like this:
- There would be the first one
- And the second one
- And the third one

I'll have to ask Marion for another copy of the brochure that has the mission statement in it. I lost it. (How could I have done that?)

I really need to find a good photograph to include in my article. You know what they say: a picture is worth a thousand words. I wonder if Marion has any good pictures at the office.

Maybe a text box could go here.

I'd probably use italics for this quote, and don't forget those quotation marks: " "

Wait a minute! I should just take my own pictures. I'd like to have some pictures anyway. These girls are so cool and so full of ATTITUDE. They may be considered "at risk," but they have a lot more nerve than I had at their age.

Maybe I'll get José to take a picture of all of us—a group shot. He actually has a digital camera, I think. Maybe we could use it.

Where would I put a picture in my article? In the middle? At the end? I don't know, but I guess I'll just make some space for it right here for now.

Here's the picture

Photo credit: José Ramirez (HA!)

Or maybe school has a digital camera. Maybe I could scan a regular picture? I'm sure that Marion deals with pictures all the time—there are lots of photos in the copies of the newsletter I've seen. I'll have to ask her.

I can't believe how little space two and a half columns is! I guess I'll have to work on being brief … hard for me.

Can't wait to print this out and see how it looks!

Maybe I should put some CONTACT INFO at the end—whom to call if someone's interested in the program. Or maybe people who read the newsletter will already know this. I'll have to think about that.

[NOTES TO MYSELF: HERE'S WHAT I KNOW:

I will have 2-1/2 columns for my article.

The columns are 2-1/4 inches wide.

There's a 1/2 inch margin at the top and bottom of the page.

The font is New York, 9 point for text, 12 point for headlines.

What size for photo credits? Or text in boxes ? I'll check.]

Acquiring permission to use an image may not be as difficult or complicated as you might think, especially when the photographs and other graphics are to be used in the publications of nonprofit agencies. Jessica Gray (see "Landmine Awareness" in the Appendix), for example, found the photographs that she used in her brochure on the Web site of the International Campaign to Ban Landmines (ICBL) (www.icbl.org). She emailed the site's webmaster and asked how she might contact the photographer in order to request permissions. Through this inquiry, she emailed Paul Hansen directly, and he granted her and the Red Cross permission to use his photographs in the brochure.

Exploring a full range of graphical possibilities takes time, and if you have to acquire permissions, it takes longer. So plan ahead as much as possible. Don't make assumptions in advance about being granted permissions. Also have a back-up plan. If you don't receive an artist's permission to use his or her work, you don't want to discover this at the last minute and have to scramble to throw together an alternate design plan.

Step Seven: Draft Your Text and Format It

There's no way around it: the time has come to draft your text and format it to accommodate your document design. If you have planned, organized, and drafted your text with format firmly in mind, it should be a beautiful fit!

Although design and format considerations are generally more crucial in practical documents than in academic ones, integration of visual elements may help you achieve more lively and compelling academic documents, without sacrificing adherence to academic format conventions. For example, information and arguments that print text conveys can often be greatly enhanced by use of digitized photographs, charts, graphs, tables, or maps. Assuming that your instructor approves your ideas, another option might be to present your paper in multimedia form—for example, on a CD or Web page—with written text enriched by hyperlinks, audio clips, or video clips.

Collectively, we are moving steadily into a world in which visual and written texts are inextricably entwined—at least in popular culture. Our educational institutions aren't far behind.

REFLECTIVE QUESTIONS
FOR JOURNAL-WRITING AND CLASS DISCUSSION

1. Select several advertisements from a variety of popular magazines. What is the denotative message and what is the connotative message of each ad? In what ways does the visual argument support the verbal argument of each? Compare your interpretations of the ads that you chose with those of other students in class.

2. If you are producing a practical document for your agency, work with a small group of your peers who are writing in a practical genre similar to yours (for example, brochures, fact sheets, or newsletter articles). Share with one another information about the specific audience and purpose for your document. Try drawing the format and layout of your project, working with various ideas about headings, bullets, photographs, and other graphical elements. Share your ideas with the group and brainstorm together additional ideas for formatting and layout in each project.

3. Over the course of a week, collect as many samples as you can of various practical documents, including flyers, brochures, newsletters, and Web sites. In a class critique session, select some of the most and least effective documents and analyze how format, including graphics and layout, contribute to their effectiveness or ineffectiveness.

TROUBLESHOOTING

WHAT IF…

you don't have access to fancy graphics software, and your agency mentor has no idea where you could format your document in the creative, professional way that he or she would like?

TRY TO…

explain your predicament to your instructor. If your college or university has an academic technology center, your instructor will probably know about it, or might have other suggestions about where you might find specialized graphics software.

bring up your problem in class. There is a good chance one or more of your classmates will have access to software that you might use.

find a copy center in town. Even a small college town will probably have a copy center that provides both computers and technical support. The problem, of course, is that someone has to pay for it.

WHAT IF…

your mentor knows the genre of your document (in other words, a newsletter article, a flyer, or a brochure) but does not have a clear picture of the format (for example, layout and graphics) that she or he wants for the project?

TRY TO…

make several sketches of possible formats for your document. Schedule a meeting with your mentor in order to review your preliminary drawings and decide together which format might best suit your document's audience and purpose.

WHAT IF...

you are closer in age to the target audience of your practical document than your mentor is and you feel strongly that your mentor's formatting ideas won't be as effective as the one you have come up with?

TRY TO...

gently explain to your mentor why you think that your idea will work better. Your mentor will probably be grateful for your input and put it to good use. Mentors usually appreciate students' unique perspectives. If, however, he or she has a specific reason for wanting the document to look or read a certain way, you will just need to accept that decision.

CHAPTER 12

Documenting

Citing your sources is important, because when something is not your idea, credit must be given, simply because of ethical issues. When you don't give credit to somebody for an idea, it is intellectual theft.
—JIMMY WU, FIRST-YEAR STUDENT

References prove or disprove the credibility of your work.
—TERENCE CHIA, SECOND-YEAR STUDENT

One of the reasons it is so important to document is so readers can investigate your sources when they want even more information.
—ANAMARIA NINO-MURCIA, SECOND-YEAR STUDENT

These three students have identified the most important reasons why documenting sources is so important, and the purposes that documentation serves. When you provide documentation in your writing, you

1. give clear and fair credit for the specific information, ideas, and perspectives that you have gathered from outside sources;

2. help establish the credibility of your own work by drawing on the credibility of others; and

3. provide the information that your reader needs if he or she wants to track down and consult your sources.

These reasons for and purposes of documentation are as important in practical writing as they are in academic writing. However, because practical and academic documents serve fundamentally different purposes, methods and styles of documentation often differ substantially between them. Furthermore, among specific practical genres as well as among particular academic disciplines, they vary even further.

It is not our intention in this chapter to discuss in depth the challenges that you face as an academic writer in developing and maintaining intellectual authority in a research essay, although that is an extremely important thing to think about. Nor is it our intention to provide you, beyond an overview, with the details of documentation format that you need to know in order to write research essays in courses in various disciplines, including the service-learning class in which you are currently enrolled. You should consult other texts for in-depth discussions and technical information in these areas.

In this chapter, rather, we provide an overview of the principles and methods of academic documentation. Having established this foundation, we address alternative principles of documentation that exist in the collaborative work culture of nonprofit and governmental agencies and suggest some documentation alternatives that might come in handy as you document the practical writing that you may have produced for your agency.

DOCUMENTING ACADEMIC WRITING

The main purpose of your academic writing is to further your education. An important aspect of what you learn through research-based writing is how to establish a critical relationship between what you know, your own insights and perspectives, and the knowledge, insights, and perspectives that you encounter through outside research. Therefore, in academic culture, where independent thinking and intellectual property are so highly valued, your careful documentation of outside sources does more than give credit to your sources where credit is due. It also helps your reader distinguish between your own ideas and analysis and those of other people, which ultimately highlights what you know and have come to learn. Documented writing in academic contexts, then, should be a kind of critical dialogue between you and your sources, and documentation style, like the identification of alternating speakers in a script, helps to clearly identify who's speaking where.

In academic writing, you are obliged to cite outside sources that you have consulted in your paper in two ways: with *internal citations* and in a *bibliography*. Students are often confused about what kinds of information they need to cite and what kinds of information they need not cite in academic writing. This decision depends on how we define *common knowledge* as opposed to specialized, or particular, knowledge.

Common Knowledge in Academic Writing

In academic writing, writers do not need to cite *common knowledge*, but they do need to cite specialized knowledge. There is no absolute or universal definition of "common knowledge" because what might be common knowledge for one reader, or in one discourse community, might not be common knowledge for, or in, another. This is one reason why consideration of audience and purpose is important, even in documentation.

Many of us were taught that we need to cite in our writing anything that we did not know before we began our research. This may have been wise advice in high school, when students are learning the very fundamentals of intellectual accountability, but it is not entirely practical in more advanced academic contexts. Perhaps a better, more useful, definition of common knowledge is required for college students: *common knowledge is information that is widely available, and replicated in many forms, in the reference section of a good library.*

Common knowledge generally has to do with *accepted facts.* Although the definition of a "fact" can be slippery, generally speaking, something is considered an accepted fact when reasonable authorities, whose expertise we generally trust, have agreed that it can be measured and confirmed in a certain way. For example, we accept Greenwich Mean Time as the standard on which everyone, worldwide, measures time.

Facts often have to do with events: for example, the U.S. presidential election is held on the first Tuesday of November every four years, or Jane Fonda won the Oscar for best actress in 1978 for the film *Coming Home.* Facts also have to do, often, with processes: for example, how photosynthesis takes place, or how an internal combustion engine works. These kinds of facts can be safely considered common knowledge as far as both general and specialized readers are concerned.

When your readers have a specialized knowledge in the field or discipline in which you are writing, however, what constitutes common knowledge shifts accordingly. For example, common knowledge among readers specialized in botany would exceed common knowledge among lay (nonspecialized) readers, and common knowledge among psychiatric social workers would exceed common knowledge among nonprofessional readers. The more specialized the reader, the higher the bar is raised on "common knowledge."

So what *do* you need to cite in documented writing in academic contexts? A good rule is that you should cite:

1. Material that constitutes specialized, as opposed to general, knowledge, according to the knowledge base of your reader.

2. Facts that are in the least bit controversial.

3. Material that involves any degree of individual interpretation, perspective, or point of view.

Plagiarism

Most students are worried about plagiarism, and they should be. *To plagiarize is to steal or represent as one's own the ideas, writings, or spoken words of other people.* An act of plagiarism can damage or entirely wreck a student's academic career. Beyond stating this simple fact, there is probably little that we could say to discourage the conscious plagiarist. However, when students who are concerned about plagiarism actually commit it, it is often because they do not clearly understand what plagiarism is, or they are being just plain sloppy in their documentation.

Even when a student's plagiarism is unintentional, there can be extremely serious consequences. So it is crucial first to understand very clearly what plagiarism is and then to take the necessary steps to avoid it. For the most part, these steps involve paying attention and being extremely careful to document clearly and correctly all of the material from outside sources that you use in your writing, from the note-taking stage on.

You are obligated … to acknowledge all borrowings … from other sources, even if you don't copy the exact words used in the original—even if you never actually quote the original. Plagiarism includes:

- Quoting material without attribution. The most obvious kind of plagiarism.
- Passing off another's idea as your own, even if it's been reworded. Changing an original's wording doesn't avoid plagiarism. The underlying idea of plagiarism is unacknowledged borrowing of ideas, not specific words.
- Imitating a passage's structure or argument without attribution. Suppose a source presents an assertion and three supporting points. If you adopt that particular structure, including the particular examples or supporting points, you need to provide a citation to the original. This holds even if you substantially revise the wording.
- Concealing the extent to which you've borrowed from a text or other source. Citing a specific passage in a work doesn't give you license to draw on the rest of the work without citation. This can be the nastiest kind of plagiarism because it's so sneaky.

—Michael Harvey, Washington College, Nuts and Bolts Guide
(http://www.nutsandboltsguide.com/plagiarism.html)

Most people clearly understand that quotations from sources must be cited. However, we have encountered more than one student who has somehow thought that she or he was not obliged to cite—or to cite fully—summarized or paraphrased material from sources. Writers need to cite and document summaries or paraphrases exactly as they would quotations from sources, minus only the quotation marks in the text. You might consider plagiarism that arises from this misconception as an honest mistake, but it is a mistake nonetheless, and one that could get you into a whole lot of trouble.

When you *summarize* or *paraphrase* a source, you state the author's idea *entirely in your own words,* although you may embed quotations from your source within a paraphrase or summary, if you use quotation marks. The difference between summary and paraphrase is essentially a matter of scope. In a summary, you state in your own words an over-arching idea from a source; for example, you might summarize a work by someone else by stating its thesis and key points in your own language. In a paraphrase, you state in your own words a much more specific idea or point from a source—something that the source author has stated in one or a few sentences, or perhaps in a paragraph.

Plagiarism can begin with sloppy note-taking. If, in your notes, you summarize or paraphrase a source, make sure that you remember to record the exact source, including the author, the publication, and page number. Summarizing and paraphrasing even at the note-taking stage of research is a good idea, as opposed to recording quotations exclusively, since in order to summarize or paraphrase you need to have an explicit understanding of the source text. Often, however, it will not only be the information, idea, or point of view that your source provides that interests you, but also the way in which the source has expressed it. When you do record quotations from sources in your notes and transcribe them in your paper, be extremely careful to replicate them with absolute accuracy, right down to the punctuation.

The same rules of citation and documentation apply to primary source material as to secondary source material. Any quotations from, or summaries or paraphrases of, material that you gather from archival research or interviews that you conduct must be cited and documented, too.

Documentation Styles and Conventions in the Disciplines

Documentation styles vary among academic disciplines. The documentation style that you choose for any given research essay is not a random choice; it is based on the discipline in which you are writing and the audience for, and purpose of, your work.

The most common and widely accepted documentation styles are:

- For documented writing in the sciences, the CBE (Council of Biology Editors) number system and the CBE name/year system.
- For documented writing in the social sciences, the APA (American Psychological Association) and the ASA (American Sociological Association) author/date style.
- For documented writing in the humanities, the MLA (Modern Language Association) author/page style in which parenthetical citations are used, and the Chicago author/page style, in which footnotes or endnotes are used.

Variations in form among these documentation styles may seem somewhat arbitrary, but the most fundamental differences, at least, are not. Within science, social science, and humanities disciplines, primary and secondary sources are documented in ways that emphasize the particular aspects of information that are most important in each discipline.

For example, because CBE documentation style for writing in the sciences is often used in reporting and documenting original research and findings, a number system is used, keying internal citations—(1), (2), (3), and so on—with entries in the bibliography, which are arranged sequentially rather than alphabetically. This system emphasizes the original research, while allowing the researcher-writer to acknowledge outside sources responsibly. In the APA and ASA styles for writing in fast-changing fields in the social sciences, where current information is so important, internal citations require author and year of publication as well as, in most cases, specific page references. In the MLA and Chicago documentation styles for writing in the humanities, internal citations require author and specific page references, emphasizing the source text itself. Whichever documentation style you choose in writing an academic research essay, be consistent; don't change documentation styles in midstream.

You will find details of academic documentation style explained and illustrated in various guides and handbooks that are available in print. If one of your course texts does not include documentation guidelines, you can find documentation style guides in the reference section of your library. You can also easily access this kind of information online. Many college and university writing centers and libraries post documentation style guides online.

Two particularly useful sites among many include one sponsored by the Writing Center at the University of Wisconsin–Madison ("Writer's Handbook: Documentation Styles" at www.wisc.edu/writing/Handbook/Documentation.html) and one by Ohio State University Libraries ("Research and Internet Aids: Citation Style Guides" at www.lib.ohio-state.edu/guides). These online resources are available to anyone. They contain detailed information about documentation styles in various academic disciplines, including guidelines to documentation of Internet and other electronic sources in these styles. Furthermore, these sites provide valuable hyperlinks to other documentation resources.

In-Text Citations

In-text citations identify sources in brief and usually specify page numbers. Complete information about the source is provided in a separate bibliography section or list of works cited. In-text citations may be made in the form of *parenthetical citations* or *notes*.

Parenthetical Citations

In parenthetical citations, you must give enough information so that your reader will be able to identify your source in your list of works cited. In most cases, parenthetical citations will also provide specific location information, such as page numbers. Place citations as close as possible to the information to which they apply, but preferably at the end of a sentence.

The fundamental information called for in parenthetical citations varies among disciplines. In the sciences, the information contained within a parenthetical citation will be either the author's name and the year of publication (in the CBE name/year citation system) or a number keyed to the source in Literature Cited (in the CBE number system). In the social sciences, parenthetical citations will include the author's last name, the year of publication, and usually a page number. Parenthetical citations in writing in the humanities include the author's last name and a page number.

Using a *signal phrase* in the text to introduce your source and indicate his or her qualifications establishes clarity and reinforces credibility. For example, if you were to write, "According to Dr. Kiesha Mack, Director of Health and Human Services for the city of...," you would accomplish two things. First, you would clearly distinguish the information, idea, or quotation cited from this source from what came before it. Your parenthetical citation, which in this case will probably consist of a page reference, will signal the end of reference to this particular source, setting it apart from what follows. Second, in supplying important information about the source's qualifications, you enhance your source's credibility, which will in turn enhance your own. If you use the source's name clearly in text, you need not repeat it in the parenthetical citation.

If you use figures (for example, tables, charts, or graphs) or photographs from outside sources in your academic papers, you must label each figure or photo accurately and cite its source.

Notes

In many disciplines and documentation styles, parenthetical citations are preferred over the general use of numbered endnotes or footnotes. (Chicago style is a major exception.) You may use informational notes in a paper that is documented with parenthetical citations, when the information that you provide in these notes is important but tangential to the idea that you are developing in your text. If you use informational notes, you cite the source of information, ideas, or quotations contained within that note with a parenthetical citation at the end of the note itself.

Bibliographies

Bibliographies go by various names—Literature Cited, Bibliography, References, References Cited, or Works Cited, for example—depending on the specific documentation style that you are using and the academic discipline in which you are writing. By whatever name, a list of works cited at the end of your paper will provide complete bibliographic information about *all* of the sources to which you have referred specifically within your paper. Your internal citations and your bibliography should, in most cases, reflect one another precisely.

Although details of bibliographic form vary depending on which documentation style you use, the essential information included in bibliographic entries is the same:

Primary Sources in the Form of Interviews
- The full name of the person you interviewed.
- Interviewee's professional position, job title, or a phrase that describes his or her qualifications in the context of your paper, along with location of his or her work or residence.
- Form of interview (e.g., personal interview or telephone interview).
- Date of interview.

Books

- The full name of the author or authors.
- The full title of the book.
- Publication data, including city of publication, name of publisher, and latest copyright date.

Articles in Newspapers, Magazines, and Journals

- The full name of the author.
- The full title of the article.
- Publication data, which varies according to the type of periodical but will include the full title of the periodical, the date of publication, and the inclusive page numbers of the article.

Sources Accessed on the Internet

- The full name of the author (if known) or sponsoring entity.
- The title of the Web page.
- The full title of the Web site; the date of its creation or latest revision.
- The date you visited the page or site and the URL.

The idea in a bibliography is to supply your reader with the information that she or he will need to track down the sources you cited in your text, whether they are primary or secondary sources.

Standards of documentation in academic writing are both extremely rigorous and extremely precise because intellectual property is very highly valued in the academic discourse community. When you participate in discourse in this community, whether through a traditional or a community-based academic paper in a service-learning class, follow the conventions of the academic community.

DOCUMENTING PRACTICAL WRITING

> I think documentation is as important in community writing genres as in academic writing. It is crucial that everything you write is accurate and that you're able to back it up.
>
> —*Louise Auerhahn, fourth-year student*

Louise is right. Documentation is at least as important in practical genres as it is in academic genres, and for essentially the same reasons: documentation serves to give fair credit to others' ideas and work, it enhances the credibility of your own work, and it provides location information to the reader who wants to investigate your sources and topic further. After all, practical documents *document.* Accuracy and credibility of information may be considered even more important in practical documents than in academic documents, since readers are relying on your authority, often basing their actions on it. However, documentation standards and conventions differ among practical writing genres, depending on who is reading a document, in what form readers encounter it, and the specific purpose a document serves.

Plagiarism and Common Knowledge in Community Writing

Service-learners who produce writing for their agencies in the community need to be just as aware of plagiarism as academic writers do. As in academic writing, you don't use other writers' or speakers' unique language without both quoting and acknowledging those sources. Nor do you use information and ideas from outside sources without fair and clear acknowledgment.

What constitutes an "outside source," however, may be somewhat different in a community context than in an academic one because in community contexts there tends to be closer collaboration among members of particular discourse communities. For example, the work (including writing) accomplished by individuals directly affiliated with your agency will probably be seen as *collective* rather than individual work. Therefore, if you reproduce your agency's mission statement in something that you write for your agency, there is no need to cite the person or people who wrote it, because it is owned by the collective, and you, after all, are writing also for the collective. Similarly, someone working within the agency who recycles parts of a document that you wrote for the agency will not be obliged to acknowledge you.

Furthermore, some agencies in the community have close working relationships with other agencies with similar missions. It is common practice for these agency *collectives* to share resources with one another, including information and various kinds of writing as well. Often, through this sharing process, information and written text are recycled liberally without specific acknowledgment. It is important, however, not to make any assumptions about agencies' collaborative or collective relationships; always ask permission before recycling information or text originally generated by another agency for your use on behalf of your agency.

As you should in all writing you do, consider carefully what constitutes "common knowledge" for your particular reader. Use the same bottom-line definition that we recommend for academic writing: *common knowledge is information that is widely available, and replicated in many forms, in the reference section of a good library.*

> We actually didn't cite our sources, since this was a large public display that provided basic information.
>
> *—Steven Fan, first-year student*

Even though Steven and his group consulted a number of outside sources in completing their project—a display board intended to educate young children about the usefulness of bacteria in the environment—their sources were general knowledge sources, and the information that they acquired from these sources qualifies as common knowledge. Had they quoted one of these general knowledge sources directly, they certainly would have been obliged to acknowledge that source. But one of their major objectives (and challenges) was to understand the principles and processes they were explaining so completely that they could translate them into the simple, direct, and lively language appropriate for their young readers. This certainly was not the kind of language they encountered in the general knowledge sources—including college textbooks—that they consulted to insure the accuracy of their information.

Documentation and Readability

Readability is important in any document, regardless of its reader and purpose. However, it is probably safe to say that readability is even more critical in public or practical documents than it is in academic ones. Remember that your instructor is obligated to read what you have written for school, regardless of how easy or difficult it is to read; you have no such automatic advantage in community writing. If your reader finds your document confusing, cluttered, or in any other respect difficult to read, she or he is very likely to simply stop reading it, defeating your purpose.

A practical document's formatting can contribute to, or interfere with, its readability in many ways, thereby facilitating or undermining its purpose. Documentation style is an aspect of document formatting that can facilitate or undermine a document's readability. In many practical genres—brochures, flyers, newsletter and newspaper articles, letters, solicitations, fact sheets, Web pages—academic documentation styles are often not appropriate because they would interfere with readability, just as an overly formal academic writing style would. Parenthetical citations with page references, notes, and formal bibliographies in these kinds of documents usually just get in the reader's way.

The fact that academic documentation styles are not always the best way to acknowledge outside sources used in practical documents does not mean that you should not acknowledge your outside sources, however. It simply means that you must be clever in figuring out other, more readable, ways to do it.

Documentation Alternatives in Practical Writing

> I basically presented evidence (quotes and explanations from the mayor's speech). I did use mostly direct quotes rather than saying *the mayor says that*....Then I referred to what he said to make an argument about the mayor's attitude towards the community.
>
> *—Louise Auerhahn, fourth-year student*

It is important to use common sense in documenting your sources clearly in practical documents, whatever the specific genre might be. Sometimes what you do in community writing is not all that different from what you do in academic writing. For example, in quoting from a primary source (in this case, the mayor's speech) in her newsletter article in order to analyze and argue from it, Louise did what students do all the time when they write analytical essays based on primary texts.

However, it would have been ridiculous for Louise to cite the mayor's speech in the more formal ways used for academic writing (with parenthetical citations and in a list of works cited). In the text of her article, though, she gives us all the information we need to track down the text of the speech ourselves: the mayor's name; the city; the date, location, and occasion for the speech.

Naming Sources in Text

> I quoted volunteers and managers at the clinic. Adding the speakers' credentials and names in the text of the article served to qualify the information.
>
> —*Katie Cameron, first-year student*

Earlier, we mentioned the usefulness of signal phrases in academic writing, even though a parenthetical citation offers the opportunity to name your source. Providing your source's full name and qualifications in the text enhances both clarity and credibility. The use of signal phrases can be crucial in practical documents because often no other means of documenting internal references are used. Not only naming but also stating the relevant qualifications of your source in a signal phrase is essential in many practical documents in which parenthetical citations would appear awkward or overly formal and may not be a feasible documentation option.

Most internal citations in academic documents provide specific page references, but this level of specificity is often lost in the more casual references provided in many practical documents. More casual, less specific references are adequate to the needs of many readers and the purposes of many practical documents, and the fact that a specific page reference is often not provided is not a great loss.

Alternatives to Academic Bibliographies

> Where appropriate, we put our sources at the end of the articles. Our unformatted works had full references and citations. It's always good to have references so that people can look up the information that you used.
>
> —*Terence Chia, second-year student*

As Terence suggests, it is a good idea to provide your agency with a complete bibliography of works that you consulted in writing your practical document, as well as any other relevant sources that you encountered in your research, even if you did not use them directly. Such a bibliography, the product of your hard work, can serve an important service to the community, because you have provided an important information resource to your agency.

A full and formal bibliography, however, will not be appropriate to include in your finished and formatted document if it would interfere with the document's overall readability. Several functional alternatives to formal bibliographies, however, more casually identify sources that you consulted in your writing and provide readers with other sources of information, without interfering with your document's readability.

- ■ ***"Sources Used"*** In many practical documents—pamphlets, newsletter articles, fact sheets, Web pages—providing a list of "Sources Used" or "Sources" in an informal bibliography at the conclusion of the document can serve as a good alternative to a more formal bibliography. These informal bibliographies are generally not complete when measured by academic documentation standards, but they provide the reader with enough information to allow him or her to locate the sources referred to in the document.

  For an example, take a look at Jenny Bernstein's indicator report for Sustainable San Mateo County, "Water Quality: Tap Water." Credibility of sources is extremely important to the overall credibility of this report. Jenny includes a "Sources" section at the end of her report, listing all the sources that she consulted and cited. This list is compact and abbreviated, and it would not suffice in an academic context. However, in the context of this practical document, this list supplies the reader with adequate information in a form that does not interfere with the document's overall readability.

- ■ ***"For More Information..."*** An even more informal way to include bibliographic information in your document—in a pamphlet, newsletter article, fact sheet, or Web page, for example—is to include a "For More Information" or "For Further Information" section at the end. You may want to include sources that you have not directly referred to in your document, if these sources promise to serve as important resources for your reader. This low-keyed alternative to a formal bibliography is especially useful in documents that will be read by young audiences.

- ■ ***"Do You Want to Help?"*** Some proactive documents, in which the writer is asking the reader to take action, end with a "Do You Want to Help?" plea. The sources listed under a proactive heading like this will provide contact information: for example, the email address of a senator or member of Congress, or the Web site of a political action group. Some of these contacts probably will be to institutions and agencies that the writer has consulted in writing the document; others will not be.

  In her brochure for the American Red Cross on "Landmine Awareness" (see Appendix), Jessica Gray included a "To HELP, you can" section in conclusion. Here she provides the URL to the International Campaign to Ban Landmines, the source of much of the information she includes in her brochure, and suggests that the reader visit the organization's Web site, as she has, in order to "stay on top of international decisions and actions."

- ■ ***"Links in Web Pages"***   Links included in Web pages provide a hypertext version of a bibliography, which is a wonderful way to connect readers directly with relevant sources and resources. If you have drawn from online sources in your research and writing for a Web page, include links to these sources at the point at which references to them occur in your Web text and in a links section at the end of your document or relevant section of your document. As with "For More Information" above, you can include links to sources that you did not refer to specifically in your document, if they promise to provide your reader with pertinent resources and information.

Formal Documentation in Practical Writing

For some kinds of practical writing, formal academic documentation may be appropriate. In fact, in some practical documents the formality and precision of academic documentation conventions may enhance the credibility of your research and the tone of what you have written, making the right impression on certain readers.

For example, some formal reports, project proposals, feasibility studies, and grant proposals that students write for their agencies target professional rather than general readers, and the situations in which readers encounter these kinds of documents tend to be more formal. These documents seek to make an impression on the reader, and the thoroughness and precision of the writer's research and documentation are part of what create that impression. Often, the primary rhetorical objective of these kinds of documents is persuasive: the professional reader is asked to give something (as in a grant proposal) or to take a certain stand or make a certain decision (as in a project proposal). A carefully documented piece of writing, with formal in-text citations and a bibliography that is complete and accurate by academic standards, may be exactly the way to go.

REFLECTIVE QUESTIONS
FOR JOURNAL-WRITING AND CLASS DISCUSSION

1. *Intellectual property* is highly valued, especially in academic communities. Intellectual property includes not only the words but also the ideas and styles of individual writers. With this in mind, discuss the meaning of plagiarism in academic and community contexts.

2. In this chapter, common knowledge is defined as *information that is widely available, and replicated in many forms, in the reference section of a good library.*

Can you think of situations in which this basic definition would not apply? To what extent do we need to adjust definitions of common knowledge depending on the rhetorical situation?

3. Bring to class a documented academic paper that you have written (preferably a draft) for this class or another and exchange it with a peer's. Between one class and the next, try to track down the sources that your classmate cited. These sources could be primary or secondary. Are the sources documented properly, both in text and in the bibliography? How easy or difficult was it for you to locate the sources based on the information provided? In class, discuss with your partner any difficulties that you encountered and how to resolve them.

4. If you are writing a practical document for your agency, bring the draft to class; if you are not working on a practical writing project, bring instead one or two sample documents from your agency. Trade these with other students in the class. How is documentation handled in these documents? Is documentation clear? Is enough information provided so that you could track down sources of information and perspective if you wished to? If documentation is not clear, how much of a problem do you consider this to be, and why?

TROUBLESHOOTING

WHAT IF…

you are unsure which documentation style to use in writing a research paper for a particular class?

TRY TO…

discuss with your instructor which style best suits research and writing in the discipline in which the class is offered, but also consider which documentation style best suits your topic and your approach to it. Your instructor may want you to use the documentation style most appropriate to the discipline in which the course is offered. If the course and the topic are interdisciplinary, discuss with your instructor the approach that you plan to take in researching and analyzing your topic. For example, if you plan to research the recent resurgence in tuberculosis infection, will you focus on the scientific or the social aspects of the disease? The answer to this question will help you determine which documentation style will best feature your research and analysis.

WHAT IF…

you have created a practical document in which a point of information is common knowledge as far as staff at your agency is concerned, but it may not be common knowledge for your reader?

TRY TO...

understand common knowledge from the point of view of your reader. Generally, it won't matter whether or not you or agency staff considers information included in public documents to be common knowledge, since neither of you is the targeted audience. Which facts will your reader need to be convinced of? For example, staff at your agency may be well aware that 11.3 percent of the U.S. population lives below the poverty line, but your reader may need the authority provided by a reference to a credible source (the 2000 Census) in order to accept this statistic as true.

WHAT IF...

when the writing that you did for your agency is finally published, you are disappointed to find that your agency has not credited you for your work?

TRY TO...

remember that you are working for a collective in which getting the agency's message across is generally more important than featuring the contribution of any individual. It is not crucial for the audience to know the author's name for most brochures, informational Web pages, flyers, or fact sheets. Since these types of documents speak for the agency as a whole. Furthermore, if you write a grant proposal for your agency, you will probably find that the executive director, as the primary representative of the agency, will sign his or her name to your work. On the other hand, if you write a feature article for the agency newsletter, your individual perspective may well be important, and your name on the finished product may indeed be relevant.

CHAPTER 13

Revising and Editing

I feel that my most significant writing improvement has come about because of revision.
—REBECCA FREELAND, FIRST-YEAR STUDENT

Many students and professional writers alike will tell you that revising a piece of writing can take more time than drafting it—and that these efforts substantially improve the finished product. Although revising and editing can be recursive (that is, to some extent you edit as you revise, and perhaps revise even as you edit), there is, or should be, a fundamental distinction between these two activities.

Some people prefer the term *re-visioning* to *revising,* because it more accurately describes what this part of the writing process really entails: the reworking of ideas, the rearrangement of fairly large chunks of writing or thinking. In revising, be prepared to: (1) Reevaluate your assumptions and the conclusions that you have drawn, testing their logic, (2) Ensure that nothing crucial is missing, and that everything that you have included is directly relevant, (3) Make sure that your points are well explained and well supported by reasons and evidence, including illiustrations and examples, (4) Reorganize portions of your draft, if necessary, so that one point leads smoothly and logically to the next and the entire essay reflects the unity of your main point, and (5) Reconsider the content, style, and format of your draft according to your reader's needs and expectations. You may find that the piece of writing you end up with is not what you originally had in mind. When you approach your writing as a relatively fluid process rather than a one-shot deal, you have room to let your perceptions evolve, sometimes even to change your mind radically. Writing is a learning process, quite apart from the written product.

Editing occurs at a much more minute level than revising. It is the final step before you declare a piece of writing done. It is your opportunity to polish phrasing and refine word choice, to catch grammatical and spelling errors, to make sure that the finished writing is free of typographical errors and correctly formatted. In editing, be prepared to: (1) Proofread for correct grammar and usage, especially for your grammatical demons. For instance, if you know that you tend to write comma

224

splices or that you don't always use the possessive form correctly or that subjects and verbs don't always agree in your writing, proofread aggressively for these errors. (2) Ask someone else to proofread your work and point out any awkward language or errors that you might have missed.

Editing is extremely important to the overall effectiveness of any formal piece of writing, but especially to writing that serves a public and practical purpose. Since readers in the community have no obligation to read what you have written, awkward language and errors may cause your reader to discard what you have written in frustration.

STRATEGIES FOR REVISING AND EDITING

One reason many people don't revise their drafts at all or as thoroughly as they might is that they lack time, especially if they put off writing tasks until the last minute. But another, perhaps even more significant reason that many writers don't revise, or don't revise productively, is that they don't know what kinds of changes to make, why a piece of writing would be more effective if it were changed in a certain way, or how to carry out these changes. This chapter will provide you with specific strategies for revising and editing your drafts for academic writing and practical writing projects.

Reviewing Your Draft

A key strategy for productive revision is to put yourself in your reader's place, adopting a reader's perspective of your work. Accomplishing this shift in perspective from writer to reader can be challenging. Whether the reader is your instructor or a reader in the community, he or she may be quite different from you, but you must nonetheless get to know your reader well in order to read from his or her perspective. Furthermore, especially at the draft stage, you may be so immersed in your own perspective that it is hard to shake it loose enough to take on a reader's point of view. There are, however, ways to approach revising both academic and practical writing that can help you gain your audience's perspective.

Let Your Draft Rest

I have learned that there is value to writing a draft, letting it sit for a couple of days, and then coming back and rereading the draft and making changes with the reader in mind. This revision technique has helped me to write better with more emphasis on audience and purpose.

—Scott Ransenberg, first-year student

The best revision effort requires that you gain some distance from your own work, since in order to judge its effectiveness you will have to approach it as your reader would. As Scott suggests, if you can spare the time, let your draft sit for a day or so before you revise it. The lapse of time allows you to see your draft in a fresh light. This new reading of your draft can offer a window of critical opportunity, if you are able to detach yourself from your draft and assume your reader's perspective.

Isolate Openings and Closings

One especially helpful method of testing the unity and coherence of most types of academic writing and some types of practical writing—letters, proposals, and reports that are developed and articulated in full paragraphs—is actually fairly simple.

1. Read the opening paragraph of your essay, then read the closing paragraph. Do these two paragraphs fit together as a kind of question and answer, or do they merely repeat each other? Is your conclusion honest and relevant? Does it reflect the subject and the main point of your writing as you set it out in the opening paragraph, or have you traveled off track?

2. Try the same strategy on the paragraph level. Try reading the first and last sentences of each paragraph to see if the paragraph is well unified around one idea and whether you have drawn a meaningful conclusion at the end of each paragraph.

3. Check paragraph transitions by reading aloud the last sentence in each paragraph together with the first sentence of the paragraph that follows. Is there a big jump, or have you related ideas from one paragraph to the next in effective paragraph transitions?

Read Your Writing out Loud

> Recently I have begun to revise and edit my papers more thoroughly. I have found that reading them aloud is helpful as is completely reorganizing them at times (something I used to avoid at all possible costs).
>
> —Pepper Yelton, first-year student

More difficult to catch than grammatical or typographical errors is awkwardness in word choice, phrasing, and sentence structure. These are sometimes especially hard for the writer to catch because they arise out of habits of speech and writing that are second nature to the writer. Sometimes, however, if you read your writing out loud, your ear will catch awkward phrasing or constructions that seem invisible on the page. It can also be especially helpful to have someone else read your work aloud to you; you may hear your reader stumble over certain words and phrases, and even if neither you nor your reader can put your finger on the reason at the time, you can mark these spots in your draft, returning to figure them out later.

Instructor Review

Some students dread receiving input on their drafts, even (or perhaps especially) from their instructors, because they are embarrassed that their writing is not perfect or they feel defensive about what they have written. Your instructor understands—probably through his or her personal experience as a writer—that a draft is not perfect; it is a work in progress.

If your instructor will discuss your draft with you, take advantage of this opportunity; if your instructor provides written comments on your drafts, pay heed. In either case, your instructor's intention, in intercepting you and your writing at the draft stage, is to provide constructive criticism, to help you formulate a better revision. Try not to get overly attached to what you have written in a draft. Drafts are *meant* to be revised, and if you cling to something that is not working for your reader, you will be undermining the ultimate effectiveness of what you write.

Peer Review

> A classmate's input on a draft can often prove invaluable, and looking over someone else's work can also allow you to approach your own from a new perspective. It often helps to see how something I have taken for granted is not entirely clear to the reader. After I become aware of the problem, I can then do my best to clarify and improve my draft.
>
> —*Julia Thornton, first-year student*

Peer review is of such great help to students in their roles as writers and critical readers that many instructors make peer review an integral part of their classes. Academic writers often struggle with the concept of audience. In an exchange of work in peer review, student writers expand their readership in real and significant ways, and have the chance to test the effectiveness of their writing on readers whose role is constructive more than evaluative. As a peer reviewer, you can help your classmates develop their thinking and writing as well as hone your own revision and editing skills. You can also compare your approach in an assignment with someone else's, and learn in the process.

In a peer review, exchange your work at the draft stage with someone in your class who is at work on the same assignment. In order for a peer review to be successful, it is important that both reviewers understand the objectives and criteria of the assignment as well as each other's individual purposes and goals in writing.

Peer reviewers often feel unsure of themselves, and each other, in their roles as reviewers. You may think, *I'm not confident about my own writing, so who am I to give advice to someone else?* Or you might think, *I'm not sure I trust another student to give me a peer review I can rely on. What kind of authority does another student have?*

It's helpful to know that there are several kinds of comments that you and your peer review partner can offer each other in a productive review, and that the most helpful kinds of comments may not be based on *authority* but rather on the kinds of response that any reader can provide, simply because she or he *is* a reader.

Reader-Based Comments

In *reader-based comments,* the reviewer offers a personal response, one that requires only careful thought and honesty, not any special skills or authority. For example, "I am confused by this paragraph. I don't understand the point that you are trying to make here" or "This description makes me feel as if I'm there!" are reader-based comments. They feature the pronoun "I," since they focus on the reader's experience of what the writer has written. These kinds of comments may also come in the form of observations and questions: "Here, you are telling me how your agency has worked with at-risk youth in the past," or "Can you tell me what your agency has done in the past to help at-risk youth?" The advantages of reader-based comments are that they provide the writer with an immediate, uncluttered response, and the reviewer does not pretend to be the final authority on anything. Reader-based comments are easy to give and easy to receive because they are nonjudgmental. Many students find them to be the most helpful kinds of responses in a peer review.

Criterion-Based Comments

In *criterion-based comments,* the reviewer will note successes or problems in accordance with set criteria, and these criteria are determined by the instructor, the specifications of the assignment, or widely accepted writing conventions. For example, "You have two comma splices in this paragraph" or "Are you writing from a neutral point of view as Prof. X asked us to do?" are criterion-based comments. Criterion-based comments take time and consideration to write because the reviewer not only must respond on a personal level, but must also analyze the reason for the effectiveness or lack of effectiveness of the writing based on an understanding of the criteria. Responding in this way is good exercise for the reviewer exactly because it requires his or her understanding of criteria. Since these kinds of comments are more pointed, and may seem more critical, it is important to remember that the reviewer is not the person who invented the criteria.

Directive Comments

Directive comments offer the writer constructive solutions. In offering a directive comment, the reviewer not only will identify a specific problem ("You have a comma splice here") but will also offer a suggestion to fix it ("Try a semicolon to separate two independent clauses that are related"). Directive comments require both an understanding of criteria and an understanding of how to fix a problem when criteria are not being met. If, as a reviewer, you are not sure what solution is correct, it is best to stick to reader- or criteria-based comments or to phrase your suggestion tentatively ("Isn't this a direct quotation? I think you need to put this sentence in quotation marks, but you'd better check with Prof. X to make sure").

The objective in reviewing another student's work is not merely to catch obvious shortcomings. In peer reviewing a classmate's draft, be honest, but be constructive as well. If you think something in the draft you are reviewing is not working well, say so, but be sure to support your criticisms with clear reasons, specific examples, and if possible, suggestions for improvement. Don't forget to let the writer know what he or she is doing effectively as well as what could be improved. In other words, try to provide to your partner the kind of peer review that you yourself would find most helpful. Try to meet in person with your peer review partner to discuss your comments, even when they are written.

Peer reviews tend to work best when they are based on specific guidelines, because student writers don't always know what questions are most pertinent to ask about a draft. Check out the peer review questions on the following page that would apply well to an academic argument or other kinds of academic writing assignments based on outside sources.

Taking It All In

As helpful as reader input can be in your revision process, it can also be confusing at times, and for various reasons. If your reviewer, whether your instructor or a peer reviewer, does not understand well enough what you are *trying* to do, the value of the feedback that he or she offers will be limited. It is crucial that you explain to your reviewer what you are attempting in a draft, and how you are trying to go about it, so that his or her comments can be based on your specific goals rather than on whatever specific goals your reader might imagine are appropriate. Informing your reader in advance about how you envision your audience and purpose in writing can help boost the relevance and applicability of the feedback you receive.

You will inevitably receive revision ideas and advice from a peer reviewer—and even sometimes from your instructor—that you disagree with. Part of what you learn in receiving constructive comments on your drafts are skills in critical evaluation of these comments. If you disagree with advice you have received from a reviewer, ask yourself *why* you disagree. Are you just being grumpy or defensive, or are there more valid reasons for your disagreement? If there seem to be more valid reasons, explore them. Perhaps in a specific case your reviewer has made a suggestion based on his or her lack of clear understanding of your intentions. Even if you don't use a specific suggestion that a reader provides, the fact that your reader has made it is an indication that you may need to revise your draft, perhaps to explain yourself better, developing and articulating your point or your line of reasoning more clearly.

Students who have multiple readers at the draft stage—for example, an instructor and a peer reviewer, or more than one peer reviewer—sometimes receive conflicting comments or advice. What do you do if one reviewer's feedback conflicts

PEER REVIEW QUESTIONS FOR ACADEMIC WRITING

1. Who is the author's audience? What is his or her purpose? Does he or she establish exigence (relevance, what's at stake, the reader's need to know) effectively in the opening paragraphs?

2. What is the author's thesis? Where is it most clearly stated? Is it clearly stated and effectively placed?

3. Does the author establish the subject or state the key issue or problem early enough? When you have finished the paper, look back at the introductory paragraphs. Did they give you a good idea of what the author actually addressed in the rest of the paper?

4. Does the paper reach a conclusion or does it merely stop? Does the conclusion repeat the introduction? Do introduction and conclusion fit together naturally as a kind of question and answer? Are conclusions well earned? Does the closing paragraph have an impact on you as well as inform you?

5. Does the author provide necessary background information? Is there enough? Is any superfluous? (Consider the author's audience.)

6. Is the essay organized in the most effective way? Do information, analysis, and argument follow each other in a logical, clear, and convincing sequence? Does the author provide clear transitions between the various focal points in the essay and between paragraphs, relating ideas clearly? Are there any places where you are confused?

7. Is the author knowledgeable and fair in his or her presentation of various or opposing points of view and arguments?

8. Are the points that the author is trying to make developed fully and clearly? Does the draft bring up any interesting points that you would like to see developed further? Is there needless material that should be omitted?

9. Is the author's analysis of the problem or issue clear and logical? Is it supported by convincing reasons and evidence?

10. Are the author's arguments clear? Is the argument supported adequately with evidence or examples? Is the evidence relevant? Is the evidence convincing? Does the author provide a clear context for the evidence, introducing it clearly and following it with comment or analysis?

11. Does the author draw on a good variety of sources for information and point of view? Are these sources credible?

12. Does the author integrate source material—facts and figures, quotes, paraphrases, and summaries—fluidly in the text? Does the author over-rely on quotations? Are there any quotations that might as well be paraphrased?

13. Are there any grammatical or mechanical errors (including problems with punctuation) that appear in the draft that the author will need to focus attention

(continued)

on in revising? Are there any consistent problems with diction, usage, or words misused that you can point out to the author?

14. Beyond mechanical and grammatical errors, comment on the author's writing style. Is the style appropriate to audience and purpose? Does the author choose precise words? Is there any wordiness?

15. Does the writer use clear and accurate internal documentation? Is the bibliography in correct form?

with another's? One obvious approach to resolving such conflict is to consider the authority of your reviewer. An instructor's feedback is very likely to be better informed than a peer reviewer's. However, this does not mean that your instructor will always be right in all ways and that your peer reviewer, if she or he disagrees, will always be wrong. Although your instructor is certainly more knowledgeable about course content and writing issues, your peer reviewer has authority in other ways and in other circumstances that your instructor may not have. Pay close attention to the kind and context of reviewers' conflicting advice as you consider what changes to make in revision.

If an instructor does not understand something you are trying to communicate, then you can always fall back on the excuse that they are "older, of another generation, and just wouldn't understand." When a peer tells you something is confusing or unclear, there is almost more of a sense of urgency concerning that particular problem.

—*Scott Ransenberg, first-year student*

Ultimately, it is up to you to decide which ideas and suggestions, whatever their source, you will use in revision (and how you will implement them) and which you will let pass. The ability to make these kinds of critical evaluations and judgments is crucial to your development as a confident and capable writer.

REVISING AND EDITING COMMUNITY WRITING

As important as your consideration of audience and purpose is in effectively revising academic work, it is even more crucial, and probably more difficult, in revising your writing for the community. Student writers are generally familiar with the readers and purposes of academic writing, but they are not as familiar with the readers and purposes of practical writing in the community.

Our project was a large public display that explained the usefulness of bacteria in the environment. The primary purpose was to provide a teaching tool. Young children, who lose attention very quickly, were going to look at our project. We had to keep our writing simple. This meant limiting the use of big words, summarizing complicated scientific data into basic descriptions. If our explanations were too long, or too complicated, no one would want to read it. We had to make sure the reader would be able to understand what we wrote or else the purpose would be lost.

—*Steven Fan, first-year student*

The impetus for revising the practical document that your community agency asks you to write is clear. More is at stake in this writing than merely a grade; many people will be reading your work and will be relying on it for important information, analysis, and point of view. Many of your readers will take action on the basis of what you write. Your writing will *count* in the community. The extent to which you revise your document well, on the basis of your understanding of its audience and purpose, often determines whether or not your document accomplishes its purpose—whether or not it *works* as far as your reader is concerned.

When revising practical documents in a service-learning context, you have the advantage of access to even more collaborators in your revision than in most academic revisions. You may also feel challenged by having to juggle all of the feedback that you receive from so many people, on so many levels. Consider this a happy problem!

Instructor Review of Community Writing

Understanding your instructor's role in providing input on a practical writing project for your agency is crucial if you want to take full advantage of his or her expertise and at the same time provide your agency with the document it wants and needs. Although your instructor has explicit authority concerning your revisions in academic projects, he or she probably understands quite well that for your practical writing projects, the instructor's role is that of advisor.

In the planning stages of your project, perhaps your instructor helped by facilitating a service-learning placement or advising you about how to locate a placement for yourself. In the early stages of planning your writing project, perhaps your instructor helped you understand the audience and purpose of your particular document, or helped you brainstorm ideas for content, basic approach, or relevant research. In the mapping or drafting stages of your project, perhaps she or he helped you think through organizational strategies or formatting ideas.

At the revision stage of your project, your instructor's most useful role might be that of an editor. Of course, it is essential that your agency mentor review your practical writing project at the draft stage, but many instructors also want to provide input on student projects at this time. Your instructor's perspective is valuable not only because she or he may have advanced writing experience or content expertise related to the subject that you are writing about, but also because she or he can offer a fresh perspective on what you write, since in a practical writing project your instructor is an outside reader. Sometimes your instructor can even more readily adopt your intended reader's perspective than you or your agency mentor can, considering how close you and your mentor are to the project.

In reviewing a draft of your practical writing project, your instructor may ask you questions about the intended audience and purpose of the document, and how the content, voice, and formatting of your draft suit that audience and purpose. Your instructor may also provide specific editing for this kind of project, for example, questioning your phrasing, diction, or choice of words, or drawing your attention to grammatical, punctuation, spelling, or formatting errors that you need to take extra care to correct before you submit the finished product.

Keep in mind that serving as a facilitator, project manager, collaborator, and editor may be a relatively new role for your teacher. It's an adjustment for some instructors to accept that, when it comes to a practical writing project, the agency mentor—not the instructor and not the student—has primary authority and the last word about what does and does not suit your project and the agency's purposes.

Peer Review of Community Writing

Peer reviewers can provide invaluable feedback on each other's drafts for community writing projects. In collaborative projects, other members of your writing group can provide extremely helpful reviews with an inside perspective. If your practical writing project is an individual one, students who are working for the same agency but on different projects can provide reviews that are well informed by an understanding of your agency's mission and its work in the community. Students who are working with other agencies can serve as excellent reviewers exactly because they have an outside perspective, which often allows them to read your draft more as your intended reader in the community might read it.

Whoever your peer reviewer might be for the draft of your practical document, he or she will not be able to provide you with relevant or useful feedback unless he or she understands exactly what you are trying to accomplish. At the end of Chapter 10, Mapping, Organizing, and Drafting, we suggested that you complete the Community Writer's Inventory and from it compose the Community Writer's Statement of Audience and Purpose. If you and your peer review partner completed these worksheets, exchange them. They should provide each of you with a good idea of what the other is trying to accomplish in his or her draft. Based on your mutual understanding, you should be able to complete well-informed peer reviews of these two draft documents.

PEER REVIEW QUESTIONS FOR PRACTICAL WRITING

1. Do you understand what kind of document the writer is producing? Describe it in your own words.

2. Is the primary rhetorical purpose of the document clear in what the writer has written? Do you understand the ways in which any secondary rhetorical purposes serve to promote the writer's primary purpose? Do any of the author's secondary purposes overwhelm or obscure the primary rhetorical purpose?

3. Do you have a clear sense of who the author's primary reader is? Are you able to picture this reader clearly? Is there anything that might characterize this reader that the author might not have thought of?

4. Do you understand clearly the situation or occasion in which the reader is most likely to encounter the document that the author has written? Can you think of any other situations in which the reader might encounter this document?

5. Is the content of what the author has written appropriate to the document's purpose, its primary reader, and the situation in which the reader might encounter the document? Do you think any material that the author has included is unnecessary in terms of audience, purpose, and reading occasion? Is any material missing?

6. Do the specific rhetorical modes of development that the author has used (e.g. description, narration, definition of terms, classification, illustration and example, process analysis, comparison and contrast, cause and effect analysis, or argument) promote the document's primary rhetorical purpose well? Are there any changes or adjustments to these that you can recommend that might make the document more effective?

7. Are the tone and style in which the author writes appropriate to the document's purpose, its primary reader, and the reading occasion? Can you suggest any changes or adjustments to the author's writing style that would make the document more effective?

8. Does the format of the document facilitate its purpose well? Does it suit the reader well? Does it suit the occasion in which the reader is most likely to encounter the document? Can you suggest any changes or adjustments to the format that would make the document more effective?

9. Do you understand clearly any secondary readers or purposes associated with the document? Are there any changes or adjustments to content, tone and style, or format that you can suggest that might make the document more effective for secondary purposes and readers without compromising the document's primary purpose for its primary reader?

10. Does the writer seem to be well informed about the subject of the document? Do the writer's sources of information seem relevant and credible? Is

(continued)

> missing from the document? Has the author found a way to credit his or her sources that acknowledges them clearly without interfering with the document's readability?
>
> 11. Are there any grammatical or mechanical errors (including problems with punctuation) that appear in the draft that the author will need to correct in revising? Are there any problems with diction, usage, or words misused that you can point out?

Try using the following questions, or your own adaptations of them, to guide peer reviews of practical documents.

Test Marketing Your Document

If you have an opportunity to run the draft of your project past someone who might be a reader of the revised document in its finished form, by all means do so!

- Explain to this reader what agency you are writing for and what its work involves.
- Explain the purpose of your document and who its targeted readers are.
- Ask for this reader's reaction to your document, and suggestions if he or she has them. Then just listen.

Obviously, your intended reader, or someone who very closely resembles your intended reader, is in the best position to tell what is and isn't working.

Mentor Review of Community Writing

> We mainly turned to our mentors for advice, because they knew best about the content we had included. Since we did not want our final product to be in any way contradictory to what they wanted, we made sure that everything in the newsletter was perfect to their satisfaction.
>
> *—Jimmy Wu, first-year student*

If your project doesn't work according to your agency's standards, needs, and expectations, it may have provided a worthwhile learning experience for you, but it will be of limited or no use to your agency. After all the work that you have probably put into the project, this would be a disappointing outcome, for you as well as for your agency.

Most agency mentors are elated by the drafts of students' practical writing projects. Remember that you are providing your agency with something that it needs and that no one else at the agency has the time or perhaps the resources to generate. But even if your draft is well-informed and relatively polished, your mentor may have suggestions for improvement. Be ready to act on them.

Your agency mentor may send you back out to do further or last-minute research. He or she may have suggestions about what to alter in terms of content to better satisfy the audience or purpose of the document. He or she may make suggestions about how the tone of the document might be adjusted to better suit its reader or the situation in which the reader encounters the document. He or she may suggest changes in format to make the document more reader-friendly. These are the kinds of suggestions that your mentor is in an especially good position to make.

Various agency mentors will have various styles in providing feedback to students on their drafts of agency documents. Some take a relatively hands-off approach, some take a relatively hands-on approach, and some fall somewhere in between.

Hands-Off Approaches

If your mentor takes a relatively hands-off approach in reviewing your draft, he or she may say, "Thank you very much for all your hard work," requesting from you few, if any, revisions. Some mentors may do this because they are grateful for the work you put into the document and are hesitant to ask you to revise it. But it is part of your job, of course, to see this project through to the end, or to whatever point that your mentor considers the end. So when you submit your project draft for review, make it clear to your mentor that you are quite willing—in fact, that you fully expect—to work further at revising and polishing the document. Your mentor may accept your offer, or thank you but decline.

There are a couple of possible reasons that a mentor would decline an offer from a student to revise. One is that the document may be in great shape and ready to go. Another is that your mentor may prefer to do the final revising and editing of the document.

Hands-On Approaches

If what you have written for your agency undergoes extensive revision by your mentor or someone else at the agency, you may think that your work was unappreciated and not up to par. If this happens to you, remember: writing in the world outside of school, especially in the workplace, is often a collaborative endeavor in which each member of the collaborative team contributes something special. Your mentor may decide that you have contributed a solid draft of the document, and that that contribution is enough. He or she may believe that it's his or her job, given his or her expertise, to apply the finishing touches. This in no way diminishes your contribution to the agency or the worthwhileness of your project; the project probably would never have gotten done if it weren't for you.

Your mentor might take another kind of hands-on approach: he or she might want to work with you, side-by-side, in revising. This can be a wonderful experience. If your mentor takes this approach to revision, you will collaborate in making the editorial choices that will transform your document from a draft to a finished product, ready to fulfill its purpose in the community.

What to Do with Conflicting Advice

We often relied on our agency mentor and teacher for advice. We did have some contrasting feedback; our agency mentor really liked our first drafts, whereas our teacher had several points for improvement. To resolve this, we simply kept our teacher's feedback in mind as we rewrote some of the articles on our display.

—Steven Fan, first-year student

Everyone involved in helping you to revise your practical writing project will have special ways in which to contribute to the process. In juggling and evaluating all this feedback, consider what uniquely qualifies the person providing the feedback. Your instructor may be a writing expert. A collaborative member of your working group may have a grasp on the way in which the whole project is developing, and how your part fits, that no one else does. A peer reviewer outside the project may be able to offer a fresh perspective. Your intended reader in the community may have an immediate and visceral reaction to what you have written and how you have written it that can tell you a great deal. Everyone in the revision collaboration has something unique and worthwhile to contribute, and almost everyone can provide good general feedback as well.

If, however, any of these reviewers' ideas and suggestions conflict in a clear and obvious way with the ideas and suggestions that your agency mentor has, your decision is clear. This, after all, is the agency's document, not yours. It is your contribution and service to your agency. The mentor has final authority.

REFLECTIVE QUESTIONS
FOR JOURNAL-WRITING AND CLASS DISCUSSION

1. As part of your review of your draft, we suggest isolating and comparing opening and closing paragraphs, first and last sentences of paragraphs, and last and first sentences of adjacent paragraphs, a strategy that is especially helpful in checking unity and coherence in an academic essay. Try this revision strategy with a draft of one of your academic essays.

2. Ask a friend or classmate to read a draft of your practical or academic writing project out loud to you. As she or he reads, listen not only for the more obvious errors (for example, in grammar or sentence structure), but also for

more subtle ones, including abrupt transitions between ideas and awkward word choices and phrasing. Often a reader will stumble when she or he encounters these incongruities in writing; you may hear it in your reader's voice, and you may even see it in her or his body language.

3. Take a look at "Peer Review Questions for Academic Writing," on page 230. If these questions can be applied appropriately to a draft of an academic assignment in your current class, exchange drafts with a classmate and begin the peer review. Be sure to let your partner know (1) the audience that you envision for your writing, (2) what effect you want to have on your reader, (3) how rough or polished you consider your draft to be, and (4) what kinds of feedback would be most helpful to you in revision. Before you begin your review of your partner's draft, try reading his or her essay through, without comment, in order to get a sense of the whole. Then read it more carefully, writing questions and comments as you go. After you have finished with running comments, respond to the peer review questions. Remember: reader-based comments are just as valuable as—perhaps more valuable than—criterion-based or directive comments.

4. If the "Peer Review Questions for Academic Writing" do not apply well to the kind of academic writing that you have been assigned, revise (as a class or in small groups) the questions so that they do apply. Then complete the peer review.

5. If you have drafted a practical project for your community agency, exchange drafts with someone else in your class. Complete the "Peer Review Questions for Practical Writing" on page 234. In order to provide your review partner with background on your project, complete the "Community Writer's Inventory" and the "Community Writer's Statement of Audience and Purpose" in Chapter 10 and give these to your partner for reference. In choosing peer review partners, consider the relative advantages, given the nature of your practical project, of exchanging drafts with one other student or exchanging drafts of collaborative projects with another group doing collaborative work. Although there are advantages of exchanging drafts within collaborative groups, try to get a peer review from a student outside of your group as well.

TROUBLESHOOTING

WHAT IF…

you have read over your draft and you think it is in really good shape and that there is no need to revise?

TRY TO…

move beyond an overly attached perspective on your draft. Remember that revision entails reconceptualizing. It is easy to become so attached to what you have drafted that you cannot imagine changing it. But every draft, no matter how sound, can improve with revision. One way to shake an overly attached perspective is to put the draft aside and out of your mind for a few days, if time allows. Chances are that when you return to your draft after some time has passed, you will be able to read it from a new perspective—one that may be closer to your reader's—and you will notice more clearly ways in which the writing might be improved. Whether or not you have the time to let your draft rest for a day or two, allowing a peer to review your draft will reveal errors that you yourself have not noticed as well as parts of the draft that may be confusing. In the best of all possible situations, you should allow time to let your draft rest for a day or two before you revise *and* have a peer review it as well.

WHAT IF…

you do not have time to revise your practical writing project because the agency needs it right away?

TRY TO…

manage your time better. Presumably, you knew of your project's deadline well before it was due. In many cases, the agency's deadline corresponds to the end of the service-learning course. Too often, students put practical projects on the back burner only to face major time crunches at the end of the quarter or semester.

make the best of the time that you do have. Occasionally, agencies have early project deadlines, and students do face unavoidable time constraints. Try to allow time nonetheless to get feedback on your draft from both your mentor and your instructor, and give yourself at least a day to complete your revisions.

WHAT IF…

your agency mentor has not yet called or emailed you to give feedback on the draft of your project, and the final document must be ready for distribution at a major agency event scheduled three days from now?

TRY TO…

adapt to less-than-ideal circumstances. Preparing for a major event, your mentor may be tearing his or her hair out trying to get all of the details in order. You might have to make the extra effort to travel to the agency on the spur of the moment. You may be able to catch your mentor on the run. If your mentor is not there or is preoccupied with other business, find someone else at the agency—perhaps someone who is familiar with your project—who might stand in for your mentor in providing feedback on your draft document. If there is no one who can help you at the agency, meet with your peer collaborators and your instructor. Make certain that they understand your document's audience and purpose, and revise based on their comments. The bottom line: however hectic this revision process might be, the document has got to be ready online. Your mentor is counting on you to be responsible, professional, and part of the agency team.

WHAT IF...

> *your mentor or the agency director revises what you have written for the agency to the extent that you barely recognize your own writing?*

TRY TO...

> *remember that writing for your agency is a collaboration.* Although you may feel a sense of proprietorship of your work, in this situation you do not own it. Remember, too, that editing agency materials before they are published and distributed may be part of your mentor's job. The fact that your work may be revised or edited extensively does not mean that your contribution has come to nothing or that it is unappreciated by your mentor, the agency, or the community that the agency serves. Without you, this document might not have been written at all.

CHAPTER 14

Assessing Your
Community-Based Writing

*I don't think there's a concrete way of defining a project as successful
or not. As long as you get something out of it, even if the project didn't turn out
as nicely as you had hoped, whether it's learning how to better relate to people,
learning a new skill, or revolutionizing your writing style, then it was a success.
If you take these lessons and apply them on a larger scale, then you've had
a successful community-based learning experience.*

—RACHEL SIEGEL, FIRST-YEAR STUDENT

In your academic work, how do you measure success? Is it the "A" that you receive on your family genealogy in your anthropology class? Is it the "C" that you receive on your oral presentation in your communications class? Most of us in the college or university system are trained to think of success in terms of hierarchical evaluation, which in many ways does a great disservice to students, because that letter grade does not tell the entire story of success.

Generally speaking, a "C" might not seem to be a very good grade. But what if you have never made an oral presentation before without freezing up? This time, however, you *made it through the entire speech*; getting through the presentation in one piece was a milestone for you. At the same time, an "A" on the family genealogy is a wonderful grade, but what if you wanted to include more information to make the project even richer but you didn't have time? What if you are on the varsity basketball team, practicing every morning at five, traveling on weekends, and you are carrying the maximum number of course units but are able to maintain a solid "B" average? What if you come from a disadvantaged background and nobody even thought that you would make it to college, but here you are, maintaining "A"s and "B"s with the occasional "C"?

The point is that each of us measures success differently, in unique and personal terms. Sure, the grade will be a part of that measurement, but it will not be the only part. Years from now, you might not even remember the grade, but you will remember the first time that you completed an oral presentation without freaking out. You will remember interviewing your aunt Gladys in Mississippi and hearing about your two Irish immigrant grandfathers—one Catholic, the other Protestant—and the arguments that they used to have in the evenings on the rickety front porch. Ultimately, the grade will not matter to you; the confidence that you gained to speak in public and the family history that you learned will be what you take with you into your future. In the short term the grade or evaluation that the *product* of your work earns may overshadow the *process* of your learning, but in the long term the ways in which your academic experience enriches your life are what count.

WHAT HAVE YOU LEARNED?

I'm an advocate of community service writing because (1) it gives students a chance to practice writing in genres other than the school essay, (2) it demonstrates how documents differ depending on their audience and purpose, (3) it gets students thinking of themselves as real writers, (4) it gets students engaged in the community, (5) it advances the work of commendable community organizations, and (6) it promotes students' personal growth, especially their confidence and their sense of agency.

—*Nora Bacon, University of Nebraska, Omaha*

Service-learning asks that you measure success not only by what you have learned in the classroom, but also within a greater context—the context of community. Service-learning promotes a "can-do" attitude because you simultaneously learn and work in *your* world, where community and classroom become synonymous.

In community-based writing, you will measure success by what you have learned, about the subject, about the community, and about yourself. For example, in her work with Food Not Bombs (featured in Chapter 10), Caitlin Corrigan not only produced a fine research paper on Food Not Bombs and anarchy, a paper that she shared with her peers and turned in to her instructor, but she also gained firsthand insight into the practical ways in which theories of anarchy can help promote community and giving. Caitlin learned about the subtle differences in the power dynamics of serving food to people on the sidewalk in front of city hall as opposed to within the confines of a homeless shelter. Regardless of her grade on the final paper, Caitlin probably will never walk near Baltimore's city hall again without thinking about the homeless and hungry, community and anarchy, concepts that she was encouraged to think about in concrete terms in her service-learning class.

On the one hand, Caitlin and other students involved in courses with a service-learning focus will be evaluated in terms of the products that they produce.

Their instructors will evaluate the writing that they do in connection with their service-learning work by the same means that they evaluate traditional academic writing: through comments and grades. Their success is measured according to academic standards of excellence. But remember, your own service-learning experience may involve measures of success that are not fully reflected in that grade.

DID YOUR WRITING WORK FOR ITS READER?

A successful community writing project is one that will prove to be effective when it is actually put to use, when the audience for whom it was created actually benefits from it. For example, if I were to see someone drive up to the park and pick up our brochure, I would know that it was a success, because it captured his or her interest.

—Renee Jacobsen, first-year student

If you write a practical document for your agency as part of your service-learning work, the *immediate* purpose of your project (the agency's need for your written work) may overshadow the *primary* purpose (your learning experience). Because your agency needs your project, you might not think of your learning experience as the primary purpose of your work in the community, but it is. This conflict between the immediate and the primary goals in community-based practical writing situations may cause some confusion about what a successful project is.

Measurement of success for community-based practical writing is more complicated than for academic writing because there are more parties involved in the process: your instructor, your agency mentor, your community audience (the intended reader), and you. It makes sense that you come to understand the success of your writing through your audience's response to it. You may never hear directly from your readers in the community, but you can gather their response—actual or projected—from your agency mentor.

In a community context, the success of a practical document is measured in practical terms. In short, did the writing that you produced work? Did it fulfill its purpose for the audience that it targeted? Did people respond to your flyer for the opening of the new homeless shelter? Did most schoolchildren pick up the scavenger hunt fact sheet and take it with them on their excursion to the marsh? How many of these children came back with drawings and questions? How many more people than usual called your local chapter of the American Red Cross to find ways to help because they happened to pick up your brochure?

If your article is published in an agency newsletter, then the publication itself is a measure of your success. If your news article is picked up by a local newspaper and reprinted, then it was doubly successful. If enrollments in a teen parenting class rise, then it is likely that the flyer you composed to publicize it was successful. If, as a direct consequence of a grant proposal that you helped to write, your agency is awarded much-needed funds or supplies, the message—loud and clear—is that IT WORKED! If any of these clear and immediate results happen in your case, consider yourself lucky.

> I had a great feeling of accomplishment seeing my brochure sitting at the chapter office next to their other informational packets.
>
> —*Jessica Gray, first-year student*

The success of many practical documents, however, is not always dramatic or immediate. Consider the students working on the medical waste incineration issue that we write about in Chapter 9, Researching. Even now, not all of their success has been fully measured; some of the students in the community-based writing course began working on this project in the spring of 1999. They may not see the complete changes and effects of the medical waste burning ban before they graduate. At the same time, though, each of them knows that she or he was key to the success of a collective effort to help a marginalized community get its needs met.

> Honestly, it was successful on the level that I completed my part well. Unsuccessful in that the book is NOWHERE near completion. I think it is important to differentiate between the successes that you can control vs. those the agency or other people control. Sometimes a project is just out of your hands, but you have to take consolation in the fact that you did your assignment well.
>
> —*Anamaria Nino-Murcia, second-year student*

Your practical project could take a year or more to see publication. We know of one case in which three different groups of students worked painstakingly on a grant proposal over the course of three academic quarters. Your project could be absorbed into a longer, ongoing piece that the organization is working on. Your project might not be published or widely distributed; instead, it could be an in-house document, such as a volunteer handbook. Even if your project has a limited number of readers, it is crucial to your agency and the community that it serves. While the ultimate goal of your practical writing may be your learning experience, the immediate goal can dictate that you need to let go of any idea of ownership of your writing. Your writing is no longer just for you and your growth as a student and a person; rather, it becomes entangled in the web of community property. This is what is so wonderful about working on practical writing projects. This is also one of the things that can be so frustrating about the endeavor.

WAS YOUR WRITING USEFUL FOR YOUR AGENCY?

The outreach materials Nicole and Terri developed are invaluable marketing tools which we will use to inform the community about our services. I was very impressed with how both Terri and Nicole really picked up on the underlying principles of empowerment that drive our work here at the Rape Crisis Center. They took in the mission and intention of our crisis services and were able to create a new, inspiring message that is both appropriate and germane. In addition, both Terri and Nicole were proactive, independent workers, punctual for meetings, attentive listeners and met all deadlines we set up. And they were superb writers. I was so glad to be able to work with them.

—Julie Maxson, agency mentor with the YWCA Rape Crisis Center

Your students Jimmy Wu, Rachel Nakauchi, and Katie Kircanski came to our organization, stepped into the task of organizing and writing a newsletter with pictures, graphics, and a calendar of events. Their work is professional, creative, concise, and truly represents the work of our organization.

—Willard W. Davis, agency mentor with the Attitudinal Healing Network

The students did terrific work! It's always a pleasure to have them take on these projects. Both students were competent, provided drafts on schedule, and willingly took directions and suggestions to complete the project. Their finished work is ready to publish with little or no revision.

—Dan Firth, agency mentor with the Palo Alto Fire Department

Obviously, the person in the best position to evaluate your practical project is your agency mentor. Since the mentor is intimately involved with the community organization and will have special insight into the project's usefulness, his or her assessment of it is invaluable for you and your instructor. The mentors' evaluations above reflect typical standards by which mentors often measure successful practical projects. Instead of a long discussion about students' use of language and writing styles (comments much more likely to come from instructors), their evaluations point to what they see as the most important aspects both of students' work styles and of the practical writing that they produce: students' independence, adherence to deadlines, professionalism, creativity, competence, and willingness to take direction; the usefulness of students' practical documents as marketing tools; students' grasp of the agency's mission and their ability to produce an agency document that accurately reflects this mission; the creation of a piece that is "ready to publish with little or no revision." Most agency mentors approach and evaluate students' work in professional terms, since a practical writing project is a professional document to be used in the world of work—the world of your agency's work.

> I think my project was successful because the agency was able to use it without major revision and they were able to use it for several different purposes. I think that the agency's satisfaction is the primary measure of success. You may have written a wonderful piece, but if the agency is unable to use it, what's the point?
>
> —Louise Auerhahn, fourth-year student

In some cases, though, you and your agency mentor may agree that you worked your best and that a project is written beautifully, but it ends up not accomplishing what you had hoped that it would. Grant proposals are an obvious example. They are probably the most stress-inducing writing that students encounter when they write for their agencies. No matter how many hours you spend and no matter how many times you revise, it still may not bring money into the agency. It is difficult to avoid thinking that if you can write the perfect grant proposal, the most persuasive argument on behalf of your agency, it will be given the green light. But the truth of the matter is that most grant proposals—especially ones for large amounts of money—are rejected. When a grant proposal is successful, it is a huge success because it is so unusual for them to be accepted. This is why many agencies apply for several grants at one time.

What happens to all of the hard work you did on a rejected grant proposal? Neither the research nor the writing is likely to go to waste. In many cases, a nonprofit will hold on to a grant proposal that was not accepted and use parts or all of it as a template for another grant at a later date. Some of your writing might wind up in a different agency document, such as a newsletter or a brochure. Although the grant might not have come through, the agency appreciates your work and will find ways to use it. Moreover, you have had a real and valuable service-learning experience.

WHAT IS YOUR ASSESSMENT?

Let's assume your instructor has given you an "A" on your service-learning project. Your agency mentor has told you how much he or she loved your work. It is clear to you that both of these parties found your community-based academic or practical writing successful. But what about you? How do you measure your own success in a service-learning context? You might be the harshest critic of all where assessment of your work in the community is concerned.

> I don't think I'll ever know if my project worked out. Perhaps in ten years, when I come back to Oakland and I see a Native American community that is better off than it is now, I'll be able to say that what I've done has made some sort of difference.
>
> —Terence Chia, second-year student

When you write for community agencies in a service-learning context, your learning and growth as a scholar are the primary objectives, but they are no longer the only objectives. Although Terence's grade indicated a successful project, he still wonders if his project had a lasting impact on the community. He's right: he may never know. We would advise him to focus, too, on the fact that he had an important learning experience, gaining insight into the urban Native American community and the struggles that this community and his agency face. Terence could have read a book about this subject, but he was successful in that he had a *lived* learning experience. Who knows where this might lead him?

> I was originally pre-med when I came to college. But, looking back on my community research and writing project, I realized that I was much more interested in social and policy issues. I am currently majoring in the field of public policy with a focus on public health.
>
> —*Megan Vanneman, second-year student*

Beyond fulfilling their course requirements, service-learning students often measure their success by evaluating the ways in which their views of and connections with their communities change as a consequence of their experience. Some students continue to volunteer for their agencies after their service-learning courses have ended. Some determine or change their majors because of an interest sparked by their agency or community work. Other service-learning graduates are now staff members at community nonprofits. And occasionally, these former students become agency mentors themselves, who in turn work with other service-learning students. Through their initial experience in service-learning, many students opt to work for social change.

> I have never accepted the distinction between the *real* and the *academic* worlds; in fact, I think it does great damage to education.
>
> —*Michael Martin, San Francisco State University*

Service-learning teaches students to understand that higher education is not just about memorizing and regurgitating facts, not just about getting through another lecture. Service-learning teaches students that their education need not be separate from their real lives. It enables students to become more accountable to themselves and to their communities. Service-learning is democratic education in practice.

REFLECTIVE QUESTIONS
FOR JOURNAL-WRITING AND CLASS DISCUSSION

1. Describe your most successful academic learning experience. What made it successful? Do you remember the grade that you received for your work? To what extent did the grade reflect your experience of success?

2. Have you ever written an academic paper that failed? If so, on what basis did it fail? What did you learn from the project?

3. In your journal, reflect on what you think makes for a successful service-learning experience.

4. Assuming that the service-learning projects for your current class are complete or nearly complete, discuss with your classmates to what extent each of you thinks your project is, or will be, successful or unsuccessful. How will you know? What will determine success or lack of it as far as you are concerned?

TROUBLESHOOTING

WHAT IF…

you think you need more time to make your practical project really excellent, but your agency needs it now?

TRY TO…

accept that many community-based writing projects must be completed within absolute time frames. Sometimes in academic work, extensions can be arranged; however, in workplace writing, extensions are often not feasible. You may not have the time to tinker with your work as much as you would like to in a practical writing project for a community agency.

WHAT IF…

your mentor says that he or she really likes the work that you produced for the agency, but your instructor gives you a "B" on the project?

TRY TO…

bear in mind that your instructor will probably take a different view of your service-learning work than your mentor will. Your mentor's assessment may be focused entirely on the *product* of your work, whereas your instructor may be concerned not only with the product but with the *process* of your learning as well. For example, your instructor may take into account the attitude with which you approached your work, the amount of time and effort that you expended on the project, and your role as a collaborator or peer reviewer.

WHAT IF…

your collaborators have not contributed as much as you have and you think that the project's success is in jeopardy because of this?

TRY TO…

share your concerns confidentially with your instructor. One hopes that you approached your instructor for help in resolving problems of unequal contribution when these difficulties first became apparent. If you did not, you will know better next time. However, even when these sorts of issues are addressed early on, occasionally problems persist. You may want to ask your instructor if he or she is willing to evaluate your work independently. Be aware, however, that your instructor may believe that collective evaluation of a collaborative project is crucial to the learning process.

WHAT IF…

you submit an incomplete project to your agency?

TRY TO…

distinguish between what is within and outside your control when it comes to completing your project. If your project is incomplete simply because you did not complete it, that's a problem—your problem. You have not met your responsibility. However, if your project is incomplete because of factors genuinely beyond your control, you must be content with the fact that you have met your obligations to your agency to the best of your ability. For example, if you were asked to write a grant proposal, and the agency has not yet determined all of the details of the proposed project, gaps will inevitably exist in the grant proposal until the agency resolves these issues. Some documents, including proposals and Web pages, consist of parts; your job may have been to complete one section while other students or agency staff work on others. In such a circumstance, you will have little or no control over others' contributions to the complete product, but you will have control over your own.

Appendix

REFLECTIVE JOURNAL

Entries 1–3
Audience: self and instructor
Agency Affiliate: Hamilton Middle School
Student Writer: Rebecca Evans

REFLECTIVE ESSAY

Mother Hubbard's Cupboard
Audience: general community
Agencies: Dr. Martin Luther King Jr. Birthday Celebration Commission of
the Community and Family Resources Department, City of Bloomington,
Indiana; Mother Hubbard's Cupboard
Student Writer: Elizabeth Cole

FACT SHEET

Baylands Nature Center Scavenger Hunt
Audience: young children
Agency: Baylands Nature Interpretive Center
Student Writer: Jennifer Washington

BROCHURE

Landmine Awareness
Audience: adults, general public
Agency: Palo Alto Chapter of the American Red Cross
Student Writer: Jessica Gray

WEB PAGE

Home Safety Plan
Audience: children and adults, general public
Agency: The Palo Alto Fire Department
Student Writer: Jordi Feliu

REPORT

Water Quality: Tap Water

    in *Indicators for a Sustainable San Mateo County: A Yearly Report Card on Our County's Quality of Life, May 2001*
    Audience: adults, public officials and general public
    Agency: Sustainable San Mateo County
    Student Writer: Jenny Bernstein

NEWSLETTER ARTICLE

An Inside Look at Platelet Donation

    Audience: adults, previous and potential platelet donors
    Agency: Stanford Blood Center
    Student Writer: Andrew Goldfarb

GRANT LETTER

    Audience: grants management board
    Agency: Helping After Neonatal Death
    Student Writer: Adryon Burton

ACADEMIC RESEARCH PAPER (BRIEF)

Grass or Astroturf:
Environmental Groups and Corporate Sponsorship

    Audience: *primary:* instructor and classmates; *secondary:* agency
    Agency Affiliate: Bay Area Action
    Student Writer: Rebecca Freeland

ACADEMIC RESEARCH PAPER (EXTENDED)

Landmines: Distant Killers

    Audience: *primary:* instructor and classmates; *secondary:* agency
    Agency Affiliate: Palo Alto Chapter of the American Red Cross
    Student Writer: Jessica Gray

REFLECTIVE JOURNAL
Entries 1–3

January 27
Journal Entry 1

I had my first community service meeting on Wednesday the 24th for the program. The organization seems well structured concerning times, rides and general purpose. The point of the organization, it seems, is tutoring middle-schoolers. When I first attended I thought we would be working on a specific project with these children. Rather, we are supposed to encourage them in their project and help them form goals and aspirations.

While this is an admirable goal, in my particular case I'm worried that the blind may be leading the blind. While I have vague goals, I don't have specific plans and have left a lot of open room to play with and change them. I wonder if I am really in a position to help directionless middle-schoolers. Furthermore, I wonder how exactly you inspire someone. In the short time we will be working with these people, I wonder if it is truly possible to have a lasting effect.

I'm a little apprehensive about the general logistics of talking to someone who is in such a different place. I am realizing how long ago I was in seventh grade, and how I am forgetting what it was like already. I hope that this will bring it back a bit so I'm not totally out of touch.

Overall, I am excited. I think it will be good for me to leave my comfort zone. Hopefully there is a possibility that I will be able to make a difference.

February 4
Journal Entry 2

The time I spent at Hamilton last week meant so much to me. I started my first day at Hamilton Middle School nervously. I think everyone in my group was a bit nervous. We all cowered together as we entered the large basic brown stone building. A group of boys remarked loudly as we came in that we were "them college kids." That remark alone turned five normally confident college students into cowering inferiors. I think we all knew that we were in their domain. We were in a world where unruly eighth graders ruled the stairwells, something I think most of us had forgotten from our own middle school days.

In a classroom-size room lined with computers and several tables, we met the ten seventh graders we would be working with. All were black with the exception of one tough-looking white girl. Carol assigned two girls to me, Miranda and Tiffany. All the children in the room came from the same class in the seventh grade so they all knew each other fairly well. Carol had given us several questions we were supposed to discuss. Although I had been thankful for them as I came in, I soon abandoned them, in favor of making friends with the girls.

The first, Miranda, has aspirations of being a doctor, specifically an obstetrician. When she proclaimed this, it took me a moment to place the word. I didn't even know what it meant offhand. It was an eye-opener and reminded me that I had a lot to learn from these kids. On the side, she hoped to have a "hobby" in modeling. Just to make a little money, she told me.

Somehow I could imagine this. Miranda reminded me of the kids I envied in middle school: those kids who seemed to always have a swarm of boys around them, get invited to the best parties and sit with the popular kids at lunch. She reveled in the fact that she got to have an unusual visitor to show around her school and yelled a noisy hello to every teacher we passed. She made sure to stop in her "boyfriend's" class. She eagerly discussed the dance that Friday. Her nails were beautifying painted, pink with white tips and intricate flowered designs, in honor of her recent birthday.

Tiffany is quieter and she claims she would like to be a teacher. She spoke less, but when she did it was more thoughtful and slower. Whereas Miranda rattled on about this and that, every word from Tiffany was like a gift, careful and caring. She moved more awkwardly, was heavyset and always very conscious of her body.

The interaction between the two was interesting and sometimes painful to watch. It was obvious that Tiffany was pleased to have been paired with Miranda. She listened carefully to everything that Miranda said, took a great interest in her boy stories and proclaimed that she wasn't even going to the dance this weekend. It was everything about middle school I had worked to avoid. I made sure that I always had a date to the dance and that I always sat with the popular kids. I tried so hard to be Miranda.

I've realized that people like Miranda are tossed aside when it comes to the things that matter, developing yourself, forming lasting friendships, and life goals. I wanted to hug Tiffany and tell her how well she was doing, how much she would appreciate knowing herself as well as she did due to all the time she spent alone.

Despite this interesting interaction I had an amazing time talking, laughing with them, recognizing all the commonalities that I still shared despite the age difference. Right before I left, Miranda said she couldn't wait to come up and see the school. Tiffany said, "Miss Becca, I thought you were doing this for a class, I was worried you would be like a teacher, but you're my friend." I felt like crying. That one sentence made my whole stressful, difficult week light and worth it. I can't wait to see them again.

February 13
Journal Entry 3

Last week, a new girl was added to my group of kids, completely changing the dynamic of things. She seems to be tough and although she will talk about shallow things, she has only said a few things about her family. She mentioned that she has moved 12 times and that there are 6 brothers and sisters at home. Other than that, she doesn't really talk about her parents, their jobs, what she would like to do professionally, or any of the other things that Miranda and Tiffany have started openly talking about.

During one incident last week I re-realized how much we, as college kids, have to learn from these middle-schoolers. Unfortunately, one of the tutor's roommates was arrested while his tutees were visiting the room. Their reaction startled me. They dealt with it so well, because they were used to seeing it. I think they come from a different world than many of us at our school do.

In addition, I just finished reading a section of the "Soul of a Citizen." I felt a connection with several of the things Loeb said. He mentioned that "a sense of purpose is impossible to attain through private pursuits alone" (34). I am beginning to agree with this more and more. As a college freshman, I face a large amount of pressure to have strict goals and desires. However, it's a struggle to go from being a directionless high-schooler to having specific dreams and goals and finding a path to pursuing them. While I think I am meant to help the middle-schoolers do just this, at the same time, the program and the kids are helping me realize that this is something I like to do. It gives me direction as well. It really has given some purpose to this semester. In addition, our school is a bit of a glass tower. Although we are in a rather impoverished city, we are placed on this green campus in one of the wealthiest parts of town. I know kids who have lived here for six months and not even been into the city. Without this interaction, how can you truly understand the issues that the city and our nation face? In addition, a great deal of personal growth comes from experiencing unusual and different situations. Staying in a glass bubble won't allow people to live.

REFLECTIVE ESSAY
Mother Hubbard's Cupboard

A Day On! Not A Day Off 2000

Essays and Photos about
Service Projects
Sponsored by the Dr.
Martin Luther King, Jr.
Birthday Celebration
Commission of the City
of Bloomington, Indiana
Supported by Funding
from
The Corporation for
National Service

City of Bloomington, IN

Mother Hubbard's Cupboard

By Elizabeth R. Cole

Deciding on which community service activity to participate in was difficult. Everything on the list seemed very interesting. However, I chose Mother Hubbard's Cupboard due to the fact that food is a basic need in our lives. When my stomach growls, I eat. What would I do if there was no food in the cabinets? I hope that someone would be there to help me.

> *"I was astounded that such a noble cause was afforded such limited space and wished others could see how little they had to work*

Thinking of hunger and my lack of it, I reflected back on my childhood. I remembered the cafeteria in grade school packed with anxious, hungry kids: children waiting for a free meal with the orange lunch cards in their small hands. The bigger, mean kids would laugh at them and call them names. I looked at those cards and was in some way afraid of them. I did not know much, but I knew that I did not want that card.

Time goes by and we grow older, forgetting about such small memories. Now I am sixteen years old and driving my first car. The radio is blasting as I drive to a nearby fast-food restaurant. The food in my refrigerator did not seem good enough. With a combo meal in my hand, a figure catches my eye across the street; his clothes are torn, his shoes muddy, and his hands hold a sign reading, "Will work for food." I cannot take my eyes off his sad gaze, so I give him the food that he needs much more than I.

*Photos in this article are of volunteers from Ivy Tech State College and the community sorting food at the **Hoosier Hills Food Bank**. – Photos by Craig Brenner.*

NOT A DAY OFF

With such recollections, Mother Hubbard's Cupboard seemed an ideal choice for my community service. Hunger is such an old problem. I knew of it even as a child. Plus, I knew that my one random act of kindness was not enough. The goodness and pride that I felt that day inspired me to do it again.

Mother Hubbard's Cupboard is a Bloomington community food pantry. It began in 1998 as a nonprofit organization. Their goal is to make a difference in the hunger needs of Bloomington and the surrounding area. Mother Hubbard's Cupboard is unique in several ways. The staff provides mostly organic foods to their recipients in order to educate families and individuals about nutrition. Also, the pantry operates on the honor system. Recipients only need meet one of the ten guidelines and no documentation is necessary. Distributing an average of 1,800 pounds of food per week, the pantry has proved successful.

When I found the pantry, I thought I had the wrong place. It looked like a very small house. Inside, it proved to be even smaller, consisting of two tiny rooms, each about 5 by 8 feet. Ten volunteers and two staff members crowded the space: we were shoulder-to-shoulder with standing room only. While I marveled at the lack of space, a woman next to me (apparently a previous vol-

45

A DAY ON!

unteer) commented on how much bigger Mother Hubbard's Cupboard was since they had added the second room. I was astounded that such a noble cause was afforded such limited space and wished others could see how little they had to work with. Despite the cramped area, Mother Hubbard's Cupboard was well supplied. Shelves lined the walls from floor to ceiling with heaping amounts of such organic food as tofu hotdogs, whole grain cereals, herbal teas, wheat bread, couscous, soups, power bars, jalapeno potato chips, and goat milk...the list goes on and on.

The volunteers and staff were all very friendly and eager to get started. Volunteers included children, high school and college students, and mothers and fathers all united in one common mission: feeding the less fortunate. It was Martin Luther King, Jr. Day, and while most others were enjoying a day off from school or work, here was a group donating its time to enhance other people's lives.

Mother Hubbard's Cupboard was participating in a community program entitled "A Day On! Not A Day Off" in observance of Dr. King. At the food pantry, the goal of the program was to carry on King's work as a promoter for self-respect and dignity. Mother Hubbard's Cupboard's mission statement includes serving the poor with free food while maintaining an atmosphere allowing recipients to keep their dignity. The Cupboard delivers food baskets with

NOT A DAY OFF

smiling faces and caring hearts. There are neither looks of disapproval nor signs of pity. Volunteers also intended to follow King's example in uncovering society's injustices while giving a helping hand to our struggling brothers and sisters. The overall goal was to mirror Martin Luther King, Jr.'s personality and life.

Although I left Mother Hubbard's Cupboard not a penny richer, I gained more on that day than on any I can remember. I dropped off a basket at a house twenty miles from Bloomington. In that home was a little girl. She had pigtails and a grin from ear to ear. She was wearing an oversized shirt long since handed down to her. She was a little shy, but warm and sweet, asking me if my mommy was waiting outside for me. She was a child from my past, one of the quiet kids who stood last in line with their orange free lunch tickets. I realized how little I had known when I was young and how my fear of the unknown and of those different from me controlled me. When

I looked into her eyes, I knew that my sorrow for her was misplaced. Her smile cheered me and her acceptance gave me peace. She will always know the value of simple things like food, joy, and hunger.

As for me, I never really knew until that moment just how many blessings I have and how important the simple things are. I will always be thankful to her for showing me the truth. I would not say necessarily that I was proud of my volunteer work, because pride should be related to achievements. Kindness and giving are not achievements, they are ways of life. I am just glad I was there.

Above: Even children were among the volunteers who helped sort food at the Hoosier Hills Food Bank 1/17/00 — Photo by Craig Brenner

"FACT SHEET
Baylands Nature Center Scavenger Hunt

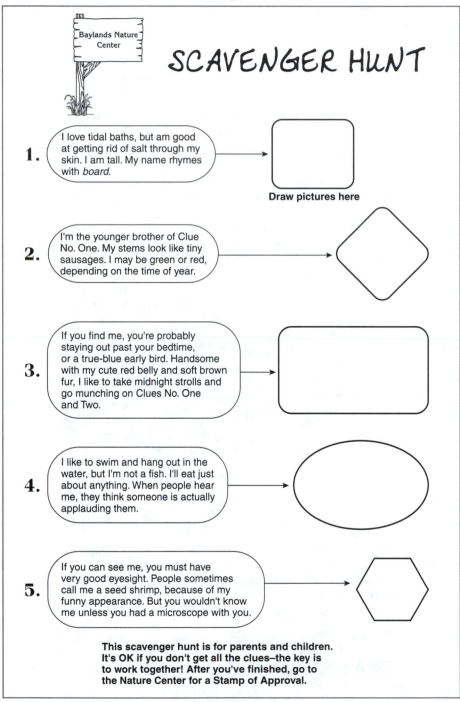

Baylands Nature Center

SCAVENGER HUNT

1. I love tidal baths, but am good at getting rid of salt through my skin. I am tall. My name rhymes with *board*.

Draw pictures here

2. I'm the younger brother of Clue No. One. My stems look like tiny sausages. I may be green or red, depending on the time of year.

3. If you find me, you're probably staying out past your bedtime, or a true-blue early bird. Handsome with my cute red belly and soft brown fur, I like to take midnight strolls and go munching on Clues No. One and Two.

4. I like to swim and hang out in the water, but I'm not a fish. I'll eat just about anything. When people hear me, they think someone is actually applauding them.

5. If you can see me, you must have very good eyesight. People sometimes call me a seed shrimp, because of my funny appearance. But you wouldn't know me unless you had a microscope with you.

This scavenger hunt is for parents and children. It's OK if you don't get all the clues—the key is to work together! After you've finished, go to the Nature Center for a Stamp of Approval.

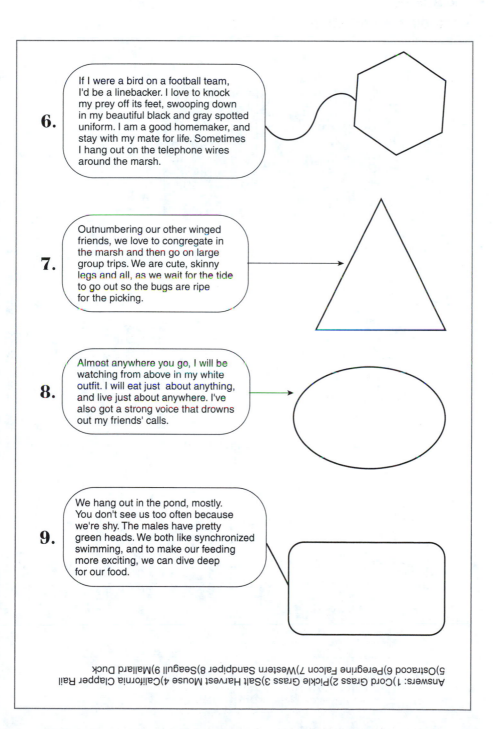

6. If I were a bird on a football team, I'd be a linebacker. I love to knock my prey off its feet, swooping down in my beautiful black and gray spotted uniform. I am a good homemaker, and stay with my mate for life. Sometimes I hang out on the telephone wires around the marsh.

7. Outnumbering our other winged friends, we love to congregate in the marsh and then go on large group trips. We are cute, skinny legs and all, as we wait for the tide to go out so the bugs are ripe for the picking.

8. Almost anywhere you go, I will be watching from above in my white outfit. I will eat just about anything, and live just about anywhere. I've also got a strong voice that drowns out my friends' calls.

9. We hang out in the pond, mostly. You don't see us too often because we're shy. The males have pretty green heads. We both like synchronized swimming, and to make our feeding more exciting, we can dive deep for our food.

Answers: 1)Cord Grass 2)Pickle Grass 3)Salt Harvest Mouse 4)California Clapper Rail 5)Ostracod 6)Peregrine Falcon 7)Western Sandpiper 8)Seagull 9)Mallard Duck

BROCHURE
Landmine Awareness

LANDMINE
Awareness

© Paul Hansen, 1996

"Landmines are being cleared – one limb at a time."

(international medical relief worker)

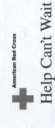

American Red Cross

Help Can't Wait

It is the Goal of the Red Cross...

To achieve a global ban on landmines as soon as feasible, using all venues possible, to provide assistance to landmine survivors today while offering hope for a world free of antipersonnel landmines tomorrow.

The American Red Cross
Palo Alto Chapter
400 Mitchell Lane
Palo Alto, CA 94301
(650) 688 – 0415
www.paarc.org

Stock No. 321111
Feb. 1996

"Mines may be described as fighters that never miss, strike blindly, do not carry weapons openly, and go on killing long after hostilities have ended. In short, mines are the greatest violators of international humanitarian law, practicing blind terrorism." (Red Cross delegate, Angola)

Landmines are hidden explosives set to detonate upon the slightest impact. Used in essentially every military conflict for decades, landmines are a threat to millions of innocent civilians in over 80 countries worldwide. Planted near populated areas, landmines outlast military conflicts, causing significant injury and death to thousands of people each year. As a result of these indiscriminant killers, individuals, families, and communities throughout the world face personal, social, and economic tragedy including the trauma of injury or death, loss of loved ones, and a destruction of the functionality of society.

Today, many individuals and organizations such as the Red Cross are working towards a mine-free world. However, given the sheer quantity of landmines already planted and the continuing use of landmines in armed conflicts worldwide, landmines remain a serious threat to millions of innocent people.

Help Can't Wait

Fact: Landmines remain active 50-100 years after they have been planted.

Fact: There are currently over 110 million landmines scattered around farmlands, roads, forests, and neighborhoods throughout the world.

Fact: Every 20 minutes another person is maimed or killed by accidentally triggering a landmine during his or her daily tasks.

Fact: For each mine cleared by a well trained professional, 20 are laid by large and small military forces from around the world.

Fact: The US Government did not ratify the 1997 Ottawa Treaty to ban land mines because of the military's refusal to forfeit the right to such an efficient weapon.

Fact: The price of a landmine is as low as $3. The cost of neutralization is anywhere from $300 to $1000.

Fact: In the last 15 years, the Red Cross has manufactured over 90,000 prostheses for over 60,000 victims of landmines in 21 countries.

© Paul Hansen 1996

Although not in your back yard,

© Paul Hansen, 1996

Landmines are in someone's back yard.

The American Red Cross is part of the International Campaign to Ban Landmines (ICBL), a humanitarian campaign that has been working to end the production, stockpiling, and implementation of landmines throughout the world as well as fund proper medical treatment and rehabilitation for victims of landmine explosions.

The ICBL initiated the 1997 Ottawa Treaty, a comprehensive treaty signed by over 100 countries that holds each signatory responsible for destroying their stockpiles and clearing their own country of landmines.

The Mine Ban Treaty and the ICBL have made a global impact; however, landmines continue to be laid and are taking far too many innocent victims.

In the past few years there has been a shift in the attention of the United States away from the landmine issue. The media has avoided it because it is not a problem that is neatly solvable.

The number of innocent victims will continue to rise unless people speak out on the issue of landmines and address it as a global crisis.

To HELP, you can:
learn the facts:
Stay on top of international decisions and actions by visiting www.icbl.org.
Raise awareness:
Write to your local newspapers about the lack of coverage of such an important issue.
Address your leaders:
 - Tell the President that the US should sign the Ottawa Treaty in 2006 and destroy the 11 million landmines we are currently stockpiling.
 - Press for a comprehensive ban on mines as well as victim assistance programs.
Get involved:
Join local organizations such as the Red Cross by calling (650) 688-0415.

"Until governments are pressed to adopt strict limits for the prohibition of weapons causing superfluous injury or having indiscriminate effects, until there is a truly effective worldwide citizens' movement concerned about wars and the conduct of warfare, the growth in suffering inflicted in armed conflicts will continue" (Eric Prokosch, author of *The Technology of Killing: A Military and Political History of Antipersonnel Weapons*)

WEB PAGE
Home Safety Plan

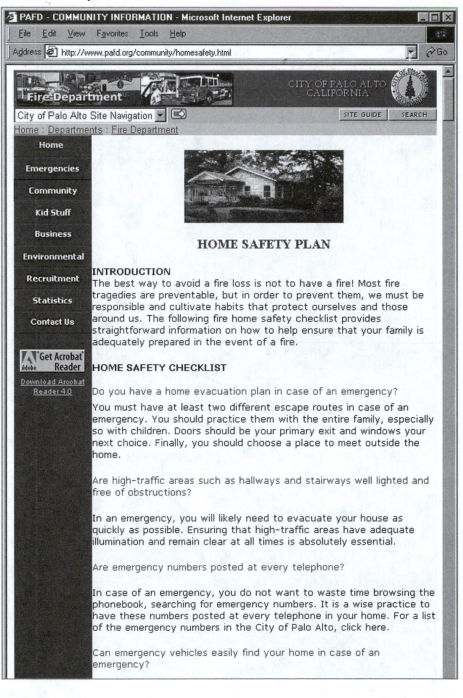

HOME SAFETY PLAN

INTRODUCTION

The best way to avoid a fire loss is not to have a fire! Most fire tragedies are preventable, but in order to prevent them, we must be responsible and cultivate habits that protect ourselves and those around us. The following fire home safety checklist provides straightforward information on how to help ensure that your family is adequately prepared in the event of a fire.

HOME SAFETY CHECKLIST

Do you have a home evacuation plan in case of an emergency?

You must have at least two different escape routes in case of an emergency. You should practice them with the entire family, especially so with children. Doors should be your primary exit and windows your next choice. Finally, you should choose a place to meet outside the home.

Are high-traffic areas such as hallways and stairways well lighted and free of obstructions?

In an emergency, you will likely need to evacuate your house as quickly as possible. Ensuring that high-traffic areas have adequate illumination and remain clear at all times is absolutely essential.

Are emergency numbers posted at every telephone?

In case of an emergency, you do not want to waste time browsing the phonebook, searching for emergency numbers. It is a wise practice to have these numbers posted at every telephone in your home. For a list of the emergency numbers in the City of Palo Alto, click here.

Can emergency vehicles easily find your home in case of an emergency?

Searching for a correct address could potentially cause rescuers to lose precious time. Your house number should be clearly visible from the street and illuminated at night so your house can be easily found.

Do you have a working flashlight within easy reach of the bed?

You should always keep a working flashlight near your bed and use it to signal for help in the event of a fire. Test your flashlight monthly to ensure it is working properly.

Are smoke detectors installed on each floor of the home?

You should install at least one smoke detector on every level of your home, including the basement and family room. A fire can potentially start in any area of the house, so the more smoke detectors you install, the better protected you are. FACT: A working smoke detector reduces the risk of dying in a home fire by nearly half.

Are the smoke detectors in your home installed in appropriate places?

Smoke detectors should NOT be placed near air outlet vents. The best locations for installing smoke detectors are in hallways and just outside bedroom doors. What good is a smoke detector that is located where no one can hear it?

Have you changed the batteries that operate your smoke detectors lately?

The IAFC (International Association of Fire Chiefs) encourages people to change smoke detector batteries at least annually. You should test your smoke detectors periodically to ensure that they are working correctly. What good is a smoke detector that does not work? FACT: Although smoke detectors are in 92 percent of American homes, nearly one-third do not work because of old or missing batteries.

Do you clean your smoke detectors of dust and cobwebs every month in order to ensure their sensitivity?

You should vacuum the grill work of all smoke detectors monthly to prevent break downs or false alarms. If the smoke sensors are blocked, the smoke detector will not function correctly. What good is a smoke detector whose sensing chamber is blocked?

Do your children understand that a smoke detector signals a home fire and do they recognize its alarm?

Make sure your children understand what smoke detectors are, what is their purpose, and how they should respond in the event of a fire. Teach them they should NEVER ignore the sound of a smoke detector alarm. FACT: Each day, an average of three kids die in home fires. 90 percent of child fire deaths occur in homes without working smoke detectors.

Have you equipped your kitchen with a fire extinguisher?

Do you know how to operate it in the event of a fire? You should have at least one fire extinguisher in your home. A fire extinguisher should be placed near or inside the kitchen to put off small fires. Be sure you know how to use a fire extinguisher – what good is a fire extinguisher if you don't know how to operate it in an emergency?

Do you have all extinguishers checked and recharged periodically?

Improper maintenance is the biggest reason fire extinguishers fail. Fire extinguishers need to be recharged periodically in order to ensure they will be useful in the event of a fire. An extinguisher that is not charged is as good as not having an extinguisher at all!

Do you have your chimney inspected annually?

Chimneys should be cleaned periodically to remove combustible soot build-up, which represents a possible fire hazard. In addition, you should use protective screens over fireplaces. Burning logs can throw sparks onto the rug and start a fire.

Do you ALWAYS keep lighters, matches, and all other smoking materials out of the reach of children?

Children are, by nature, curious about fire. You should explain to them the dangers of playing with matches or lighters, and you should always keep these and other smoking materials out of their reach. FACT: One-fourth of all fire deaths of children are from fires started by children.

Do you know how to react if your clothes catch fire?
If your clothes catch fire, do not run! If you run, the air will actually make the flames burn more rapidly. Instead, you should STOP, then DROP to the floor, and ROLL to smother the fire. Remember: STOP, DROP, and ROLL.

Do you handle flammable liquids carefully?

Are you aware of the dangers surrounding them? Volatile liquids, such as oil paints, cleaning solvents, and gasoline should be stored in tightly capped metal containers. In addition, they should be stored away from and never used near ignition sources. Flammable liquids should NEVER be stored in the home.

IS YOUR HOME SAFE? TAKE THE TEST!

- Do you have a home evacuation plan in case of an emergency?
- Are high-traffic areas such as hallways and stairways well lighted and free of obstructions?
- Are emergency numbers posted at every telephone?
- Can emergency vehicles easily find your home in case of an emergency?
- Are smoke detectors installed on each floor of the home?

- Are smoke detectors installed on each floor of the home?
- Are the smoke detectors in your home installed in appropriate places?
- Have you changed the batteries that operate your smoke detectors lately?
- Are the smoke detectors in your home installed in appropriate places?
- Have you changed the batteries that operate your smoke detectors lately?
- Do you clean your smoke detectors of dust and cobwebs every month in order to ensure their sensitivity?
- Do your children understand that a smoke detector signals a home fire and do they recognize its alarm?
- Have you equipped your kitchen with a fire extinguisher? Do you know how to operate it in the event of a fire?
- Do you have all extinguishers checked and recharged periodically?
- Do you have a working flashlight within easy reach of the bed?
- Do you have your chimney inspected annually?
- Do you ALWAYS keep lighters, matches, and all other smoking materials out of the reach of children?
- Do you know how to react if your clothes catch fire?
- Do you handle flammable liquids carefully? Are you aware of the dangers surrounding them?

We would like to thank Jordi Feliu, a student at Stanford University in the Community Service Writing Program, for developing the content of this announcement.

<u>Return to Top</u>

| ▲ Top | Acceptable Use Policy | Accessibility Guidelines | Site Guide | Site Search | Home |

REPORT
Water Quality: Tap Water

WATER QUALITY ▪ TAP WATER

Indicators Used

The most potentially dangerous impurities likely to be found in drinking water were measured. Levels of trihalomethanes (THMs), methyl tertiary butyl ether (MTBE), copper and lead in water delivered by San Mateo County's two largest suppliers of water, the San Francisco Public Utilities Commission (SFPUC) and the California Water Service Company (CalWater) are reported. Well water supplies a small percentage of the county's water and is not measured. The water quality reports for the SFPUC and for the California Water Service Company for 1998 and 1999 were reviewed. The SFPUC supplies most of San Mateo County's water, while the California Water Service Company supplies water for the communities of South San Francisco, Colma, Broadmoor, Atherton, and portions of Redwood City. The California Water Service Company and the SFPUC both supply water for Menlo Park, Portola Valley, and Woodside. The water in San Mateo and San Carlos is SFPUC water but is served by the California Water Service Company. The state and federal governments assign a maximum contaminant level (MCL) for many of the chemical and biological pollutants found in water, and these were used as standards for comparison.

Importance

THMs are chemicals which arise in the chlorination process of water and are suspected to be carcinogenic and mutagenic, possibly causing damage to DNA. MTBE, an oxygenate, is used to help gasoline burn cleaner, but recent studies show that it is a neurotoxin and possibly a carcinogen. Lead, a metal, can cause severe learning disabilities in children, blood pressure and neurological ailments in adults, and complications in pregnancy. Copper is a metal that can cause nausea, vomiting, and even death when ingested in large quantities. Because of these risks associated with lead and copper ingestion, the U.S. Environmental Protection Agency (EPA) places special emphasis on the monitoring of lead and copper levels in drinking water.

The quality of drinking water is one of many factors contributing to the environmental health of a community and to personal well-being. Contaminated water can bring disease, birth defects, increased infant mortality, and increased occurrence of cancer.

Findings

The data show that the drinking water of San Mateo County residents and businesses is essentially pollutant free.

Of the 21 contaminants that were found to be present in the water supplied by the California Water Service Company, only THMs ap-

continued

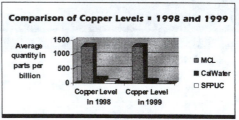

Comparison of Lead Levels ▪ 1998 and 1999

Comparison of Copper Levels ▪ 1998 and 1999

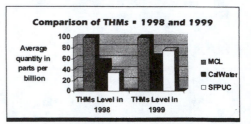

Comparison of THMs ▪ 1998 and 1999

peared at levels approaching the standard maximum level. The average level of THMs for 1999 was 64.3 parts per billion (ppb), which is 64.3 percent of the 100 ppb MCL. The level of THMs in the water supplied by the SFPUC varied from community to community. The San Francisco Water System contained 75 ppb of THMs, 75 percent of the MCL. Both water suppliers meet the federal standards for THMs levels. To comply with stricter federal regulations, the SFPUC will use new disinfectant chloramines in early 2003 to further lower THMs levels.

MTBE, which has proven problematic in neighboring Santa Clara County, is virtually nonexistent in the drinking water of major suppliers to San Mateo County, but probably does exist in well water. For 1999, the level of MTBE detected in the San Francisco Water System was below 0.5 ppb, and no MTBE was detected in water supplied by the California Water Service Company. The federal government has not yet set a standard for MTBE levels in the public drinking supply. State and federal officials have recently lowered the advisory level at which MTBE can be detected in the water by its odor, taste and appearance to 4 ppb, but this advisory serves only as a warning level, not a standard maximum level, for water managers.

There is no MCL for lead and copper levels, but there are Action Levels, serving as advisories for water managers. The average amount of copper in the water supplied by the California Water Service Company, in 1999, was 97 ppb, less than 8 percent of the Action Level, which is 1,300 ppb. No copper was detected in the SFPUC water. Lead concentrations in San Mateo County's drinking water were also very low. California Water Service provided water that contained, on average, 3.8 ppb, less than 25 percent of the 15 ppb Action Level. Lead concentrations were undetectable in SFPUC water.

Direction

Although there was a notable increase in the THMs levels in both California Water Service and SFPUC water from 1998 to 1999, the quality of water supplied to San Mateo County remains excellent. MTBE, THMs, lead and copper levels all remain below their MCLs or Action Levels.

Sources: *1999 Water Quality Report*, California Water Service Group; *Lead in Drinking Water*, Environmental Research Foundation; Rebbeka Grossman, *Tap Water: The Last Taboo*; www.plumbingsupply.com; *1999 Water Quality Report*, San Francisco Public Utilities Commission; http://www.epa.gov/ow/; David Quinones, Sanitary Engineer, San Francisco Public Utilities Commission, Water Quality Bureau
Researcher: Jenny Bernstein

The world is too much with us;
late and soon,
Getting and spending,
we lay waste our powers:
Little we see in nature
that is ours.

William Wordsworth, 1806

NEWSLETTER ARTICLE
An Inside Look at Platelet Donation

A NEWSLETTER FOR STANFORD MEDICAL SCHOOL BLOOD CENTER APHERESIS DONORS · SPRING 2001

An Inside Look at Platelet Donation
by Andrew Goldfarb

*Andrew is a Stanford student and part of the
Community Service Writing Program.
He interviewed Blood Center Administrator Vince Yalon for this article.*

Platelet donors represent a unique and important constituency of blood donors. While donors are well informed about the apheresis procedure, they may not be aware of what happens to their platelets after they leave the Blood Center.

After Donating, Where Do Platelets Go?

Once your platelet donation is complete, your platelets are processed and tested in the Blood Center's laboratories. Each day, about 25 units of apheresis platelets are collected. Samples collected at the time of donation are tested for pathogens and they are HLA (white cell) typed at the first donation. After testing is complete, all products are labeled with the appropriate blood and HLA type. Depending on the platelet count, products may be split into two separate units, for use by two different patients. Apheresis platelet units are then sent to Stanford Hospital, Lucile Salter Packard Children's Hospital at Stanford, El Camino Hospital in Mountain View, or O'Connor Hospital in San Jose.

Are My Platelets Altered Before they are Given to a Patient?

Yes, platelets are irradiated to prevent transfusion reactions in the recipient. Since blood is unique to each individual, a platelet recipient may experience a mild transfusion reaction due to the difference in antigens between the patient's and the donor's blood. Such a reaction may include, but is not limited to a mild fever, lower back pain (in the kidneys) and fluid build up in the lungs. The more transfusions a patient receives, the greater the chance for him/her to reject future transfu-
continued on page 2

Donor Buddy Days in April and May

Yes, Donor Buddy Days are here again! Here's how it works: As a Stanford platelet donor, you may recruit someone to try platelet donation. You must come in with them and donate at the same time they give their first platelet donation. New platelet donors must have previously donated whole blood at Stanford at least once in the last fours years.

Or, you can recruit a whole blood donor who has never given blood at Stanford
continued on page 4

Inside this Issue

PERSON to PERSON is a newsletter for the Apheresis donor. If you have any comments or would like further information regarding any part of this newsletter, please call 650-723-8237 or write:

Stanford Medical School Blood Center
c/o Apheresis Dept./Person to Person
800 Welch Road, Palo Alto, CA 94304

1

Letter from the Editor

This is my last letter from the editor. After almost twelve years at Stanford Medical School Blood Center, I will be leaving in mid-April in order to write children's books.

It has truly been a privilege to work at Stanford Blood Center. The cause is a noble one. My colleagues are talented, hard working and interesting. But best of all, you, our apheresis donors, are extraordinary individuals. I feel that your model for living, your dedication and selflessness, has been a constant and valuable inspiration to me.

My tradition teaches that each of us is here to help repair the world. That is our purpose in life. I know of no finer example of people repairing the world (drop by precious drop) than you.

I wish you all good health, satisfaction in donation, joy and success in all you do.

Sincerely,

Caryn Huberman

please stay in touch!

yackybooks@hotmail.com

An Inside Look at Platelet Donation

continued from page 1

sions (since the patient's body has built up antibodies).

For nearly 25 years cesium has been used to safely irradiate blood. According to Vince Yalon, while cesium has continued to be used, "modern microprocessors have allowed us to become much more refined in radiation dosage."

Who Receives My Platelets?

On a typical day, 10-30 units of apheresis platelets are used at Stanford Hospital. This amount varies according to the number of patients requiring platelets and their individual needs. A patient's clinician determines whether platelets are needed and how many units the patient requires. The patient's attending physician, surgeon, transplant surgeon, and/or anesthesiologist (who is responsible for monitoring various blood levels during surgical procedures), may determine whether a platelet transfusion is required. Cardiovascular surgeons occasionally request platelet transfusions for their patients to reduce bleeding, while platelets are seldom used during orthopedic surgeries where bleeding is usually minor.

Close to 70% of platelet transfusions go to cancer and leukemia patients. When these patients receive chemotherapy and irradiation treatments, their diseased and cancerous cells are destroyed, however, the treatment also destroys their platelets and the ability to make more platelets. These patients may be unable to produce healthy platelets of their own for up to two weeks. Their platelets and bone marrow (where the body makes platelets) have been damaged. Platelet donations rescue many oncology patients and bolster their blood clotting abilities.

Additionally, platelets are transfused to patients who are awaiting bone marrow transplant and following marrow transplant. These patients may be unable to produce healthy platelets of their own for two or three weeks after transplant. Without platelets and other transfusion products, these patients may suffer life-threatening hemorrhages or infections.

Slighty less than 30% of platelet donations go to multi-organ and liver transplant patients. These patients may require between 3 and 200 units of platelets and other blood products.

Before the system was developed to isolate and con-

continued next page

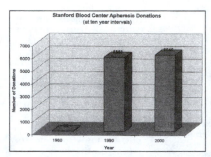

Stanford Blood Center Apheresis Donations
(at ten year intervals)

As technology improves, the harvesting efficiency for platelets is improving as well. New technology has contributed to more efficient platelet donation procedures. Currently, the apheresis donation process takes about 75 minutes, as compared to over 100 minutes just a few years ago.

What Can Apheresis Donors Look Forward to in the Future?

Presently, a cholesterol screen is performed at each donation and donors are informed of the results within a few weeks. In the future, using protein columns to remove proteins from a donor's blood, apheresis donors could possibly have their cholesterol safely *reduced* during the apheresis procedure! Wouldn't that be nice?

centrate platelets (prior to 1970), some patients died because they lacked the platelets required to maintain their clotting capabilites during surgeries, transplants and therapies.

Some less common cases, including patients suffering from Thrombotic Thrombocytopenic Purpura (TTP), a disease characterized by a deficiency of platelets, requires enormous amounts of plasma (that may be donated concurrently with platelets). These patients may require twice-daily treatments of 15 units of plasma each time.

Additionally, trauma patients may also require large amounts of platelets to stop bleeding.

While apheresis is predominantly used to acquire platelets, it is occasionally used to collect white blood cells. These blood cells are used for academic purposes by researchers at Stanford Blood Center studying white cell functions. White cells form the basis of our immune system. Stanford researchers are examining ways to train specific white cells to fight cancers and tumors.

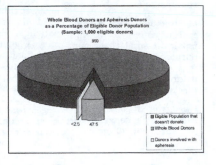

Whole Blood Donors and Apheresis Donors as a Percentage of Eligible Donor Population (Sample: 1,000 eligible donors)

3

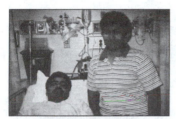

*Marrow Donor Miguel Ramirez
with his wife, Anna*

PBSC Donor Erin Brown

*Matt McCarty,
soon to be two-time marrow donor*

*George Andrews, PBSC Donor and
Marrow Donor*

DID YOU KNOW??

by Andrew Goldfarb

◆ On average, platelet donors give approximately 5 times per year, while whole blood donors give 1.7 times per year.

◆ Platelets are replenished within 48 hours of donating. Plasma is replaced within 24 hours. Red cells are replaced within 4-6 weeks.

◆ Platelets can be separated from whole blood donations by centrifuge, separating the cells by cell density. It takes 4-6 units of whole blood to yield the equivalent amount of platelets from one apheresis donation.

◆ Up to 2 units of platelets can be donated each time.

◆ As per FDA regulation, platelets must be used within 5 days of donation. After this period of time, bacteria may replicate and infect the platelets, rendering them unusable. At Stanford, platelets are usually transfused within 2.3 days of donation.

◆ Stanford is one of 6 locations involved in a phase III clinical trial using psoralen. Psoralen is a naturally occuring substance which may extend platelet shelf life to 7 days by inactivating bacteria.

APPOINTMENTS

650-723-7831

toll-free: 1-888-723-7831

online:

http://bloodcenter.stanford.edu

select "Donate Platelets"

5

GRANT LETTER

November 26, 2000
P.O. Box 341
Los Gatos, California 95031

Grants Management Board
The XYZ Foundation
1 Main Street, Suite 234
San Francisco, CA 98765

Dear Grants Management Board,

I am writing on behalf of HAND (Helping After Neonatal Death) of the Peninsula. HAND's mission is to provide support for families in the North County, Mid County, South County and Coastside region of the San Francisco Peninsula who have suffered the death of a child before, during, or after birth. These deaths result from miscarriage, the genetic termination of a much-wanted baby, stillbirth, "preemies" too little to survive, neonatal death due to congenital abnormalities, or sudden infant death. The loss of the child is often very unexpected, and the parents who had anticipated such joy are suddenly faced with extreme grief, complicated by feelings of guilt, confusion and isolation.

At the time when parents are most in need of support, they often do not find it. The bereaved couple no longer attends the prenatal classes and is unable to find solace among other expectant couples with whom they previously associated. In our loose and mobile society, many couples are far away from their relatives and have no extended family to offer them support or solutions. Additionally, for young couples the loss of their baby may be their first exposure to a death in the family. They find themselves in a bewildering situation that they could have never foreseen—they are forced to choose a casket at a time when they expected to be choosing a crib.

HAND of the Peninsula is a community based nonprofit 501(c)3 organization. We have been offering support to bereaved parents since 1981, and we have established a very successful long-term record and an excellent reputation within the community. We are the only organization in the Peninsula offering these services to those who have lost their babies. The organization is governed by a Board of Directors and has an advisory council comprising professionals with expertise in working with families. HAND's programs and service delivery are provided exclusively by volunteers.

Neonatal death afflicts nearly one in eight pregnant women. In addition to the shock, horror and grief that a mother experiences when her infant dies, she also has hormonal and physical changes to cope with after her pregnancy. Postpartum blues or recovery from a Caesarean without the consolation of a new baby can seem insurmountable. The feeling of having breast milk to feed a baby that is no longer alive is a constant and depressing reminder of the happiness and life that has been lost.

HAND is a volunteer group of parents who have experienced the loss of a baby and who wish to support other parents, along with their relatives and friends, who are undergoing a similar mourning process. HAND seeks to improve service delivery and accessibility to programs for bereaved parents and to expand outreach by providing information and support to health care providers and others in contact with families who are in their childbearing years and who may experience the death of an infant. HAND offers support and education for health care workers as well, for whom feelings of confusion and helplessness can be debilitating. It can be a great relief for staff to know they have been able to provide appropriate support to bereaved parents before they leave the hospital.

HAND's program addresses issues in the following two categories:

- *Family support and parent education:* Assisting parents in understanding and working through the grief process following the loss of a baby.
- *Health and well being:* Addressing the mental and emotional health of families in their childbearing years and increasing bereaved families' access to care and related support services.

HAND's goals are as follows:

- To help families work through their grief.
- To facilitate a support network in the San Francisco Peninsula.
- To provide multilingual printed materials with relevant information regarding the needs of those who are experiencing the loss of an infant.
- To act as a resource for a bereaved and grieving community.
- To maintain a well-staffed hot line and a Web site.
- To assist families with funeral and/or burial arrangements, including financial assistance if needed.
- To provide support for those planning on going through a subsequent pregnancy.

To achieve these goals, HAND currently offers phone support, grief support meetings twice a month, subsequent pregnancy support meetings once a month, an extensive resource library on a variety of topics (including pregnancy and infant loss, grief in general, helping children cope with grief, and relevant information for subsequent pregnancies), and an informative Web site (www.HANDsupport.org). HAND assists with funeral arrangements for families in need. We provide hospital visits, labor coaching for parents who anticipate a stillbirth or other delivery complications, and assistance in making funeral or burial arrangements. We produce and distribute a quarterly newsletter. We train our own volunteers and make in-service training presentations for health care professionals and other interested groups about the process of grief and the specific needs of parents whose expectations of a new life coming into the world have been suddenly smashed.

The number and scope of the programs that HAND runs to alleviate the mourning process dictate that the organization's limited funds be very well catalogued. The role of treasurer for such an organization is already very complicated, as money must be distributed to the printing of informational materials, including a quarterly newsletter for parents and families, general office expenses, salary of a part-time administrative assistant, purchase of library resources such as books and videos, distribution of information to hospitals, burial and funeral subsidies for families in need, monthly Internet fees, and paying for doctors or professional counselors to train HAND volunteers or give classes for bereaved parents who are expecting another child. The vital duties fulfilled by the treasurer cannot be effectively carried out without the proper technology, and therefore HAND is seeking a donation of a laptop computer or funds to purchase a laptop for this purpose.

In order to keep track of finances and the organization's numerous documents, HAND is in need of a notebook computer. After researching options and prices, we have found that an ideal model is the Dell Inspiron 5000e, with the exact requirements listed below.

Specifications:

> CPU (Pentium III) 700 MHz
>
> RAM memory 128 MB
>
> Hard drive capacity 10 GB
>
> Screen 14.1" TFT
>
> Video RAM 8 MB
>
> Floppy 3.5"
>
> CD Drive 24X
>
> Internal fax modem 56k
>
> Battery 3 hours
>
> Weight 6.75 lb.
>
> Operating system Windows 98, second edition

The prices (directly from Dell) for this model are listed below.

Prices:

Basic system with memory upgrade	$2259
External keyboard and mouse	$49
External 250 MB Zip drive (USB)	$169
Carrying case	$49
3-year service plan from purchase date	(included)

Norton Anti-Virus	(included)
Approximate sales tax (8.25%)	$208
Approximate shipping cost	(none, promo)
Total cost:	$2734

In addition to this, we will also need Microsoft Office Professional (containing Word, Excel, Outlook, Publisher, PowerPoint, Access) for the notebook, which sells for approximately $500. HAND must also purchase several additional cables, a Y-adapter for the external keyboard/mouse, and a supply of 250 MB Zip disks, as well as some additional software such as Quickbooks.

A donation from the San Francisco Foundation of $3500 to obtain this vital technology (or a donation of the technology itself if that is preferable) would greatly benefit the organization. With the help of the San Francisco Foundation, HAND may more effectively maintain records, financial and otherwise, in order to continue providing education, aid and emotional support to the unfortunate families who have suffered the death of an infant.

Thank you for your time in considering this proposal.

Sincerely,

Celia Hartnett
Coordinator
Helping After Neonatal Death

ACADEMIC RESEARCH PAPER (BRIEF)

Rebecca Freeland

Grass or Astroturf? Environmental Groups

and Corporate Sponsorship

Bay Area Action's online wish list starts off with a tongue-in-cheek request for "a million dollars, so we can create an endowment and allow the organization to live off the interest for years to come without continually worrying about financial woes (lottery tickets, anyone?)." The page goes on to list needed supplies; the agency hopes for donations of everything from garden loppers to iMacs (BAA "Wish List"). As a nonprofit organization, BAA depends on these kinds of donations—of money, goods, and services—in order to stay in operation. But, in spite of "financial woes," something else takes priority. BAA volunteer Mark Bult explains that the agency's members have "placed the organization's ideology ahead of fundraising, or at least have made the latter reliant on a clear definition of the former" (interview). That decision may seem obvious or insignificant, but it actually relates to a much larger debate over corporate sponsorship and who controls environmental activism.

Bult also wrote BAA's advertising policy, a document that clearly reflects the agency's ideology. BAA only accepts advertising that "does not promote practices, products, services, and/or companies whose primary business practices represent a negative impact on the earth or our environment." And the policy makes it very clear that "advertising and/or underwriting is separate from and different than affiliation, partnering, co-presentation, and/or endorsement" (BAA "Advertising/Underwriting Policy"). Most of these rules, as they relate to advertising, have very little practical application: BAA gets almost none of its income from selling ads. But corporate sponsorship can often result in something like advertising. Bult says that when a company makes "donations over a certain amount, we typically try to place their logo on our Web site." Sponsorship of specific events works in a similar way: "companies receive increased notoriety for an increased amount" (interview).

The advantages of corporate sponsorship are obvious: the agency gets funding and supplies. BAA, for example, recently received donations of computer equipment from Hewlett-Packard. There are nonmonetary advantages as well: working with local companies helps environmental agencies develop community ties. Such alliances may exert a positive influence on corporations, encouraging them to adopt environmentally friendly policies. Many environmental agencies rely heavily on corporate sponsorship; the local group Bay Area Alliance for Sustainable Development, for example, receives funding not just from the usual foundations and government agencies but also from Gap Inc., Bank of America, and Pacific Gas and Electric (BAASD Home Page). Larger organizations have received corporate funding as well: in one prominent 1980s case, the Environmental Defense Fund entered into a partnership with McDonald's. Hal Dash, a McDonald's representative, supported the relationship: "Companies need the environmental movement, and environmental groups take a lot of money from companies. What they want is access or cooperation, and why not?" (qtd. in Helvarg).

In fact, there are many reasons why not, especially when ideologies conflict. Far from accepting the sponsorship of Gap Inc., the BAA Schools Group actually organized protests at Palo Alto Gap stores last December. The protesters called for an end to human rights abuses and asked the Fisher family, which owns both Gap Inc. and the Mendocino Redwood Company, to stop clear-cutting redwoods in Sonoma and Mendocino counties (Vargas). These differing attitudes toward Gap's business practices reflect the emerging issue of "greenwashing," defined by the organization Corporate Watch as "the phenomenon of socially and environmentally destructive corporations attempting to preserve and expand their markets by posing as friends of the environment and leaders in the struggle to eradicate poverty" (qtd. in Klaas). Gap Inc. may support sustainable development, but is that just a way of masking environmental abuse?

According to critics like <u>E/The Environmental Magazine</u>'s David Helvarg, greenwashing depends upon "high profile partnerships with mainstream environmental groups"—not unlike McDonald's partnership with the EDF. More recent culprits were awarded Corporate Watch's Earth Day 2000 Greenwashing Awards (also known as the "Don't be fooled" awards); they include Ford, Home Depot, Exxon, and Pacific Lumber. All presented themselves as environmentally friendly—whether through token groups like Exxon's Tiger Protection Fund, or with advertising campaigns like Chevron's "People do" series—while continuing to engage in environmentally destructive behavior (Wendlant). Wendy Wendlant, president of Earth Day 2000, calls them "Astroturf environmentalists—green, fake, and rootless" (qtd. in Helvarg). Environmental organizations that accept funding from these corporations become "fake and rootless" by association; their credibility is drastically reduced by the appearance of hypocrisy. Earth Day 1990 provides a good example of this phenomenon: in many places, Earth Day events were tainted by their sponsors, which included such environmental villains as biotechnology company Monsanto (Drekmeier interview). (To avoid a repeat of these problems, Earth Day 2000 actually adopted a policy of no corporate sponsorship.)

Greenwashing is not only an issue for large corporations and national environmental groups. It may be even more of a concern for smaller, more financially vulnerable nonprofits. BAA seems very aware of that concern. Its advertising policy specifically requires that ads "not constitute a recognizable attempt at greenwashing or misrepresentation of facts" (BAA "Advertising/Underwriting Policy"). Mark Bult acknowledges that BAA has had to take an ideological stand against such attempts in order to live up to its mission: "Because most environmental organizations' objectives are in the public's interest as a whole, not merely in the interest of a small segment (say, a given company's shareholders), it is our responsibility to operate under a set of principles that are sometimes aligned in opposition to corporate interests" (interview).

Although BAA does sometimes seek out corporate sponsorship, it does so carefully, relying on its knowledgeable members to judge whether a given company has a clean environmental record and sincere intentions. For example, the leader of BAA's Environmental Eating Action Team has experience and expertise in the field of vegan and macrobiotic food; when planning an event, she can be trusted to solicit sponsorship from companies that behave responsibly in those areas (Bult interview). Even when BAA does solicit donations, it makes no guarantee of publicity for the sponsoring company. Instead, any use of the company's name or logo is what Bult calls "an acknowledgement and thank you" (interview). This perspective removes any sense that BAA <u>owes</u> something to the company, and reduces the chance that the organization could be taken over by corporate influence. (The fact that the majority of BAA's funding comes from foundations, not corporations, also helps.) Perhaps most important of all, BAA simply tries to stand firm in its goals. BAA co-executive director Peter Drekmeier explains that BAA sets up its goals in a given area long before corporations get involved, and notes, "You have to be certain in your head and your heart that donations won't affect what you want to do" (interview).

While BAA holds corporations at arm's length through these measures, it also attempts to foster positive relationships with businesses. The Peninsula Conservation Center Foundation, an environmental group with which BAA plans to merge, sponsors the Bay Area's annual Business Environmental Awards. The awards honor companies and organizations in categories like "Commute and Transportation," "Pollution Prevention/Resource Conservation," and "Sustainable Built Environments," and past winners range from Sun Microsystems to Stanford University Transportation Programs. PCCF also works with the Business Environmental Network, an organization for businesses interested in improving environmental performance (PCCF Home Page).

BAA appears to remain independent of corporate influence. The agency is popular with grassroots activists and people who, as Mark Bult points out, know whether particular companies really live up to their claims of environmentalism (interview). At the same time, BAA maintains effective relationships with local corporations. This balance suggests that the organization's strategy for dealing with the issues of corporate sponsorship and greenwashing is a good one. The key to cooperation between corporations and environmental groups is information. It is information that allows BAA members to evaluate potential sponsors or advertisers. Knowledge of a corporation's business practice can help distinguish between a greenwashing attempt and a genuine desire to help the environment. It is also information that makes it possible for BAA to acknowledge businesses that <u>do</u> act responsibly. By addressing the issue on a case-by-case basis, an agency avoids extremes: it neither allows itself to be manipulated by greenwashing nor alienates companies that might be legitimately helpful.

Granted, the case-by-case solution still leaves plenty of room for mistakes—it is, after all, dependent on individual, fallible decisions. But that may be the point: the risk posed by corporate greenwashing is that environmental groups will lose control over their images, policies, and ability to effect real change in the world. In turning the matter over to individuals, agencies like BAA/PCCF know that they at least won't be swept along by corporate power. In respect to corporate sponsorship, environmental groups might take as their motto the Greenwashing Awards' nickname—"Don't be fooled." Living up to that motto—and fulfilling a responsibility to the public as a whole—depends on staying informed and knowledgeable.

Works Cited

Bay Area Action. "Advertising/Underwriting Policy." 7 Feb. 2000.
      <http://www.baaction.org/advertising/index.html> (25 Oct. 2000).
      _____ . "Wish List."<http://www.baaction.org/wishlist/index.html>
      (25 Oct. 2000).
Bay Area Alliance for Sustainable Development Home Page.
      <http://www.bayareaalliance.org/aboutus.html> (29 Oct. 2000).
Bult, Mark. Email interview. 25 Oct. 2000.

Drekmeier, Peter. Co-director, BAA/PCCF, Palo Alto, CA. Phone interview. 29 Oct. 2000.

Helvarg, David. "Perception Is Reality: Greenwashing Puts the Best Public Face on Corporate Irresponsibility." E/The Environmental Magazine Nov.–Dec. 1996. <http://www.emagazine.com/november-december_1996/1196feat2.html> (25 Oct. 2000).

Klaas, Michael. "End Game: Week 1—Greenwash." Chronically Deficient Productions 30 May 2000.

<http://www.deficient.net/news/mk_2.asp> (29 Oct. 2000).

Peninsula Conservation Center Foundation Home Page.

<http://www.pccf.org/> (30 Oct. 2000).

Vargas, Jose Antonio. "Falling Out of the Gap: Local Students Protest Alleged Human Rights Abuses." Mountain View Voice 17 Dec. 1999. <http://www.baaction.org/news/12-99/MVVoiceGapProtest.html> (27 Oct. 2000).

Wendlandt, Wendy. "USA: Earth Day Greenwashing Awards Announced." Corporate Watch 14 April 1999. <http://www.corpwatch.org/trac/corner/worldnews/other/379.html> (27 Oct. 2000).

ACADEMIC RESEARCH PAPER (EXTENDED)

Jessica Gray

Landmines: Distant Killers

Nhia Yeurng, a 65-year-old father and grandfather living near the Thai-Cambodian border, awoke one morning to the sound of an explosion and his grandson's voice crying for help. Yeurng rushed to see what had happened. While tending cattle only two hundred meters from his house, Yeurng's grandson had triggered a landmine. Yeurng could not believe what he saw. His grandson was sprawled on the road, his left leg riddled with fragments from an antipersonnel mine. In an attempt to pick up his pain-stricken grandson and bring him to a hospital, Yeurng lost his balance and triggered another mine (American Red Cross, Factsheet).

Unfortunately, this story and others like it are not only shockingly true, but also extremely common. Every twenty minutes an antipersonnel mine maims or kills another victim (Human Rights Watch 6). With over one hundred million land mines planted in 64 countries around the world, the possibility of triggering a mine is a reality for millions of people (American Red Cross, Factsheet). In fact, the UN estimates that there is one mine in the ground for every 50 humans on earth (Capello and Cusac 18). With numbers so phenomenally high, it is clear why civilians in mine-infested countries such as Angola, Cambodia, Afghanistan, Sudan, Iraq, Bosnia, Ethiopia, and Mozambique regularly suffer casualties.

Although a life-altering fact for millions of people worldwide, the issue of landmines seems to be a distant threat to most Americans. Very few people in our country are aware of the devastation that landmines cause in civilian populations and know little about past or present involvement by U.S. companies, the U.S. military, and U.S. political leaders in this issue. Although landmines do not directly threaten American soil, as citizens of a global community it is our duty to be informed about the current issues surrounding landmines, to vocalize our outrage as members of this community, and to publicize the atrocities caused by landmines in order to eliminate them as a worldwide threat. The American Red Cross, a subsidiary of the International Committee of the Red Cross, is one of the better-known humanitarian organizations working toward educating the public about the dangers of landmines, aiding victims of landmines, and encouraging government and community involvement in the complete elimination of all existing landmines. If there is to be any progress made in the worldwide humanitarian struggle against mines, public awareness and involvement in the issue are crucial.

Ever since their creation in the mid-nineteenth century, antipersonnel mines have been a fundamental component of military strategy that revolutionized infantry tactics. There are four basic types of antipersonnel mines—blast, fragmentation, directional, and bounding devices—each of which describes a different method of explosion. The blast mine is the most common. Hidden underground, the blast mine is activated when the victim steps on it. When not instantly deadly, these mines almost always require surgical amputation (Boutros 8).

Originally, landmines were planted by hand and were defensive weapons to protect military installations and resources, or to impede enemy advance. In the 1960s, when armies began delivering mines by rocket, they became offensive weapons used for saturating target areas and to prevent enemy retreats (Cameron 275). Remotely delivered (air-dropped) landmines tend to be more dangerous than planted ones because they can be mass deployed; their use increases the probability of major amplification of post-conflict casualties because of their arbitrary landings and sheer numbers (Capello and Cusac 19).

Two major differentiations between mines are between "smart" mines and "dumb" mines. Smart mines are a technological innovation in which the landmine self-destructs after a prescribed length of time. These mines, though significantly more expensive, are more humane than "dumb" mines because they do not remain a threat for generations. According to Army statistics, smart mines are 99.99% accurate at deactivation, and have a built-in back-up deactivation mechanism when the battery runs out (Capello and Cusac 20). Although appealing, smart mines have significant drawbacks; the name does not remove their function as deadly weapons, they are not always short-lived, and they can be reprogrammed. Caleb Rossiter, the director of Demilitarization for Democracy, articulated the humanitarian point of view: "Nobody who understands weaponry should use the term 'smart mines.' 'Smart' implies a computer that makes an intelligent discrimination between targets. Landmines aren't smart. They are triggered by anything—children, animals" (qtd. in Capello and Cusac 21).

For decades the U.S. has played a significant role in the deployment and distribution of both smart and dumb landmines and has only recently been curbing use of the weapon. Until 1996, the United States was one of the world's largest producers and exporters of landmines. From 1969 to 1992 alone the U.S. exported 4.4 million mines for military deployment and for use by other countries ("Landmines: Another Pro Life Issue" 3). In 1992, however, the U.S. ratified the Antipersonnel Landmine Moratorium Act in which it placed a one-year ban on the sale, export, and transfer abroad of landmines (Boutros 9). This moratorium was extended until 2000 (Human Rights Watch 11). The moratorium on landmines ensures that the U.S. does not make more mines than it has at the present time. In 1997, countries from around the world ratified the Ottawa Treaty to ban landmines. The U.S., however, would not sign this treaty because of military reasons and has only destroyed 3 million of its stockpile of 15 million landmines (Human Rights Watch 2). Currently, the U.S. maintains a stockpile of 11 million smart mines that can be used and replenished whenever necessary.

Tactically speaking, landmines are efficient defensive weapons for the military because they deter an oncoming infantry. Although some landmines kill, their primary purpose is to maim soldiers in order to slow the encroaching army. A wounded person also has a "detrimental psychological effect on his fellow soldiers" (Human Rights Watch 5). Another "benefit" to landmines is their price. The cheapest antipersonnel mines cost as little as three dollars each (American Red Cross, Factsheet). In both the Vietnam War and the Persian Gulf War, the United States deployed countless landmines. The Department of Defense estimates that in this century, 100,000 Americans have been injured or killed in landmine accidents during or after these two wars. The irony is that most of these casualties have been self-inflicted. In Vietnam, ninety percent of all mine and booby trap components used against the U.S. were from our own weapons, while in the Persian Gulf War, thirty-four percent of all U.S. casualties were caused by landmines (Human Rights Watch 6). From looking at these statistics, it appears that the landmines we used escalated the number of American casualties causing excessive harm to our own soldiers. In fact, the landmines we placed throughout those wars are still harming U.S. soldiers today. According to Human Rights Watch, "the terrible irony of modern day peace keeping for U.S. troops is that their lives are sometimes threatened by landmines manufactured, sold, and shipped out from their own nation a few years or a generation ago" (6). American landmine parts sold to other countries as well as nondetonated U.S. mines leftover from previous battles have continually come back to haunt U.S. soldiers. Some landmines, especially older versions, have an average life span of 50 to 100 years, claiming victims long after fighting has ceased (Human Rights Watch 6).

John F. Troxell, the director of national securities studies at U.S. Army War College, believes that the strategic value of landmines overrides the humanitarian costs. He asserts that "while there are legitimate humanitarian concerns related to indiscriminate and undisciplined use of the weapons ... there are equally valid concerns relating to the effectiveness and security of U.S. forces and their ability to accomplish assigned missions throughout the world." With no effective alternatives to landmines, Troxell argues that all mines should remain in the U.S. arsenal; landmines are too vital a battlefield tool in channeling enemy forces, defending flanks, or restricting terrains and border zones to be eliminated as a weapon (103). Although the need to protect American soldiers is important, Troxell downplays the statistics indicting U.S. landmines as a major cause of American casualties. Troxell also neglects to acknowledge the obvious reality that civilians are primary victims of mines, especially after conflicts are over. According to Eric Prokosch, author of The Technology of Killing: A Military and Political History of Antipersonnel Weapons, "those who fall victim to [mines] are the most vulnerable in society: the innocents, the poorest of the poor. They are the ones who forage into the countryside, knowing that there are mines out there, because they are driven to do so by economic necessity" (ix).

Because of the unbelievable destruction inflicted on millions of innocent civilians, in 1994 the President of the International Committee of the Red Cross (ICRC), Cornelio Sommaruga, called for a complete ban on landmines (American Red Cross, Factsheet). The ICRC is a Swiss-based organization that works for the application and development of international laws that regulate the conduct of armed conflict, known as "international humanitarian law" (Prokosch 148). The American Red Cross joined the ICRC in the fight against landmines and set out specifically "to achieve a global ban on landmines as soon as feasible, using all venues possible, to provide assistance to landmine survivors today while offering hope for a world free of antipersonnel landmines tomorrow" (American Red Cross, Factsheet). Individual chapters of the Red Cross educate the public on the impact and danger that landmines present to civilian populations, the long-term health consequences and social costs surrounding the mines, and the victim assistance programs that the Red Cross provides (American Red Cross, Factsheet).

The Red Cross's efforts to encourage support for the ban on landmines have faced difficult setbacks in the United States. Public support in the U.S. has declined since the Ottawa Conference to ban landmines in 1997 because people assumed that the conference would bring about an effective solution. Support continues to decline as the U.S. government makes distant promises to sign the Ottawa Treaty in the year 2006, presuming that technology has advanced to a reasonable degree so that landmines can be replaced as an effective military weapon. Because government officials are able to sidestep the issue so often without public resistance, it is difficult to ensure that the U.S. will actually take action against the use of landmines (American Red Cross, Factsheet). Until the government comes through on its promises to sign in 2006, no action will be taken to rid the world of landmines, and until American citizens show their resolution to oppose the existence of landmines, the government will remain vague in its landmine deliberations.

Governments around the world are active in the ban against landmines. There are two ways in which governments get involved in the landmines issue: through international demining efforts and through supporting the passage of an international treaty banning the production and use of landmines. The earliest international landmines conference, the Conference of Government Experts on Weapons That May Cause Unnecessary Suffering or Have Indiscriminant Effects, was held in Lucerne in 1974. Its goal was to regulate the use of mines. The only humanitarian agency allowed in the conference was the ICRC, where forty-nine countries were present. The conference came up with six requirements to be enforced upon ratification; however, these requirements were seen as unrealistic and were shot down without any replacement measures, thereby terminating the conference without a ratified treaty. Two more conferences followed the Lucerne Conference. Neither was successful in establishing a code of conduct regarding the use of landmines that could be followed worldwide, although the 1980 Conventional Weapons Convention did create the first formal U.N. Treaty ban on conventional weapons since 1899 (Prokosch 161–162).

It was not until 1992 when the International Campaign to Ban Landmines (ICBL) gained enough worldwide support to establish a prominent voice in the landmine issue that governments began to address humanitarian problems surrounding landmines. The landmines campaign developed from the efforts of nongovernmental organizations concerned with human rights and overseas medical assistance. The six founding members of the ICBL are the French Handicap International, the German Medico International, the Mines Advisory Group from Great Britain, and the American organizations Human Rights Watch, the Vietnam Veterans of America Foundation, and Physicians for Human Rights (Prokosch 182). These groups recruited over 1000 other organizations and numerous individuals to campaign to rid the world of landmines. The ICBL approached the humanitarian issue by acting boldly; it fought for a complete ban on exports and a complete ban on landmine use rather than searching for a balance between humanitarian and military needs. The justification for such a complete ban is that the adverse effects on society are so high that they outweigh any possible military needs (Prokosch 184).

The ICBL has been a prominent voice in the efforts to ban landmines. As a large international organization, it has the ability to conduct field research quickly and efficiently, as well as to publicize its results in a timely manner all around the world (ICBL Home Page). The ICBL also has access to national decision-makers worldwide and has the information and credibility necessary to persuade them to act quickly and decisively. In 1992, the U.S. Congress adopted legislation imposing a moratorium on the sale, transfer, and export of mines from the United States as a direct result of effective lobbying by the ICBL (Prokosch 183).

The campaign's successes are due to its ability to "attract public sympathy and favorable treatment of its cause by the news media through its forthright portrayal of the sufferings of mine victims," according to Eric Prokosch (182). Individuals such as Princess Diana, Elizabeth Dole, and Nobel Peace Laureate and ICBL coordinator Jody Williams have dedicated countless hours to raising awareness and significant funding for landmine victims (Vidulich 14). At Princess Diana's tragic death, the American Red Cross stated that "the Princess brought the power of her presence, her compassion and her position to some of the most important humanitarian issues of our time, saving countless lives and bringing comfort to countless others. Her work to bring about a global ban on the landmines did more to galvanize the world opinion on this issue than any other single individual" (American Red Cross, News Release). After Diana's death, Queen Nor of Jordan continued Diana's role as a powerful voice in the campaign. It is only through the significant public support by such prominent individuals and organizations and through the campaign's ability to galvanize public opinion that the ICBL has been influential in its proposal to ban landmines.

As a result of the ICBL's efforts to focus worldwide attention on the damage landmines were causing to innocent civilian populations, the Ottawa Treaty was written in 1997. Formulated at the Convention on the Prohibition of the Use, Stockpiling, Production, and Transfer of Antipersonnel Mines and on Their Destruction, the treaty declared the use of landmines violation of international law, outlawed the production of mines, mandated the destruction of existing mines over the next four years, and blocked any transfer of landmines between participating countries (CNN). One hundred of the 137 signatories have ratified the treaty. However, the United States is among countries such as Turkey, Russia, China, India, Pakistan, and others who refuse to sign, thereby delaying the worldwide elimination of landmines (American Red Cross, "Guidance"). Although the Ottawa Treaty demands that signatories destroy their stockpiles within four years and clear mines within their own territories in ten years (Vidulich 14), realistically the onus to follow through on these commitments is on individual countries as there are not substantial criteria established for enforcing the treaty.

Although the U.S. supports the Ottawa Treaty in theory, it cited several reasons that it could not sign. The primary excuse made by the U.S. was the claim that "the U.S. has 'special needs' for land mines in South Korea, where 37,000 U.S. troops face a one-million-man North Korean Army" (CNN). The U.S. uses landmines in conjunction with antitank mines not mentioned in the treaty, and the military asserts that it is essential to maintain this tank protection system until a better alternative can be found ("Landmines: Another Pro Life Issue" 3). Whoever is the president in 2006 will review the treaty once again, provided that the Pentagon has developed alternatives to antipersonnel mines (Vidulich 14).

Another factor in the political actions of the U.S. government surrounding landmines is the substantial economic pressure on the government to maintain production of landmines because of the lucrative profits found in manufacturing. In 1996, a Human Rights Watch Report identified forty-seven U.S. companies involved in mine manufacture or delivery. These companies, including Motorola, General Electric, Alliant Techsystems, and Ratheon, all were involved in some aspect of mine manufacture and shipment (Human Rights Watch 2). After publication of the Human Rights Watch Report, Motorola and sixteen other U.S. companies terminated their involvement in the production process. The majority, however, including Alliant Techsystems of Hopkins, Minnesota, refused to halt production since profits are so large. From 1985 to 1995, Alliant earned $336,480,000 in production contracts and sales, a profit that the company refused to part with (Human Rights Watch 3). In producing their report, the HRW's goal was to initiate protests from the general public against companies involved in the creation of landmines in the form of letters, statements of protest, and divestment and shareholder resolutions of protest. However, because government facilities are the only locations where landmines are assembled, many companies that produce landmine parts do not feel morally responsible for the overall production. The creation of landmine parts is so lucrative for these companies that eliminating the production of landmines in the U.S. remains an ongoing struggle (Human Rights Watch 5).

American political leaders have not been pressured enough by public opinion for the ban on landmines to outweigh the significant military and economic arguments for their continued production. The U.S. government has tried to appease humanitarian pressure through increased contributions to the international effort on de-mining and raised its monetary contribution from forty to eighty million dollars in 1998 (American Red Cross, "Guidance"). However helpful these contributions are, they do not effectively address the extremity of the landmine crisis because there are still countless numbers of mines in existence. By maintaining the right to produce smart mines that self-destruct, the U.S. neutralizes its antilandmine efforts, creates more work for de-miners, and ensures that more victims will be claimed by landmine accidents.

Ridding the world of landmines is a struggle so difficult that it seems almost impossible. Obstacles surrounding mine clearance include technological limitations of detection and removal techniques, a shortage of sufficient funds, and a lack of a definitive knowledge of the extent of the problem. Although the idea that technology will solve our landmine crisis is appealing, it is unrealistic; technological advances are in fact worsening the global mine crisis. As landmine technology advances, the mines become more difficult to detect and remove because of new materials and a higher level of sophistication in electronic fuses. Unlike landmine technology, mine clearance technology has advanced little since the 1940s. Currently, detection equipment is just sixty to ninety percent effective in finding mines made with a minimum of metal (Boutros 9). Until governments of developed countries, who are usually not directly affected by landmines, become fully involved in the detection and removal process, new technologies will not be developed and mine clearance will remain slow and dangerous work.

Landmines are extremely expensive to remove. While they cost as little as three dollars to make, mines cost anywhere from three hundred to a thousand dollars each to remove, not including the medical costs associated with accidents caused in the process (American Red Cross, Factsheet). The United Nations funds many mine clearance programs around the world, and it has found that the most cost-effective and successful method of de-mining is to train locally recruited clearers (Boutros 8). Clearance costs are so high because they include management, training, equipment, communications, medical support, casualty evacuation, insurance, and compensation for the workers. Beyond the monetary cost, de-mining is a slow and dangerous process because of the precision it requires. Each time an individual faces a landmine, he or she puts his or her life at risk by attempting to deactivate it. In Kuwait, 84 experts were killed or injured while removing mines that were laid during the Gulf War (American Red Cross, News Release).

The most fundamental impediment to mine clearance, however, is that it is impossible to determine the full extent of the problem. Although there are an estimated one hundred million active mines in the world today, this number cannot be more than an approximation given the lack of information about the location and number of mines planted. There is no way to determine accurately the number of landmines planted in the world today; many armies do not create maps of their minefields, and if the maps are created, they are usually inaccurate (Boutros 8). In Afghanistan, for example, the Soviet Union scattered mines across the countryside by plane, making Afghanistan the most heavily mined country in the world. These mines were not recorded and did not contain self-neutralizing devices, causing the long-term problems that Afghanistan faces today (Prokosch 182). Understanding the magnitude of injuries caused by landmines is crucial for the development of appropriate interventions and optimal use of resources. However, organizations such as the ICRC have difficulty accumulating complete data because the regions most affected by landmines are generally poor and inaccessible areas that are sometimes even at war (Krug et al. 465).

Although helpful to know the exact number of mines planted in the world, the number will not diminish the threat that landmines pose to individuals and communities worldwide. According to Chris Giannou's article "Antiperonnel Landmines: Facts, Fictions, and Priorities," published in the British Medical Journal in 1997, "The absolute number of mines is of little consequence. Whether a square kilometer of rural Angola contains 10 mines, 10,000 mines, or 10,000,000 mines is not important: it is one square kilometer of farmland that cannot be used to grow crops to feed families. That is what is important" (1453). Angola suffers from countless landmine accidents. Anna Catildi, in her article "Resilient People Amidst an Armed Truce," states that in Angola "it's not a case of teaching people to avoid mines. Every Angolan knows that somewhere there is a mine with his name on it. We [the U.N.] try to ensure that the meeting is postponed for as long as possible. It's like telling someone that they've got cancer and may live for a few months or twenty years. All we can do is offer help to prolong that." Physicians Against Landmines estimates that at the current rate of de-mining, it will take over a century to rid Angola of all of its landmines ("Landmines: Another Pro Life Issue" 3).

Cambodian citizens also face incredible odds in their struggle against landmines. Cambodia is one of the most heavily mined countries in the world today. With a population of 9.9 million, landmine deaths and injuries total over 700 per month. Although there is no exact count of the number of deaths from landmines, it is estimated that one out of every 236 people is an amputee. In the United States, on the other hand, one out of every 22,000 people is an amputee (Krug et al. 465). According to the American Red Cross,

> With an estimated eight to ten million mines scattered throughout the country, Cambodia remains one of the world's most mine affected countries. Mines have affected almost every aspect of Cambodia life, destroying lives and families, rendering valuable fertile land too dangerous to farm, endangering roads, bridges, and rail lines throughout the country and posing a constant threat to civilians trying to reconstruct their lives after years of civil war. (Factsheet)

Although there are currently 1,400 trained mine cleaners in the country, the de-mining process is slow because mines are overgrown by one foot of grass and each blade must be removed individually in order to prevent pulling tripwires (Boutros 9). In 1991, the Red Cross began its rehabilitation program in Cambodia. The 3.6 million dollars in funding that the program utilizes covers the renovation of hospital facilities and an upgrade in surgical and nurse training programs, as well as the construction of a rehabilitation center for landmine victims and other disabled civilians (American Red Cross, Factsheet).

In Central America, countries affected by landmines allied under the support of the United States in 1995 to create PADCA, the Assistance Program for De-mining in Central America. PADCA's objectives include assistance to member countries in building a national capacity for de-mining, a strengthening of inter-American cooperation in the clearance problem, and a support of the actual de-mining. PADCA also sponsors a public awareness campaign and rehabilitation programs for victims. The goal of PADCA was to eliminate all existing mines on Central American soil by the year 2000. Although the work is not yet completed, countries

such as Honduras, Nicaragua, and Costa Rica have all undergone major
de-mining efforts. Honduras has successfully cleared a one-hundred mile
area of 1,145 landmines and concluded an intensive awareness and
educational program. Nicaragua speculates that there are 90,000 mines
still in place and clearing operations will continue (Coimbra and Dorio 53).

In Central America, as in all mine-infested areas, landmines are so
devastating because they adversely affect individuals in society as well as
the community as a whole. Landmines render their victims unable to
work—to plough fields or carry heavy loads—so they become an economic
burden to their families. In the last fifteen years, the Red Cross has
manufactured over 90,000 prostheses for over 60,000 amputees in 21
countries (American Red Cross, Factsheet).

Prosthetic limbs, when individuals are lucky enough to get them, are
extremely expensive to maintain, especially in a poor community.
According to the ICRC, most prostheses must be changed every six
months for a child and every three to five years for an adult (American
Red Cross, Factsheet). Such regular medical attention creates a heavy
medical bill for victims' families to cover, especially since the families
have most likely lost breadwinners to landmine accidents. Communities
suffer for years after the fighting has ceased because they are unable to
rebuild. In many armed conflicts, mines were planted around key
economic installations such as power plants, water treatment plants, and
market centers. Through the neutralization of essential infrastructure,
landmines create a virtually insuperable obstacle to post-conflict peace-
building and economic revitalization (Boutros 12).

Of course, considerable health consequences surround communities
that have been tormented by landmines. Beyond the fact that they kill
and maim, cause long-term psychological problems because victims feel
useless and burdensome, and impose financial burdens on the affected
families and entire communities, landmines have devastating indirect
consequences. Because they block access to roads, arable land, and health
facilities, landmines may stimulate an increase in waterborne diseases,
malnutrition, and infectious diseases (Krug et al. 465). They also

undermine the health care system because the demands for care are too high. Crucial services such as first aid, patient transport, and qualified staff become overburdened due to the large number of emergency patients, and materials such as sanitary operating rooms and large supplies of blood are unavailable. All these constant setbacks render the health care system ineffective (Giannou 1453).

Landmines have been a worldwide humanitarian problem for many years; however, it is only within the past decade that the global effort to remove landmines has begun to take shape. Armed with overwhelming evidence of destruction and millions of horror stories, supporters of an international ban on landmines have been working to publicize the detrimental effect that landmines have on individuals, families, and entire countries. Because public health agencies are unable to follow the lives of landmine victims after their accidents, determining the most effective use of rehabilitory resources is exceedingly difficult (Krug et al. 466). Without a full understanding of the true extent of the problem, care providers must speculate on the most effective use of their efforts. For the ICRC and other humanitarian organizations, finding a complete and effective solution to the landmine crisis is proving to be impossible because of the scarcity of information on the location of landmines, the influx of advanced mines, and the lack of cooperation from many countries. As one of the most influential and powerful nations worldwide, the United States' commitment to the campaign against land mines is critical for the campaign's ultimate success.

While dealing with information gaps, humanitarian organizations must also deal with the politics of de-mining. Government leaders are continuously faced with pressure from military and economic interests, and they need substantial public and media involvement to balance the scales. Ever since the United States vaguely promised to ratify the Ottawa Treaty in 2006, support for the landmine ban from the media and the public has been on a rapid decline. Whether it is due to lack of interest, or a sentiment that the problem will solve itself, the American public chooses to ignore the threat that landmines pose to the rest of the globe. Eric Prokosch highlights the need for an active public by remarking,

> Until governments are pressed to adopt strict limits for the prohibition of weapons causing superfluous injury or having indiscriminate effects, until there is a truly effective worldwide citizens' movement concerned about wars and the conduct of warfare, the growth in suffering inflicted in armed conflicts will continue. (195)

Without public awareness and support, organizations such as the ICRC face overwhelming barriers in their attempts to prevent needless destruction and injury and to help victims. Through establishing a public voice on the issue of landmines now, we can work to eliminate them as a threat for generations to come.

Works Cited

American Red Cross. "American Red Cross Statement on the Death of the Princess of Wales." News Release. 18 July 1997. <https://corpweb. redcross.org/comm/media/fy98/press/083197.html> (20 April 2001).

_____ . "The Red Cross Movement and Landmines." Landmines Factsheet. May 1997. <https://corpweb.redcross.org/intl/landmine/ factsheet.html> (20 April 2001).

_____ . "Guidance to Chapters Interested in Landmine Use." May 1997. <https://corpweb.redcross.org/intl/refcent/landmns.html> (20 April 2001).

Boutros, Ghali. "The Land Mine Crisis: A Humanitarian Disaster." Foreign Affairs v73 n5 (Sept.–Oct. 1994): 8–12.

Cameron, Maxwell A., Robert J. Lawson, and Brian W. Tomlin, eds. To Walk Without Fear: The Global Movement to Ban Landmines. Toronto: Oxford UP, 1998.

Capello, Catherine, and Anne-Marie Cusac. "Meet the People Who Make Landmines." <u>Progressive</u> v61 (Nov. 1997): 18–25.

Cataldi, Anna. "Resilient People Amidst an Armed Truce." <u>Landmines: Demining News From the United Nations.</u> Dec 1997. <http://www.un.org/depts/dpko/mine/Newsletter/2_4/cataldi.htm> (20 April 2001).

CNN Interactive, "Signing of Historical Land Mine Treaty Begins." 3 Dec. 1997. <http://www.cnn.com/WORLD/9712/03/land.mines.ban/> (20 April 2001).

Coimbra, Luiz, and Jorge Dorio. "Reclaiming the Poisoned Land." <u>Americas</u> (English Edition) v49 n5 (Sept.–Oct. 1997): 53–55.

Giannou, Chris. "Antipersonnel Landmines: Facts, Fictions, and Priorities." <u>British Medical Journal</u> v315 (Nov. 29 1997): 1453–1454.

Human Rights Watch Arms Project. <u>Exposing the Source: US Companies and the Production of Antipersonnel Mines.</u> April 1997: vol. 9.

International Campaign to Ban Landmines. <u>Home Page.</u> 15 May 2001. <http://www.icbl.org>.

Krug, Etienne G., Robin M. Ikeda, Michael L. Qualls, Mark A. Anderson, Mark L. Rosenberg, and Richard J. Jackson. "Preventing Land Mine–Related Injury and Disability". <u>JAMA</u> v280 n5 (Aug 5 1998): 465–467.

"Land Mines: Another Pro-Life Issue." <u>America</u> v180 n6. America Press, Inc. (Feb. 27, 1999): 3.

Prokosch, Eric. <u>The Technology of Killing: A Military and Political History of Antipersonnel Weapons.</u> New Jersey: Zed Books, Ltd., 1995.

Troxell, John F. "Landmines: Why the Korea Exception Should Be the Rule." <u>Wilson Quarterly</u> v24 n2 (Spring 2000): 103–104.

Vidulich, Dorothy. " 'Ban Mines' Activists Urge Clinton, Congress." <u>National Catholic Reporter.</u> v36 n35 (July 28 2000): 14.

Credits

Index